THE FOUR GOSPELS

An Introduction
for Teaching and Preaching

J. SAMUEL SUBRAMANIAN

The Four Gospels: An Introduction for Teaching and Preaching

The General Board of Higher Education and Ministry leads and serves The United Methodist Church in the recruitment, preparation, nurture, education, and support of Christian leaders—lay and clergy—for the work of making disciples of Jesus Christ for the transformation of the world. Its vision is that a new generation of Christian leaders will commit boldly to Jesus Christ and be characterized by intellectual excellence, moral integrity, spiritual courage, and holiness of heart and life. The General Board of Higher Education and Ministry of The United Methodist Church serves as an advocate for the intellectual life of the church. The Board's mission embodies the Wesleyan tradition of commitment to the education of laypersons and ordained persons by providing access to higher education for all persons.

Wesley's Foundery Books is named for the abandoned foundery that early followers of John Wesley transformed, which later became the cradle of London's Methodist movement.

HIGHER EDUCATION & MINISTRY
General Board of Higher Education and Ministry
THE UNITED METHODIST CHURCH

Contents

3. THE GOSPEL ACCORDING TO MARK

4. THE GOSPEL ACCORDING TO LUKE

5. THE GOSPEL ACCORDING TO JOHN

6. CONCLUSION: THE LIFE OF JESUS IN FOUR DIMENSIONS

Foreword

We live in turbulent times. Nowhere is this more evident than with the major changes we see taking place in the mission and ministry of the local church. One arena where we see major changes is in the liturgical life in local churches. But some things remain constant. Today the format of the sermon may be quite different from what we were accustomed to in earlier years, but there is still a text read and an exposition given on its importance to the people of God. This still stands at the center of what takes place in the worship assembly.

As a retired seminary professor, I now sit toward the rear of the congregation. Here I am regularly impressed by the response of congregations when the text is read. Whether they are following carefully what is written in their Bibles or turning to a translation on an electronic device, people will seek to access the text. When the sermon comes, they expect a coherent exposition that makes the word relevant to some aspect of their lives.

At this point we connect with the work that is before us. At the heart of the Scriptures are the four Gospel accounts of the life and teachings of Jesus. On a regular basis in the church year we will hear expositions on texts from these accounts. Will the words of exposition match the expectations of those who seek to hear God's word on the basis of these texts?

Professor J. Samuel Subramanian is a preacher. With practiced regularity, he steps behind the pulpit and shares the eternal Word with his hearers. His background is in United Methodism, and his service in these circles is impeccable. Trained in academic studies at Southern Methodist University in the era of Dr. Albert C. Outler, Dr. John W. Deschner, Dr. Schubert M. Ogden, Dr. Jouette M. Bassler, Dr. Victor Paul Furnish, and Dr. William R. Farmer, Subramanian received a sterling education in biblical studies. He knows how to put together sermons on the Gospels. In this work he goes out of his way to point out to one who is less comfortable in the circles of biblical studies what one needs to know before public exposition on these critical texts. There are some things anyone needs to know when preaching from the Gospels, and Subramanian shows what they are.

Without being too detailed, if one is about to preach, for example, on a text from Luke, one can be introduced to a basic strategy by reading the relevant chapter in Professor Subramanian's book. There, one can learn quickly what is the Lukan theological dictum and how the particular text in the intended discourse connects with this strategy.

Of course, there are a multitude of commentaries on the Gospels, and this work is not meant to supersede them. It is more like a workbook. It gets the preacher directly to the point of the text so that he or she may avoid the periphery and be guided to preach its central word confidently.

One final word: In working through the book myself, I found one particular worthwhile feature that is unique for works of this genre. In each chapter, Professor Subramanian underscores important points that John Wesley drew from the Gospel texts in his preaching. From this latter-day Methodist preacher, it doesn't get any better than that.

Allan J. McNicol
A. B. Cox Professor Emeritus of New
   Testament and Biblical Theology
Austin Graduate School of Theology
Austin, Texas
February 10, 2020

Preface

> Long ago God spoke to our ancestors in many and various ways by the prophets, but in these last days he has spoken to us by a Son, whom he appointed heir of all things, through whom he also created the worlds. He is the reflection of God's glory and the exact imprint of God's very being, and he sustains all things by his powerful word. When he had made purification for sins, he sat down at the right hand of the Majesty on high, having become as much superior to angels as the name he has inherited is more excellent than theirs. (Heb 1:1–4)

The author of the Letter to the Hebrews sums up the gospel in a nutshell. The four Gospels—Matthew, Mark, Luke, and John—bear witness to the gospel of Jesus Christ from four different perspectives. They provide a coherent narrative on how God's acts of salvation became fulfilled in Jesus. That is why all four Gospels are necessary to understand the course of salvation history (*Heilsgeschichte*). The purpose of this book is to present the life and ministry of Jesus as seen from the witness of the four Evangelists. It can be construed that the four Evangelists stand at four different corners of an intersection and thus view from four dimensions Jesus, who stands at the center of the intersection. Each Evangelist is true to what they witnessed and what they saw, although they stood at different places from one another. And these four witnesses continue to undergird the ongoing mission of the church in the proclamation of the gospel of Jesus Christ. This book provides basic tools for teachers and preachers alike. Both teachers and preachers need to know some background of the Gospels in terms of authorship, date, purpose, provenance, major themes, and theology. Whether one teaches apart from preaching or one combines both teaching and preaching, this book will serve as a valuable asset in authentically articulating the gospel of Jesus Christ in both church and society. Every aspect of the book can be integrated into teaching and preaching ministries of the church.

While in seminary, I was introduced to Gospel studies by Dr. Hermann Klaus, Dr. Clement Morrow, Dr. Mrs. E. Banerjee, Deacon George Joy, Dr. J. G. Frank Collison, and Dr. K. James Carl. While in graduate school, I worked closely with Dr. William R. Farmer, Dr. Stephen R. Westerholm, Dr. Eileen M. Schuller, Dr. Alan Mendelson, and Dr. Ben F. Meyer on Gospel studies, the Septuagint, the Dead Sea Scrolls, Philo, and hermeneutics. I eventually became associated with the research team of the International Institute for Gospel Studies, where I had the opportunity to work with Dr. William R. Farmer, Dr. David L. Dungan, Dr. Philip L. Shuler, Dr. O. Lamar Cope, Dr. Thomas R. W. Longstaff, Dr. David B. Peabody, and Dr. Allan J. McNicol on Interrelations of the Gospels. I coedited a volume with Dr. David B. Peabody and Dr. Allan J. McNicol, *Resourcing New Testament Studies: Literary, Historical, and Theological Essays in Honor of David L. Dungan* (London: T. & T. Clark, 2009). All those scholars helped me understand the complexities involved in Gospel research. They all have contributed to my research, teaching, and preaching on the four Gospels.

This book has six chapters. Chapter 1, "Four Gospel Accounts of the Witness of Jesus," deals primarily with the placement of the four Gospels in early Christian tradition and the canon, the centrality of Jesus, sources, the role of John, and the placement of the Gospels in the New Testament. Each subsequent chapter focuses on one Gospel, examining authorship, date, purpose, place of writing, main themes, theology of each Gospel writer, John Wesley's explanatory notes on each Gospel, important points to consider when preaching and teaching from each Gospel, summary, and questions for discussion. The conclusion, "The Life of Jesus in Four Dimensions," sums up the witness of the four Gospel accounts on the life and ministry of Jesus.

A special aspect of this book is that it makes extensive use of the testimony of the early Church Fathers, who knew and used the earliest versions of the four Gospels. Their testimony is considered especially reliable in relation to authorship and composition of the Gospels. Their articulation of Christian faith rooted in the apostolic tradition greatly contributed to the formation of the New Testament canon. Another unique aspect is that I have sought to bring John Wesley into conversation with the four Gospels. Wesley, an important biblical scholar in his own right, articulated the meaning of the text in its original historical and authorial contexts before he drew implications for daily living. His method of interpreting the biblical text has great significance not only for teachers and preachers in the Wesleyan tradition but in the wider ecumenical community. Only by setting the Bible in its historical context will one be able to interpret the message of the Gospel writers in the contemporary setting. Teachers and preachers will find ample resources in this book to engage in teaching and preaching ministries in the church and beyond. Questions placed at the end of each chapter will generate great interest for group discussion among wider audiences. It is the intention of the author to present the academic research of the four Gospels in plain language. The average person can use this book in both academic and church settings to enlarge his or her understanding of the Gospels and to authentically teach and preach the gospel of Jesus Christ.

I owe a debt of gratitude to Dr. Allan J. McNicol of Austin Graduate School of Theology both for his encouragement and his insightful comments on the research underlying this volume. I extend my gratitude to my faculty colleagues at United Theological Seminary of the Twin Cities for their support. I express my gratitude to Dr. Dale C. Dobias, associate professor of theological research and bibliography and director of the library at United, for his assistance in providing library resources that were extremely helpful. My gratitude also extends to The General Board of Higher Education and Ministry of The United Methodist Church for publishing this book.

I have dedicated the book to the late Dr. William R. Farmer, professor of New Testament, Southern Methodist University, in Dallas, Texas. It is he who invited me some years ago to Perkins School of Theology to work with him on Gospel research, and for this I will always be grateful.

J. Samuel Subramanian, PhD
February 17, 2020

Abbreviations

AB	Anchor Bible
Ant.	*Jewish Antiquities*
ASNU	Acta Seminarii Neotestamentici Upsaliensis
Autol.	*Ad Autolycum*
Bib	*Biblica*
BAR	*Biblical Archaeology Review*
BBR	*Bulletin for Biblical Research*
BETS	*Bulletin of the Evangelical Theological Society*
BJRL	*Bulletin of the John Rylands University Library of Manchester*
BT	*Biblical Theology*
CBQ	*Catholic Biblical Quarterly*
CBR	*Currents in Biblical Research*
Comm. Matt.	*Commentarium in evangelium Matthaei*
Cons.	*De consensu evangelistarum*
ConBNT	Coniectanea Neotestamentica or Coniectanea Biblica: New Testament Series
Did.	*Didache*
Ep. fest.	*Epistula festales*
ET	English translation
ETL	*Ephemerides Theologicae Lovanienses*
EvJTh	*Evangelical Journal of Theology*
Haer.	*Adversus Haereses* (*Elenchos*)
Hist. eccl.	*Historia ecclesiastica*
Hom. Luc.	*Homiliae Lucam*
HTR	*Harvard Theological Review*
Ign. Eph.	*Ignatius, Epistle to the Ephesians*

Ign. Phld.	Ignatius, *To the Philadelphians*
Ign. Pol.	Ignatius, *To Polycarp*
Ign. Smyrn.	Ignatius, *To the Smyrnaeans*
Int	*Interpretation*
JBL	*Journal of Biblical Literature*
JBR	*Journal of Bible and Religion*
JETS	*Journal of the Evangelical Theological Society*
JSNT	*Journal for the Study of the New Testament*
JSNTSup	Journal for the Study of the New Testament Supplement Series
JTS	*Journal of Theological Studies*
J.W.	*Jewish War*
LCL	Loeb Classical Library
LNTS	Library of New Testament Studies
Marc.	*Adversus Marcionem*
Neot	*Neotestamentica*
NovT	*Novum Testamentum*
NTS	*New Testament Studies*
Pan.	*Panarion (Adversus haereses)*
PIBA	*Proceedings of the Irish Biblical Association*
PRSt	*Perspectives in Religious Studies*
ResQ	*Restoration Quarterly*
RevExp	*Review and Expositor*
RHT	*Revue d'histoire des textes*
SBLMS	Society of Biblical Literature Monograph Series
SNTSMS	Society for New Testament Studies Monograph Series
TB	*Tyndale Bulletin*
TC	*A Journal of Biblical Textual Criticism*
ThSt	Theologische Studiën
TJ	*Trinity Journal*
USQR	*Union Seminary Quarterly Review*
Vir. ill.	*De viris illustribus*
WThJ	*Wesley Theological Journal*

Four Gospel Accounts of the
Witness of Jesus

Introduction

THE Gospel (that is, good tidings) means a book containing the good tidings of our salvation by Jesus Christ. St. Mark in his Gospel presupposes that of St. Matthew, and supplies what is omitted therein. St. Luke supplies what is omitted by both the former: St. John what is omitted by all the three."[1] Thus writes John Wesley, who taught

---

1 John Wesley, *Wesley's Notes on the New Testament* (Oxford: Benediction Classics, 2010), 5. John Wesley (1703–1791) was an Anglican clergyman, Bible scholar, theologian, preacher, social activist, and founder, along with his brother Charles Wesley, of the Methodist movement in the Church of England. In 1735 both Wesleys accompanied James Oglethorpe and sailed to Savannah, Georgia, where John attempted to convert Native Americans. But he ended up mostly ministering to European settlers. The journey to America produced the first Anglican church in Savannah and the first Anglican hymnbook in America (*Collection of Psalms and Hymns*, 1737), written by John Wesley. It also affected the early stages of Methodism with the establishment of the first "Methodist" religious society meeting in Frederica, Georgia in 1736. In 1737 he returned to England. At a small religious meeting in Aldersgate Street, London on May 24, 1738, John Wesley had a spiritual experience in which his "heart was strangely warmed." After the spiritual transformation, he devoted his life to evangelism and social justice. Beginning in 1739 he established Methodist societies throughout England. He traveled and preached, especially in the London-Bristol-Newcastle triangle, with frequent forays into Wales, Ireland, and Scotland. He became a leader in many areas of social justice, including prison reform and the abolition of the slave trade. In 1744 he wrote a tract called "Thoughts on Slavery." He preached a powerful sermon in Bristol, attacking the slave trade and the slave traders. In 1746 he set up a free medical dispensary in London to give out free medicine to the poor. He continued throughout his life a regimen of personal discipline and ordered living. He is said to have preached 40,000 sermons and to have traveled 250,000 miles. In 1784 John Wesley gave the Methodist societies a legal constitution, and in the same year he ordained Thomas Coke for ministry in the United States; that action signaled an independent course in the history of Methodism. Some of his last words were "The best of all is, God is with us." See R. Hattersley, *The Life of John Wesley: A Brand from the Burning* (New York: Doubleday, 2003).

New Testament at Oxford University and who eventually became the founder of Methodism along with his brother, Charles Wesley.

The four Gospels—Matthew, Mark, Luke, and John—that are placed at the beginning of the New Testament canon speak of the life and ministry of Jesus. Jesus occupies the central place in the testimony of the Gospel writers. It is the gospel of Jesus that is presented in four dimensions. The word *gospel* (Gk: *euangelion*) means "good news" or "good tidings." It is often used to describe a word announcing "good news." The word is used in the major Greek translation of the Hebrew Bible known as the Septuagint (LXX).[2] It occurs in the context of conveying the news of Saul's death to David, which is not the good news that David expected: "As the LORD lives, who has redeemed my life out of every adversity, when the one who told me, 'See, Saul is dead,' thought he was bringing good news [Gk: *eugangelizomenos*], I seized and killed him at Ziklag—this was the reward I gave him for his news" [Gk: *euangelia*] (2 Sm 4:9b–10 LXX).[3] The apostle Paul primarily uses the word *gospel* in terms of the message he preached. Writing on the resurrection of Christ, Paul says, "Now I would remind you, brothers and sisters, of the good news [Gk: *euangelion*] that I proclaimed to you, which you in turn received, in which also you stand, through which also you are being saved, if you hold firmly to the message that I proclaimed to you—unless you have come to believe in vain" (1 Cor 15:1–2). Speaking on the divine origin of the gospel, Paul writes, "For I want you to know, brothers and sisters, that the gospel [Gk: *euangelion*] that was proclaimed by me is not of human origin; for I did not

---

2   The word *septuagint* comes from the Latin *"septuāgintā,"* meaning "seventy," which refers to the seventy Greek translators of the Hebrew Bible. The Roman numerical LXX (seventy) is widely used as an abbreviation for the Greek text of the Hebrew Bible. For a discussion on the influence of the Septuagint in the early Christian writings, see T. M. Law, *When God Spoke Greek: The Septuagint and the Making of the Christian Bible* (New York: Oxford University Press, 2013). For a complete English translation of the Septuagint, see Albert Pietersma and Benjamin G. Wright, eds., *A New English Translation of the Septuagint* (New York: Oxford University Press, 2007).

3   Unless otherwise stated, all biblical quotations are taken from The New Revised Standard Version (NRSV).

receive it from a human source, nor was I taught it, but I received it through a revelation of Jesus Christ" (Gal 1:11–12).

Early in the second century CE the word *gospel* came to be associated with the collection of the four Gospels together in one book. Ignatius, Bishop of Antioch (15 CE–110 CE), seems to use "gospel" as a book that contains the advent, death, and resurrection of the Savior, Lord Jesus Christ.[4] Irenaeus, Bishop of Lyons (130–202), also refers to the "gospel" as the book that is the "four pillars" of the earth.[5]

---

4 In his letter to the Philadelphians, Ignatius writes, "But the gospel [Gk: *euangelion*] possesses something distinctive, namely, the coming of the Savior, our Lord Jesus Christ, his suffering, and the resurrection. For the beloved prophets preached in anticipation of him, but the gospel is the imperishable finished work. All these things together are good, if you believe with love" (*Ign. Phld.* 9.2). See *The Apostolic Fathers: Greek Texts and English Translations of Their Writings*, trans. J. B. Lightfoot and J. R. Harmer, ed. and rev. M. W. Holmes, 2nd ed. (Grand Rapids, MI: Baker Book House, 1992), 182–83. Born in Syria, Ignatius Theophorus, or Ignatius Nureno, converted to the Christian faith and eventually became bishop of Antioch. He represented the Christian religion in transition from its Jewish origin to its assimilation in the Greco-Roman world. He laid the foundation for church dogmas that would be formulated in succeeding generations. Tradition suggests that he was a disciple of John the apostle along with Polycarp. Tradition also says that when Ignatius was a little boy, Jesus hugged him and said, "Truly I tell you, unless you change and become like children, you will never enter the kingdom of heaven" (Mt 18:3). He is well known for his advocacy of a hierarchical structure of the church with emphasis on episcopal authority, his insistence on the real humanity of Christ, and his ardent desire for martyrdom. He was the first outside the Gospels to speak of Jesus's virgin birth (*Ign. Eph.* 18.2). He was also the first to use the term *catholic* to describe the universal church (*Ign. Smyrn.* 8.2). In the year 107, Emperor Trajan visited Antioch and forced the Christians there to choose between death and apostasy. Ignatius openly confessed Christ and was condemned to be put to death in Rome. On the way to Rome, he wrote six letters to the churches of Ephesus, Magnesia, Tralles, Rome, Philadelphia, and Smyrna and also addressed a letter to Bishop Polycarp of Smyrna. See W. J. Burghardt, S.J., "Did Saint Ignatius of Antioch Know the Four Gospels," *ThSt* 1 (1940): 1–26.

5 Irenaeus, *Haer.* 3.11.8: "It is not possible that the Gospels can be either more or fewer in number than they are. For, since these are four zones of the world in which we live, and four principal winds, while the Church is scattered throughout all the world, and the 'pillar and ground' of the Church is the Gospel and the spirit of life; it is fitting that she should have four pillars, breathing out immortality on every side, and vivifying men afresh." Quoted from *The Apostolic Fathers with Justin Martyr and Irenaeus*, ed. A. C. Coxe, vol. 1 of *Ante-Nicene Fathers*, ed. A. Roberts and J. Donaldson (Peabody, MA: Hendrickson Publishers, 1999), 428. See T. C. Skeat, "Irenaeus and the Four-Gospel Canon," *NovT* 34 (1992): 194–99. Irenaeus was a leading Christian theologian in the early church. Tradition says that he heard the preaching of Polycarp, bishop of Smyrna. He acted as mediator between various contending factions. His work *Adversus Haereses* ("Against Heresies"), written in about 180 CE, was a refutation of gnosticism. In the course of his writings Irenaeus advanced the development of the New Testament canon, the creed, and the authority of the episcopal office. He died as a martyr.

Since this time, the words *gospel* or *gospels* came to be associated with the fourfold collection of the four Gospels. The visions of the prophet Ezekiel recorded in Ezekiel 1:10–11a and that of John of Patmos in Revelation 4:6b–7 include four living creatures that stand in the presence of the throne of God.[6] In both visions these heavenly creatures appear like a man, a lion, an ox, and an eagle, though their detailed descriptions differ. In the early church, these four creatures came to be identified with the four Gospels. Irenaeus connected the four Gospels with four living creatures in this combination: man with Matthew, eagle with Mark, ox with Luke, and lion with John.[7] Jerome (345–420)—a Christian theologian from Stridon, Dalmatia (modern Croatia or Slovenia)—made the following identification based on Ezekiel's vision: man with Matthew, lion with Mark, ox with Luke, and eagle with John.[8] Augustine (354–430), an early Christian theologian,

---

6   "As for the appearance of their faces: the four had the face of a human being, the face of a lion on the right side, the face of an ox on the left side, and the face of an eagle; such were their faces" (Ez 1:10–11a). "Around the throne, and on each side of the throne, are four living creatures, full of eyes in front and behind: the first living creature like a lion, the second living creature like an ox, the third living creature with a face like a human face, and the fourth living creature like a flying eagle" (Rv 4:6b–7).

7   Irenaeus, *Haer.* 3.11.8, in *Ante-Nicene Fathers*, 1:428–29.

8   See Jerome's *Commentary on Matthew*, Preface 3: "The book of Ezekiel also proves that these four gospels had been predicted much earlier. Its first vision is described as follows: 'And in the midst there was a likeness of four animals. Their countenances were the face of a man and the face of a lion and the face of a calf and the face of an eagle.' The first face of a man signifies Matthew, who began his narrative as though about a man: 'The book of the generation of Jesus Christ the son of David, the son of Abraham.' The second [face signifies] Mark in whom the voice of a lion roaring in the wilderness is heard: 'A voice of one shouting in the desert: Prepare the way of the Lord, make his paths straight.' The third [is the face] of the calf which prefigures that the evangelist Luke began with Zechariah the priest. The fourth [face signifies] John the evangelist who, having taken up eagle's wings and hastening toward higher matters, discusses the Word of God." Quoted from *St. Jerome Commentary on Matthew*, trans. T. P. Scheck, The Fathers of the Church, vol. 117 (Washington, DC: The Catholic University of America Press, 2014), 55. Jerome was recognized as an important Bible scholar and monk. He was ordained a presbyter. However, he never ministered in a church, preferring the monastic life. In Rome, he served as the theological advisor and secretary to Pope Damasus I. Jerome translated the Bible into Latin, which is called *Vulgate* (meaning, "Common"). He repeatedly exhorted others to saturate their minds with the Scriptures: "Make knowledge of the Scripture your love. . . . Live with them, meditate on them, make them the sole object of your knowledge and inquiries." He died in Bethlehem.

philosopher, and bishop of Hippo in North Africa, correlated the four living creatures of the Apocalypse (Revelation) to the Gospels in this order: lion with Matthew, man with Mark, ox with Luke, and eagle with John.[9] In this chapter, the following four points will be discussed in order to set the four Gospels in context: the four Gospels and the canon of the New Testament; Jesus and the witness of the four Gospels; relation of the synoptic Gospels to John's Gospel; and the four Gospels and the rest of the New Testament.

Four Gospels and the Canon of the New Testament

The New Testament canon consists of twenty-seven books: Matthew, Mark, Luke, John, Acts, Romans, 1 Corinthians, 2 Corinthians, Galatians, Ephesians, Philippians, Colossians, 1 Thessalonians, 2 Thessalonians, 1 Timothy, 2 Timothy, Titus, Philemon, Hebrews, James, 1 Peter, 2 Peter, 1 John, 2 John, 3 John, Jude, and Revelation. The order of these works has varied in various segments of the church throughout its history, but the Gospels always stand at the head of the order. Other gospels, such as the *Gospel of Thomas*, the *Infancy*

---

9 See Augustine, *Cons.* 1.6.9: "For these reasons, it also appears to me, that of the various parties who have interpreted the living creatures in the Apocalypse as significant of the four evangelists, those who have taken the lion to point to Matthew, the man to Mark, the calf to Luke, and the eagle to John, have made a more reasonable application of the figures than those who have assigned the man to Matthew, the eagle to Mark, and the lion to John. For, in forming their particular idea of the matter, these latter have chosen to keep in view simply the beginnings of the books, and not the full design of the several evangelists in its completeness, which was the matter that should, above all, have been thoroughly examined." Quoted from Augustine, *The Harmony of the Gospels*, trans. S. D. F. Salmond, ed. M. B. Riddle, vol. 6 of *Nicene and Post-Nicene Fathers*, ed. P. Schaff (Peabody, MA: Hendrickson Publishers, 1995), 80. Augustine was ordained a presbyter and later became bishop at Hippo. He came from Thagaste in the Roman province of Numidia (now Annaba, Algeria). He systematically synthesized classical thought with Christian teaching, which created a theological system of great authority and lasting influence. His teachings and writings contributed to the practice of biblical exegesis and the foundation of medieval and modern Christian thought. Some of his most important works are *Confessiones* ("Confessions") and *De civitate Dei* ("The City of God"). He worked on the harmonization of the four Gospels in his treatise *De consensus evangelistarum* ("The Harmony of the Gospels"). He argued that Matthew was the first written Gospel and that the other Gospel writers—Mark, Luke, and John—reworked Matthew to emphasize different aspects of the life of Jesus.

Gospel of Thomas, the *Gospel of Mary*, the *Gospel of Peter*, and the *Gospel of Judas*, were circulated in the ancient church but were never included in the canon.[10] One might wonder why only four Gospels are included in the canon and not the other gospels. Very early on in the second and third centuries CE, the Church Fathers made the determination that only these four Gospels were worthy of reading and determining practice in the church. Papias, Bishop of Hierapolis (70–163), who was knowledgeable of the tradition of the primitive elders (presbyters), said that "Matthew collected the oracles in the Hebrew language, and each interpreted them as best he could."[11] Papias's testimony presumes that Matthew's Gospel served as the foundational text for other Gospel writers.[12] Clement of Alexandria (150–215), who taught at the Catechetical School of Alexandria, also testified to the existence of the four Gospels on the basis of the testimony of the primitive elders.[13] Eusebius states,

---

10 For a list of noncanonical gospels, see B. D. Ehrman and Z. Pleše, *The Apocryphal Gospels: Texts and Translations* (Oxford: Oxford University Press, 2011). Hal Taussig has included ten apocryphal New Testament writings along with twenty-seven canonical New Testament writings in order to present a Bible for the twenty-first century. See H. Taussig, ed. with comm., *A New New Testament: A Bible for the 21st Century Combining Traditional and Newly Discovered Texts* (New York: Houghton Mifflin Harcourt, 2013).

11 Eusebius, *Hist. eccl.* 3.39.16. All quotations from Eusebius are taken from Eusebius, *Ecclesiastical History, Books 1–5*, trans. K. Lake, LCL 153 (Cambridge, MA: Harvard University Press, 1926); Eusebius, *Ecclesiastical History, Books 6–10*, trans. J. E. L. Oulton, LCL 265 (Cambridge, MA: Harvard University Press, 1932). Eusebius of Caesarea (260 CE–339 CE) was the bishop of Caesarea and an early church historian. He produced a fully documented history of the Christian church. For that reason, he is known as "the Father of Church History." At the Council of Nicaea (325 CE), Eusebius was more concerned about church unity than about anti-Arianism. For a new translation of Eusebius's works, see *Eusebius' Ecclesiastical History: Complete and Unabridged, New Updated Edition*, trans. C. F. Cruse (Peabody, MA: Hendrickson Publishers, 2006).

12 Papias was a hearer of the apostle John and a disciple of Bishop Polycarp of Smyrna. He was known to have compiled the sayings and teachings of Jesus, which made up his *Expositions of the Sayings of the Lord* in five books. Unfortunately, only fragments of this work have survived in the writings of Irenaeus and Eusebius.

13 Clement's main contribution to the development of church dogmas was his attempt to reconcile Christian teachings with the ancient Greek philosophers. Three of his works survive: the *Protreptikos* ("Exhortations"), which presents the Christian faith in contrast with paganism; the *Paedagogus* ("The Instructor"), which encourages Christians in the disciplined pursuit of holiness; and the *Stromata* ("Patchworks"), which

> He [Clement] said that those Gospels were first written which include the genealogies, but that the gospel according to Mark came into being in this manner: When Peter had publicly preached the word at Rome, and by the Spirit had proclaimed the Gospel, that those present, who were many, exhorted Mark, as one who had followed him for a long time and remembered what had been spoken, to make a record of what was said; and that he did this, and distributed the Gospel among those that asked him. And that when the matter came to Peter's knowledge he neither strongly forbade it nor urged it forward. But that John, last of all, . . . composed a spiritual Gospel.[14]

From the Clementine tradition, Eusebius proposes to account for the order of the four Gospels: Matthew and Luke preceded Mark and John. From Eusebius's reading of Clement's testimony, one might assert that the four Gospels came to be considered the authoritative documents in the early church.

Irenaeus also noted the existence of four authoritative Gospels and alludes to all four. Quoting from Irenaeus, Eusebius writes, "Now Matthew published among the Hebrews a written gospel also in their own tongue, while Peter and Paul were preaching in Rome and founding the church."[15] Irenaeus seems to have known the existence of a Hebrew Gospel of Matthew, and probably the same Gospel was produced in Greek as well. Then Irenaeus goes on to say, "But after their death Mark also, the disciple and interpreter of Peter, himself handed down to us in writing the things which were preached by Peter, and Luke also, who was a follower of Paul, put down in a book the gospel which was preached by him."[16] Irenaeus seems to associate both Mark's and Luke's Gospels with Peter and Paul respectively. Although Mark and Luke were not earthly followers of Jesus, their association with Peter and Paul lends authority to their writings. Irenaeus continues to

---

address the subject of faith in relation to human reason. See E. Osborn, *Clement of Alexandria* (Cambridge: Cambridge University Press, 2008).

14 Eusebius, *Hist. eccl.* 6.14.5–7.

15 Eusebius, 5.8.2.

16 Eusebius, 5.8.3.

testify, "Then John, the disciple of the Lord, who had even rested on his breast, himself also gave forth the gospel, while he was living at Ephesus in Asia."[17] Irenaeus used the four Gospels to defend his theological doctrine of the One God and of the Sonship of Christ Jesus.[18] Again, the four Gospels emerged as the authoritative documents for use in the early church.

Origen, Presbyter of Alexandria (184–253), attested that he only knew of four Gospels, "which alone are unquestionable in the Church of God under heaven."[19] Of the four Gospels, Origen writes "that first was written that according to Matthew, who was once a tax-collector but afterwards an apostle of Jesus Christ, . . . Secondly, that according to Mark, who wrote it in accordance with Peter's instructions, . . . And thirdly, that according to Luke, . . . the Gospel that was praised by Paul. After them all, that according to John."[20] Origen vigorously defended the four Gospels as the authoritative documents of the church. He went on to state, "The Church has four Gospels. Heretics have very many."[21] Origen seems to be aware of other gospels, but he defended the four Gospels as the gospels of the church. Origen writes, "I know one gospel called *According to Thomas*, and another *According to Matthias*. We have read many others, too, lest we appear ignorant of anything, because of those people who think they know something if they have examined these gospels. But in all these questions we

---

17 Eusebius, 5.8.4.

18 Cf. Irenaeus, *Haer.* 3.9–11 in *Ante-Nicene Fathers*, 1:422–29.

19 Eusebius, *Hist. eccl.* 6.25.4. Origen was famous for his *Hexapala*, an extensive work of Old Testament analysis written to answer Jewish and gnostic critics of Christianity. It was an examination of biblical texts arranged in six parallel columns: one in Hebrew and the other five in various Greek texts. He was the first Bible scholar to explore the Scriptures on three levels: literal, moral, and allegorical. His exegetical writings consist of commentaries, homilies (sermons), and scholia (marginal notes). His main work, *De Principiis* ("On First Principles"), was the first systematic elucidation of Christian theology ever written.

20 Eusebius, *Hist. eccl.* 6.25.4–6.

21 Origen, *Hom. Luc.* 1.2, in Origen, *Homilies on Luke*, trans. J. T. Lienhard, The Fathers of the Church, vol. 94 (Washington, DC: The Catholic University of America Press, 1996), 5.

approve of nothing but what the Church approves of, namely only four canonical Gospels."[22]

With Origen vigorously defending the authority of the four Gospels, the canonical listing of the authoritative accounts of Jesus's life was sealed.

Athanasius, Bishop of Alexandria (298–373), was also influential.[23] The four Gospels were again affirmed as the authoritative writings of the church. In his Thirty-Ninth Festal Epistle, written in 365 or 367, Athanasius mentions the four Gospels along with the other books of the New Testament: "Again it is not tedious to speak of the [books] of the New Testament. These are, the four Gospels: according to Matthew [*kata Matthaion*], according to Mark [*kata Markon*], according to Luke [*kata Loukon*], according to John [*kata Yōannēn*]."[24] Bishop Athanasius's Festal Epistle clearly indicates that the four Gospels and the rest of the New Testament books, totaling twenty-seven in number, form a uniform canon for the "orthodox" church and excludes other gospels and writings known as the Apocrypha that originated in the early church.[25]

---

22 Origen, *Hom. Luc.* 1.2, in Origen, *Homilies on Luke*, 6.

23 Bishop Athanasius's dogmatic and historical writings are almost all polemic, directed against every aspect of Arianism, the teaching by Arius that Jesus was not truly divine. Athanasius was exiled five times for his defense of the doctrine of Christ's divinity. As bishop of Alexandria, Athanasius used to send his annual letters to the churches in his diocese, called a "festal letter." Such letters were used to fix the dates of Christian festivals such as Lent and Easter and to discuss matters of general interest. In one of his festal letters, Athanasius listed what he believed were the books (twenty-seven in number) that should constitute the New Testament canon. One of his major contributions is his *Life of St. Anthony*, which helped to shape the Christian ideal of monasticism. See P. Schaff, ed., *Athanasius: Select Works and Letters by Athanasius* (Grand Rapids, MI: Christian Classics Ethereal Library, 1892).

24 Athanasius, *Ep. fest.* 39.5, in J. Kirchhofer, *Quellensammlung zur Geschichte des Neutestamentlichen Kannons bis auf Hieronymus* (Zurich: Meyer and Zeller, 1844), 7–9; ET: *Canonicity: A Collection of Early Testimonies to the Canonical Books of the New Testament*, trans. A. H. Charteris (Edinburgh: William Blackwood, 1880), 13–15. For a discussion of Athanasius's Festal Letter, see D. Brakke, "A New Fragment of Athanasius's Thirty-Ninth Festal Letter: Heresy, Apocrypha, and the Canon," *HTR* 103 (2010): 47–66.

25 For the study of the development of the biblical canon in early Christianity, see W. R. Farmer†, "Reflections on Jesus and the New Testament Canon," in *Resourcing New Testament Studies: Literary, Historical, and Theological Essays in Honor of David L. Dungan*, ed. A. J. McNicol, D. B. Peabody, and J. S. Subramanian (London: T. & T. Clark, 2009), 161–78; E. L. Gallagher and J. D. Meade, *The Biblical Canon Lists from Early Christianity: Texts and Analysis* (Oxford: Oxford University Press, 2019).

The inclusion of the four Gospels and the exclusion of all other gospels in the canon of the New Testament affirm what the Church Fathers fought for. The canon of the New Testament was not ultimately decided by any council of the church. However, Bishop Athanasius's Festal Epistle carried great authority, and it remains an important document in the canon of the New Testament in early church history.

Jesus and the Witness of the Four Gospels

Jesus remains the central figure in the accounts of the four Gospels, but the way Jesus is presented differs from one Gospel to another. Although the first three canonical Gospels seem to have used a common source, they differ from one another in the portrayal of Jesus, and John's Gospel narrates the life of Jesus from a considerably different perspective. What does it all mean?

Jesus's Call of the First Disciples

Jesus's call of the first disciples is recorded in all four Gospels (Mt 4:18–22; Mk 1:16–20; Lk 5:1–11; Jn 1:35–51). According to Matthew's Gospel, Jesus called disciples in pairs. First, he called two brothers, Simon and his brother Andrew (Mt 4:18–16). Second, he called another pair, James and his brother John (Mt 4:20–22). Matthew mentions "two brothers" first and then their names individually (Mt 4:19, 21). According to Mark's Gospel, Jesus called Simon and his brother Andrew, and then James and his brother John (Mk 1:16–20). Mark does not use the phrase "two brothers" to introduce them by name. In both Matthew and Mark, the call story occurs by the Sea of Galilee (Mt 4:18; Mk 1:16). According to the Gospel of Luke, Jesus called Simon along with James and John (Lk 5:9–11). Luke does not include Andrew in the first call. In Luke's Gospel the call takes place at the lake of Gennesaret (Lk 5:1). According to John's Gospel, the first disciples of Jesus include an unnamed disciple who was a former disciple of John the Baptist, Andrew, Simon, Philip, and Nathaniel (Jn 1:35–51).

In both Luke and John, the call story is considerably detailed, whereas in Matthew and Mark, the call story is brief. One may conclude that each Gospel writer seems to witness the life of Jesus in similar yet different ways. As Rudolf Schnackenburg says, "The historical Jesus, from whom all the Gospels emanate and whom they reflect from the post-Easter standpoint, is reflected in each Gospel in a different way."[26] The church has chosen the four Gospels as authentic witnesses to the life and ministry of Jesus.

The Confession of the Disciples and Peter

The story of the confession of the disciples and Peter is found in Matthew, Mark, and Luke (Mt 16:13–25; Mk 8:27–33; Lk 9:18–22). It is found in John's Gospel in a different form (Jn 6:66–69). According to Matthew, the event takes place in the district of Caesarea Philippi (Mt 16:13a). In Mark's Gospel it is placed in the villages of Caesarea Philippi and on the way there (Mk 8:27a). In Luke's Gospel it takes place when Jesus was praying alone with his disciples nearby (Lk 9:18a). The question Jesus asked differs slightly from Gospel to Gospel. In Matthew's Gospel Jesus asked, "Who do people say that the Son of Man is?" (Mt 16:13b). In Mark's Gospel, Jesus asked, "Who do people say that I am?" (Mk 8:27b). In Luke's Gospel, Jesus asked, "Who do the crowds say that I am?" (Lk 9:18b). All three Gospels agree on the response the disciples gave, which was that people say that Jesus is John the Baptist, Elijah, or one of the prophets (Mt 16:14; Mk 8:28; Lk 9:19), except Matthew mentions Jeremiah or one of the prophets. When Jesus asked the disciples, "But who do you say that I am?" Simon Peter responded in Matthew's Gospel, "You are the Messiah, the Son of the living God" (Mt 16:16). In Mark's Gospel, Peter answered, "You are the Messiah" (Mk 8:29). In Luke's Gospel, Peter answered, "The Messiah of God" (Lk 9:20).

For Matthew, Jesus is not only the Messiah, but he is the Son of God. For Mark, Jesus is the Messiah. For Luke, Jesus is the Messiah

---

26 R. Schnackenburg, *Jesus in the Gospels: A Biblical Theology*, trans. O. C. Dean Jr. (Louisville: Westminster John Knox Press, 1995), 14. German: R. Schnackenburg, *Die Person Jesu Christi im Spiegel der vier Evangelien* (Freiburg im Breisgau: Verlag Herder, 1993).

of God. In John's Gospel the confession of Peter is placed in the context of Jesus's teaching. Not only the twelve, but also many of Jesus's disciples found his teaching hard to follow, so many of them left Jesus (Jn 6:66). Jesus asked the twelve if they also wished to go away (Jn 6:67). But Simon Peter answered, "Lord, to whom can we go? You have the words of eternal life. We have come to believe and know that you are the Holy One of God" (Jn 6:68–69). All four Gospels testify to the personhood of Jesus in similar yet different modes.

Through the confession of Peter, both Mark and Luke identify Jesus as the Messiah. But the crowds failed to perceive the messianic identity of Jesus. They thought that Jesus was John the Baptist or Elijah or one of the prophets. Herod himself was concerned about the identity of Jesus (Mk 6:14–16; Lk 9:7–9; cf. Mt 14:1–2). Mark and Luke do not contrast the perception of others with the confession of Peter. They simply present the different understandings of Jesus along with Peter's grasp of who Jesus is. As Frank J. Matera comments, "It would appear that the Evangelist envisions a narrative movement from the faulty speculation of Herod and others to Peter's recognition of Jesus's messiahship."[27] So, the Gospel writers are trying to establish the true identity of Jesus. In Matthew's Gospel, in the confession of Peter, Jesus is not just the Messiah, but he is more than the Messiah, namely the Son of the living God. Matthew seems to work backwards. From the point of view of the resurrection, Jesus is recognized as the Son of God, and he was already the Messiah in his earthly existence. As Paul S. Berge says, "For the Evangelist, Peter's confession represents the proclamation of the Easter faith. Jesus is confessed as the Anointed One; the one for whom the eschatological prophets prepared. As the Anointed One, Jesus is confessed as the Son of God, the one in whom God lives among us eschatologically (cf. Mt 1:23)."[28]

Each Gospel writer operates from a particular standpoint from which they attempt to describe the identity of Jesus in light of multiple

---

27 F. J. Matera, "The Incomprehension of the Disciples and Peter's Confession (Mark 6:14–8:30)," *Bib* 70 (1989): 165.

28 P. S. Berge, "Exposition of Matthew 16:13–20," *USQR* 29 (1975): 285.

witnesses to the gospel tradition. In the confession of Peter in John's Gospel, the author seems to urge his readers to look beyond a simple messianic expectation of Peter's confession. For John, Jesus is already the Lord. Jesus is the bearer of words of eternal life. Jesus is the Holy One of God, a divine representative. As William R. Domeris asserts, "Peter's confession forms an ascending trio of claims. Jesus is Lord. He has the words of eternal life. Finally as the true object of belief and knowledge, he is the Holy One of God."[29] By reading the witnesses to Jesus in the four Gospels, one will gain a fuller understanding of the personhood of Jesus.

Jesus's Commissioning of the Disciples

After the resurrection, Jesus himself commissioned his disciples to bear witness and take the gospel to the ends of the earth. Jesus's disciples not only preached what Jesus preached, but they also bore witness to Jesus, who became the content of the Gospel. In Matthew's Gospel, Jesus commanded his disciples to go and make disciples of all nations; baptize them in the trinitarian name of the Father, the Son, and the Holy Spirit; and teach them to observe what Jesus taught (Mt 28:19–20a). He also promised that he would be with them in their mission (Mt 28:20b). In Mark's Gospel, Jesus commanded his disciples to proclaim the gospel to the whole world and to the whole creation and to baptize the believers (Mk 16:15–16). In Luke's Gospel, Jesus commissioned his disciples to bear witness to the gospel of repentance and forgiveness of sins offered in Jesus's name (Lk 24:47–48). In John's Gospel, Jesus commissioned his disciples with these words: "As the Father has sent me, so I send you" (Jn 20:21b). The four Gospels stand as a testimony to what the early apostles preached about Jesus. Although the writers Mark and Luke were not apostles, their association with the apostle Peter and the apostle Paul respectively made their writings apostolic along with the writings of the apostle Matthew and the apostle John.

---

29 W. R. Domeris, "The Confession of Peter According to John 6:69," *TB* 44 (1993): 165.

The Synoptic Gospels and the Source Question

The first three Gospel writers share a common source in addition to sources found in only two Gospels and sources found in only one Gospel. Furthermore, there are many verbal agreements and similar arrangements of the order of materials between Mark and both Matthew and Luke. That is why the first three Gospels are grouped together as the synoptic Gospels. The Greek word *synopsis* (Lat.: *synopticus*) means "seeing together." Johann Jakob Griesbach (1745–1812), in the course of doing textual criticism of the first three Gospels, was the first one to use the word *synoptic* (Ger.: *Synoptisch*).[30] Since that time, the first three Gospels came to be referred to as the "synoptic Gospels."

The first three Gospels are so similar that they can be read side by side in parallel columns.[31] More often John's Gospel is studied independently because its major source is different from that of the synoptic Gospels. The search for the literary sources used by the synoptic Gospel writers has become a vexed and complicated issue. In scholarly circles, it has become known as the "Synoptic Problem." A literary relationship between the synoptic Gospels is based on the following pieces of information: (a) the agreement in order and wording, including verbatim agreement; (b) Triple Tradition materials shared by all three synoptic Gospels (86 pericopes appear in all three Gospels); (c) Double Tradition materials shared by Matthew and Mark (16 pericopes), Luke and Mark (3 pericopes), and Matthew and Luke

---

30 In 1776 J. J. Griesbach published *A Synopsis of the Gospels of Matthew, Mark, and Luke*. In 1789 Griesbach published his defense (Mark was compiled from Matthew and Luke) of the thesis as "A Demonstration that the Whole Gospel of Mark Is Excerpted from the Narratives of Matthew and Luke" (*Commentaio Qua Marci Evangelium totum e Matthaei et Lucae commentariis decerptum esse monstratur*).

31 See B. H. Throckmorton Jr., *Gospel Parallels: A Comparison of the Synoptic Gospels, New Revised Standard Version* (Nashville: Thomas Nelson, 1992); J. B. Orchard, ed., *A Synopsis of the Four Gospels in Greek Arranged According to the Two-Gospel Hypothesis* (Edinburgh: T. & T. Clark Limited, 1983); K. Aland, ed., *Synopsis of the Four Gospels* (New York: American Bible Society, 1985).

(50 pericopes); (d) Special Tradition materials often called *Sondergut* found in Matthew (40 pericopes), Luke (61 pericopes), and Mark (4 pericopes).[32]

In the current textual study, the literary dependence of all three synoptic Gospels came to be explained in four major hypotheses: the two-source hypothesis, the Farrer hypothesis, the two-Gospel hypothesis, and the orality and memory hypothesis.[33] A brief explanation of each hypothesis is furnished here simply to provide basic awareness of this scholarly discussion. Students are advised to peruse the bibliography of the book in note 33 in order to formulate their own conclusions on those matters.

The Two-Source Hypothesis

According to the two-source hypothesis, Matthew and Luke used Mark independently and, in addition, they also used an unknown source called "Q" (Ger.: *Quelle*, meaning "source") to make up their Gospels.[34] As the reader can see, this hypothesis assumes an unknown source (Q) not available to Mark but available to both Matthew and Luke. Extracted from Matthew and Luke it only exists to bolster Markan priority. This hypothesis does not adequately explain the minor agreements between Matthew and Luke if Mark was copied independently by both Matthew and Luke.

The Farrer Hypothesis

According to the Farrer hypothesis, Matthew and Luke used Mark, and Luke also used Matthew.[35] By dispensing with Q, this hypothesis eliminates the need for postulating a nonexistent source to account

---

32　The word *pericope* comes from the Greek word *perikope*, which means "a cutting-out." In biblical context, pericope refers to a passage or a section that serves as a narrative block.

33　For the current discussion on the Synoptic Problem, see S. E. Porter and B. R. Dyer, eds., *The Synoptic Problem: Four Views* (Grand Rapids, MI: Baker Academic, 2016).

34　See C. A. Evans, "The Two Source Hypothesis," in *The Synoptic Problem*, 27–46.

35　See M. Goodacre, "The Farrer Hypothesis," in *The Synoptic Problem*, 47–66.

for the common source shared by Matthew and Luke. This hypothesis makes Luke dependent on Matthew to address the problem of the minor agreements between Matthew and Luke against Mark. However, this hypothesis does not explain why both Matthew and Luke jointly omitted the Special Tradition materials found only in Mark. This hypothesis also does not consider all the Double Tradition materials found only in Matthew and Mark but not shared by Luke, if Luke knew both Matthew and Mark.

The Two-Gospel Hypothesis

According to the two-Gospel hypothesis (also known as the Griesbach hypothesis), Matthew was written first, Luke copied Matthew, and Mark used both Matthew and Luke to produce an abridged version.[36] This hypothesis dispenses with the Q source because Matthew already composed a full Gospel with all the sources that were made available to Luke and Mark.

The two-Gospel hypothesis argues that Mark's Gospel is an abridgment or harmonizing summary of the Jewish-Christian Gospel of Matthew and the Gentile-Jewish-Christian Gospel of Luke. In this way, Mark's Gospel emerged as a Gentile Gospel out of Matthew and Luke.[37] Moreover, this hypothesis takes patristic evidence into consideration. The early Church Fathers unanimously testified that Matthew was the first written Gospel, which became the source for Luke and Mark.[38] However, this hypothesis has been deemed

---

36 See D. B. Peabody, "The Two Source Hypothesis," in *The Synoptic Problem*, 67–88. Recently, Allan J. McNicol wrote about the legacy of William R. Farmer, who advocated for the two-Gospel hypothesis. See A. J. McNicol, "After Fifty Years: The Legacy of William Farmer's Solution to the Synoptic Problem in Memory of David Barrett Peabody," *ResQ* 61 (2019): 193–205. For the solution to the Synoptic Problem proposed by William R. Farmer, see W. R. Farmer, *The Synoptic Problem: A Critical Analysis* (Dillsboro, NC: Western North Carolina Press, 1976).

37 Allan J. McNicol persuasively argues how Mark seems to move from the mission to Israel into predominately a Gentile mission. See A. J. McNicol, "The Importance of the Synoptic Problem for Interpreting the Gospels," *EvJTh* 1 (2007): 13–24.

38 For a summary of the patristic testimony on the priority of the Gospels, see D. B. Peabody et al., *One Gospel from Two: Mark's Use of Matthew and Luke. A Demonstration*

problematic by some, because one wonders why a shorter Gospel was needed in the early church if Matthew and Luke already existed.

The Orality and Memory Hypothesis

According to the orality and memory hypothesis (also known as the multiple-source hypothesis), all three Gospels used multiple sources along with the oral tradition available to the authors. The problem is that it multiplies the number of hypothetical works used by the Gospel writers. It often assumes that there was a proto-Mark (the Triple Tradition Source) that was used by Matthew, Mark, and Luke.[39] Matthew, Mark, and Luke may not even be dependent on one another. This hypothesis does not prove the existence of multiple sources prior to the composition of the synoptic Gospels. One can always explain something by creating multiple sources.

The Healing of Peter's Mother-in-Law—A Test Case

Let us see how close examination of a pericope in the synoptic Gospels opens up the possibility that they are interconnected. The healing of Peter's mother-in-law occurs in all three synoptic Gospels (Mt 8:14–15; Mk 1:29–31; Lk 4:38–39). According to scholars, this is based on the Triple Tradition common to Matthew, Mark, and Luke, to which the Q source does not apply. The text is presented below with solid underline that represents agreements by all three Gospel writers, dotted underline that illustrates agreements between Luke and Mark, dashed underline that indicates agreements between Matthew and Mark, wave underline that shows agreements between Matthew and Luke, and bold text that shows differences from other passages.

---

by the Research Team of the International Institute for Gospel Studies (Harrisburg, PA: Trinity Press International, 2002), 46–54.

39 See R. Riesner, "The Orality and Memory Hypothesis," in Porter and Dyer, eds., The Synoptic Problem, 89–112.

Mt 8:14–15

[14] When Jesus entered Peter's house, he saw his **mother-in-law** lying in bed with a **fever**; [15] he touched her hand, and the fever left her, and she got up and **began to serve** him.

Lk 4:38–39

[38] After leaving the synagogue he entered Simon's house. Now Simon's **mother-in-law** was suffering from a high **fever**, and they asked him about her. [39] Then he stood over her and rebuked the fever, and it left her. Immediately she got up and **began to serve** them.

Mk 1:29–31

[29] As soon as they left the synagogue, they entered the house of Simon and Andrew, with James and John. [30] Now Simon's **mother-in-law** was in bed with a **fever**, and they told him about her at once. [31] He came and took her by hand and lifted her up. Then the fever left her, and she **began to serve** them.

Just looking at the three passages, Mark has more words than Matthew and Luke. Although Mark is the shortest synoptic Gospel, one may be surprised to know that often Mark gives the longest account for many of his pericopes. In this particular story, Mark uses fifty-nine words, Luke uses forty-five words, and Matthew uses thirty-three words. If Mark is copied by both Matthew and Luke independently, one would expect both Matthew and Luke to produce a narrative somewhat closer to what Mark wrote. But the way the narrative appears in the Gospels shows that Mark seems to be aware of both Matthew and Luke. Mark seems to switch between following Matthew and Luke, which is only possible if Mark was writing third. Mark starts by agreeing with Luke (Mk 1:29; Lk 4:38) and ends the narrative by aligning with Matthew (Mt 8:15; Mk 1:31).[40] In addition, Mark alone maintains some of the disciples' names, such as "Andrew, with James and John"

---

40 See Peabody et al., *One Gospel from Two*, 90–91.

(Mk 1:29); those names are missing in both Matthew and Luke. Several other descriptions in Mark, such as "He came . . . and lifted her up," are jointly omitted by both Matthew and Luke (Mk 1:31). The joint omission of the materials of Mark by both Matthew and Luke could suggest that Mark was writing third. Otherwise, either Matthew or Luke most likely would have produced verbatim portions of the Markan narrative. On the other hand, in other parallel narratives Mark seems to conflate both Matthew and Luke and decorates his narratives with additional materials. The example here is typical of his editorial procedure.

The similarities and differences that exist among the synoptic Gospels lead to the conclusion that the first three Evangelists utilized sources. The interrelations between the synoptic Gospels suggest that one Gospel became a major source for the second Gospel and that the first and second Gospels became the major source for the third Gospel. Readers are encouraged to work through the pericopes and choose a hypothesis that best takes into account both the literary and patristic evidence. No single hypothesis is unanimously agreed upon among scholars. In studying the Gospel accounts for teaching and preaching, readers are encouraged to do their research and raise questions similar to those noted above. This process of inquiry and research explains the complexities of the Gospel narratives (cf. 2 Tm 2:15).

Relation of the Synoptic Gospels to John's Gospel

To complete the sources on the life of Jesus, one must study the Gospel of John. Although John uses sources independent of the synoptic Gospels, John has a number of parallels with the synoptic Gospels, mostly with Matthew's Gospel, but differs considerably from them in content. Therefore, John's Gospel is seldom drawn into conversation on the source question in the same way as the synoptics are compared. Scholars like Raymond E. Brown agree that John's Gospel presupposes the synoptic Gospels, but at the same time John is not directly dependent on them.[41] The Gospel of John is similar to the synoptic Gospels in that all four witness to the life and ministry of Jesus, and all four cover the major categories of Jesus's life and ministry: his birth (Matthew and Luke; John, theologically), his public ministry, and his death and resurrection (Matthew, Mark, Luke, and John). John's Gospel agrees especially with Matthew's on the overall framework of the life of Jesus.[42] However, John's way of tracing the itinerancy of Jesus's ministry makes it extremely difficult to display in all Gospel synopses.[43] Therefore, the literary dependence of the synoptic Gospels is usually studied independently of the Gospel of John.

The following parallels are found between the synoptic Gospels and John's Gospel:

John the Baptist (Mt 3:1–6; Mk 1:2–8; Lk 3:1–6; Jn 1:19–23)

John's Preaching (Mt 3:11–12; Mk 1:7–8; Lk 3:15–18; Jn 1:24–28)

Baptism of Jesus (Mt 3:13–17; Mk 1:9–11; Lk 3:21–22; Jn 1:29–34)

Journey into Galilee (Mt 4:12; Mk 1:14a; Lk 4:14a; Jn 4:1–3)

Ministry in Galilee (Mt 4:13–17; Mk 1:14b–15; Lk 4:14b–15; Jn 4:43–46a)

Healing of the Paralytic (Mt 9:1–8; Mk 2:1–12; Lk 5:17–26; Jn 5:8–9a)

Healing of the Centurion's Son (Mt 8:5–13; Lk 7:1–10; Jn 4:46b–54)

Woman with the Ointment (Mt 26:6–13; Mk 14:3–9; Lk 7:36–50; Jn 12:1–8)

---

41 R. E. Brown, *The Gospel According to John I–XII: A New Translation with Introduction and Commentary* (New York: Doubleday, 1966), XLIV–XLVII. For other theories of John's dependence on the synoptics, see J. D. Dvorak, "The Relationship Between John and The Synoptic Gospels," *JETS* 41 (1988): 201–13.

42 For John's use of Matthew's Gospel, see J. Barker, *John's Use of Matthew*, Emerging Scholars (Minneapolis: Fortress Press, 2015).

43 John Bernard Orchard, who vigorously defended the two-Gospel hypothesis, produced a synopsis of all four Gospels according to this hypothesis. See Orchard, *A Synopsis of the Four Gospels in Greek Arranged According to the Two Gospel Hypothesis*.

Feeding the Five Thousand (Mt 14:13–21; Mk 6:32–44; Lk 9:10a–17; Jn 6:1–15)

Jesus's Walking on the Water (Mt 14:22–33; Mk 6:45–52; Jn 6:16–21)

Jesus's Healings at Gennesaret (Mt 14:34–36; Mk 6:53–56; Jn 6:22–25)

Peter's Confession (Mt 16:13–20; Mk 8:27–30; Lk 9:18–21; Jn 6:67–71)

Jesus's Entry into Jerusalem (Mt 21:1–9; Mk 11:1–10; Lk 19:28–40; Jn 12:12–19)

Jesus's Cleansing of the Temple (Mt 21:10–17; Mk 11:15–17; Lk 19:45–46; Jn 2:13–17)

Anointing at Bethany (Mt 26:6–13; Mk 14:3–9; Lk 7:36–50; Jn 12:1–8)

Jesus's Prediction of His Betrayal (Mt 26:21–25; Mk 14:18–21; Lk 22:21–23; Jn 13:21–30)

Jesus's Prediction of Peter's Denial (Mt 26:30–35; Mk 14:26–31; Lk 22:31–34; Jn 13:36–38)

Jesus's Arrest (Mt 26:46–56; Mk 14:43–52; Lk 22:47–53; Jn 18:2–12)

Jesus before the Sanhedrin (Mt 26:57–68; Mk 14:53–65; Lk 22:54–71; Jn 18:13–24)

Peter's Denial (Mt 26:69–75; Mk 14:66–72; Lk 22:56–62; Jn 18:25–27)

Jesus's Trial before Pilate (Mt 27:11–14; Mk 15:2–5; Lk 23:2–5; Jn 18:29–38)

Jesus or Barabbas? (Mt 27:15–23; Mk 15:6–14; Lk 23:17–23; Jn 18:39–40)

Jesus's Crucifixion (Mt 27:33–37; Mk 15:22–26; Lk 23:33–34; Jn 19:17b–27)

Jesus's Death (Mt 27:45–54; Mk 15:33–39; Lk 23:44–48; Jn 19:28–30)

Jesus's Burial (Mt 27:57–61; Mk 15:42–57; Lk 23:50–56; Jn 19:38–42)

Women at the Tomb (Mt 28:1–8; Mk 16:1–8; Lk 24:1–12; Jn 20:1–13)

Jesus's Appearance to the Women (Mt 28:9–10; Mk 16:9–11; Lk 24:10–11; Jn 20:14–18)

The above parallels between the synoptic Gospels and John's Gospel only appear to show that John would have been aware of the general content of the synoptic Gospels, whether Matthew only, or Matthew and Luke, or Matthew, Luke, and Mark. Since John was probably writing after the publications of the synoptic Gospels, it would be reasonable to conclude that he was aware of what at least some of the synoptics said, even if his task appears to be to place Jesus's life in a more theological dimension.

Four Gospels and the Rest of the New Testament

Other New Testament writings, such as the Acts of the Apostles, Paul's letters, Hebrews, the Catholic letters, and the book of Revelation, do echo some things in the Gospel tradition. What appears in the rest of the New Testament seems to be theologically compatible with the gospel tradition, although it is very difficult to determine the literary connection between the canonical Gospels and the rest of the New Testament. There are only a few places where Jesus's tradition in the synoptic accounts is explicitly echoed. The first one is Paul's letter to the Corinthians (1 Cor 11:23–26). Paul refers to the Lord's Supper tradition, which has parallels in the synoptic Gospels (Mt 26:26–28; Mk 14:22–24; Lk 22:19–20). The text in 1 Corinthians 11:23–26 reads:

> For I received from the Lord what I also handed on to you, that the Lord Jesus on the night when he was betrayed took a loaf of bread,

and when he had given thanks, he broke it and said, "This is my body that is for you. Do this in remembrance of me." In the same way he took the cup also, after supper, saying, "This cup is the new covenant in my blood. Do this, as often as you drink it, in remembrance of me." For as often as you eat this bread and drink the cup, you proclaim the Lord's death until he comes.

Paul claims that he received the Lord's Supper directly from authoritative tradition stretching back to the Lord. The phrases such as, "Do this in remembrance of me" and "the new covenant in my blood" are found only in the Lukan account of the Lord's Supper (1 Cor 11:24b, 25; cf. Lk 22:19b, 20b). It is generally regarded that Paul's quotation is from early tradition since the synoptics were probably written after Paul's death. Even if the synoptics did exist prior to Paul's death, Paul probably did not have access to the canonical Gospels.

Second, the transfiguration of Jesus is echoed in 2 Peter 1:16–18 (cf. Mt 17:1–9; Mk 9:2–10; Lk 9:28–36). The text in 2 Peter 1:16–18 reads,

For we did not follow cleverly devised myths when we made known to you the power and coming of the Lord Jesus Christ, but we had been eyewitnesses of his majesty. For he received honor and glory from God the Father when that voice was conveyed to him by the Majestic Glory, saying, "This is my Son, my Beloved, with whom I am well pleased." We ourselves heard this voice come from heaven, while we were with him on the holy mountain.

The second letter of Peter claims to be closing words to the church. It echoes a Matthean version of the transfiguration of Jesus. The words of the heavenly voice in 2 Peter 1:12 comes close to the Matthean version of the transfiguration narrative (cf. Mt 17:5). The voice from heaven reads as follows,

2 Peter 1:17b: "This is my Son, my Beloved, with whom I am well pleased."

Matthew 17:5: "This is my Son, the Beloved; with him I am well pleased."

Mark 9:7: "This is my Son, the Beloved."

Luke 9:35: "This is my Son, my Chosen."

It seems that the author of 2 Peter uses the Matthean version of the transfiguration story not as an event of the past but as a foreshadow or prophecy of the *parousia* (second coming) of Jesus Christ.[44]

Apart from those two direct references to the synoptic tradition, the following are typical of some of the allusions to the Gospel tradition found in the rest of the New Testament:

Let us not fall asleep (1 Thes 5:6; cf. Mt 24:42; Mk 13:17; Lk 21:34, 36)

The Lord's command on divorce (1 Cor 7:10–11; cf. Mt 5:31–32; Mk 10:11–12; Lk 16:18)

Jesus as a descendant from David (Rom 1:2; cf. Mt 1:1)

Love one another (Rom 13:8–10; cf. Mt 22:34–40; Mk 12:18–36; Lk 10:25–28; Jn 13:34; 15:12, 17)

Clean and unclean (Rom 14:14; cf. Mt 15:11; Mk 7:15)

Jesus's teaching on human conduct (Rom 12:14–21; cf. Mt 5:38–48; Lk 6:27–36)

Jesus's teaching on worry (Phil 4:6; cf. Mt 6:25; Lk 12:22)

Jesus's exaltation (Heb 1:3; cf. Mt 22:44)

Jesus's prayer (Heb 5:7; cf. Mt 26:44; Mk 14:32–43; Lk 22:40–46)

Curtain of the temple (Heb 6:19; cf. Mt 27:51; Mk 15:38)

Christ's intercession (Heb 7:25; cf. Jn 17:9)

Hospitality to strangers (Heb 13:2; cf. Mt 25:35)

Jesus's crucifixion outside the city gate (Heb 13:12; cf. Mt 21:39; Lk 20:15)

---

44 See J. H. Neyrey, "An Apologetic Use of the Transfiguration in 2 Peter 1:16–21," *CBQ* 42 (1980): 504–19.

Walk in darkness, walk in light (1 Jn 1:6–7; cf. Jn 3:19–21)

No one has ever seen God (1 Jn 4:12; cf. Jn 1:18)

The coming of the Son of Man (Rv 1:7; cf. Mt 16:27; Mk 8:38; Lk 9:26)

Judas's death (Acts 1:18–19; cf. Mt 27:3–10)

John's baptism (Acts 19:3–4; cf. Mt 3:11; Mk 1:8; Lk 3:16; Jn 1:26)

Thus, even though the exact wording of the Gospels is hardly quoted precisely in the rest of the New Testament, the gospel tradition is regularly echoed by them. In other words, the rest of the New Testament writings do bear witness to the life of Jesus in an indirect way. The New Testament writers build on the foundation that has already been laid in the four Gospel accounts.

Summary

1. The four Gospels—Matthew, Mark, Luke, and John—serve as a witness to the life and ministry of Jesus Christ. The inclusion of the four Gospels in the canon of the New Testament represents the work of the early Church Fathers who fought to include only these four that represented "orthodoxy" and to exclude all other gospels that deviated from the orthodox doctrine of the early church. They also argued strongly that only the four Gospels authentically bear witness to the actual Jesus of history.

2. Each Gospel writer looks at the life of Jesus from a different perspective. That is why one will find four attestations to the same Jesus, who remains the central figure in the gospel story. Four accounts make the proclamation of the good news of Jesus Christ authentic in the life of the church. Thus it is necessary to study all four Gospels in order to get a comprehensive understanding of who Jesus is in relation to faith and proclamation of the church.

3. The question of the priority of the Gospels continues to occupy a unique place in scholarly circles. Anyone who reads the four

Gospels, especially the synoptics, will encounter the priority question because those Gospels are similar yet different from one another. Various hypotheses are proposed to account for the interrelation of the synoptic Gospels. This issue is important. If it could be resolved we could be more certain how the events of Jesus's life were preserved and transmitted. So it is necessary for readers to be aware of each hypothesis and arrive at a viable explanation as to how the earliest accounts of the sayings and deeds of Jesus were transmitted.

4. The fourth Gospel is seldom drawn into the source question, be-cause John's Gospel uses different sources to compose a gospel that would dwell upon a Christology higher than the synoptics. However, the fourth Gospel seems to be dependent on some of the materials in the synoptics.

5. Paul and other New Testament writers echo traditions that are found in the four Gospels. There is little doubt that the Gospels are foundational. The early Church Fathers placed the four Gospels at the beginning of the canon of the New Testament to show that the gospel of Jesus Christ should be read first before the other writings of the New Testament.

For Discussion

1. Should we include other apocryphal gospels, such as the *Gospel of Thomas*, the *Gospel of Mary*, the *Infancy Gospel of Thomas*, and the *Gospel of Truth* in the New Testament canon? Why or why not?

2. Read the Healing of the Paralytic in parallels (Mt 9:1–8; Mk 2:1–12; Lk 5.17–26) and discuss which gospel account could have been written first and then copied by the other two Gospel writers. What is your conclusion about the priority of the synoptic Gospels?

3. Read Jesus's Cleansing of the Temple as it appears in each Gospel (Mt 21:10–17; Mk 11:15–17; Lk 19:45–46; Jn 2:13–17). Note the similarities and differences. What does each Gospel writer try to

communicate to the readers in the first century? Describe a place where you want Jesus to act the way he acted in the Temple. How will you imitate Jesus in your life, in church, and in society?

4. Read the Letter of Jude. Can you find any allusions to any one of the four Gospels?

5. Do you agree with John Wesley that Mark presupposes Matthew? In what ways would Mark have used Matthew? Discuss your findings.

2

The Gospel According to
Matthew

Introduction

C oncerning the four Gospels which alone are uncontroverted in
the Church of God under heaven, I have learned by tradition
that the Gospel according to Matthew, who was at one time a publican and afterwards an Apostle of Jesus Christ, was written first; and
that he composed it in the Hebrew tongue and published it for the
converts from Judaism."[1] Thus writes Origen in his *Commentary on
the Gospel of Matthew* (*Commentarium in evangelium Matthaei*).
The Greek canonical Gospel of Matthew may very well represent
the Hebrew Gospel of Matthew, which possibly eroded in influence
during the process of transmission from the Palestinian Jewish audience to the Gentile audience. Even in the Greek version, Matthew's
Gospel is very much Jewish in its portrayal of Jesus as the promised
Messiah of Israel.

The purpose of Matthew's Gospel is to demonstrate to readers
that Jesus is the Messiah as foretold in the Scriptures and that Jesus is
the one who saves people from their sins (cf. Mt 1:21). This Gospel
was written for people familiar with the Jewish Scriptures, both the
Law of Moses and the Prophets. Matthew's Gospel quotes more from
the Old Testament than any other Gospel. It is the perfect book to
bridge the gap between the Old Testament and the New Testament.
In his famous Sermon on the Mount, highlighting the importance

---

1   Origen, *Comm. Matt.*, Book I, in *Ante-Nicene Fathers*, vol. 9, trans. J. Patrick, ed. A.
    Menzies, 4th ed. (Peabody, MA: Hendrickson Publishers, 1999), 412.

of the Torah, Jesus says, "Do not think that I have come to abolish the law or the prophets; I have come not to abolish but to fulfill" (Mt 5:17). It is an artistically written Gospel that comprises the entire life and ministry of Jesus Christ.

Authorship

Traditionally, the church identified the author of Matthew's Gospel as Matthew the tax collector. The first canonical Gospel records the call of Matthew this way: "As Jesus was walking along, he saw a man called Matthew sitting at the tax booth; and he said to him, 'Follow me.' And he got up and followed him" (Mt 9:9). The parallel passages found in Mark and Luke omit Matthew's name but identify him as "Levi sitting at the tax office" (Mk 2:14; Lk 5:27). Further, in the listing of the names of the twelve apostles, only the Gospel of Matthew attributes the title "the tax collector" to Matthew, whereas Mark and Luke mention only Matthew's name without the title (Mt 10:3; cf. Mk 3:18; Lk 6:15). Among the synoptic Gospels, only Matthew's Gospel reports the payment of tax to the Romans: "When they reached Capernaum, the collectors of the temple tax came to Peter and said, 'Does your teacher [Jesus] not pay the temple tax?'" (Mt 17:24). It suggests that the author of the Gospel of Matthew is interested in the work of Matthew as the tax collector and worker in financial details.

In general, the author of Matthew's Gospel is thoroughly rooted in Judaism. The author often quotes from the Old Testament and shows that Jesus is the fulfillment of the messianic prophecy (Mt 1:23 // Is 7:14; Mt 2:6 // Mi 5:2; Mt 2:15 // Hos 11:1; Mt 2:18 // Jer 31:15; Mt 2:23 // Is 11:1; Mt 4:15–16 // Is 9:12; Mt 8:17 // Is 53:4; Mt 12:1821 // Is 42:14; Mt 13:14–15 // Is 6:9–10; Mt 13:35 // Ps 78:2; Mt 21:5 // Zec 9:9; Mt 26:56 // no parallel text; Mt 27:9–10 // Zec 11:13).[2]

---

2 For a discussion of the fulfillment quotations in Matthew's Gospel, see K. Stendahl, *The School of St Matthew and Its Use of the Old Testament*, ASNU 20 (Lund, Sweden: C. W. K. Gleerup, 1954; Philadelphia: Fortress Press, 1968); J. Nkhoma, *The Use of*

The author emphasizes obedience to the law and the prophets as normative for the disciple of Jesus (Mt 5:17–20; 7:12; 28:16–20).[3] The author also focuses on Jesus's ministry within Galilee and does not pay much attention to his work with Gentiles as does Luke. Thus, the author is mostly concerned with Jesus's ministry to the Jews. Among the synoptic Gospels, only Matthew's Gospel mentions Jesus's charging the twelve disciples not to go to the Gentiles in his initial commission to the Twelve. Matthew shows Jesus saying, "Go nowhere among the Gentiles, and enter no town of the Samaritans, but go rather to the lost sheep of the house of Israel" (Mt 10:5–6). From the details considered above, Matthew the tax collector best matches the author of the first canonical Gospel.[4]

The early church is unanimous in their acceptance of Matthew as the author of the first Gospel. As stated in chapter 1, Bishop Papias of Hierapolis was the first one to testify that Matthew wrote the oracles (Gk: *logia*) in the Hebrew language, and each one interpreted them as best he could. Other Church Fathers, like Clement of Alexandria, Irenaeus, and Origen, confirmed the widespread belief that Matthew was the author of the first Gospel. Scholars like the nineteenth-century German Ferdinand Christian Baur argue that the first canonical Gospel of Matthew constitutes the basic text (Ger.: *Grundschrift*) written in the Hebrew language from which the Greek text evolved.[5] Baur goes on to say that the Gospel bearing the name of the apostle Matthew assumes Matthew as the author of the basic text or as the author

---

the *Fulfillment Quotations in the Gospel According to Matthew*, Kachere Theses, no. 4 (Malawi: Mzuni Publications, 2006).

3 Cf. D. B. Peabody et al., *One Gospel from Two: Mark's Use of Matthew and Luke. A Demonstration by the Research Team of the International Institute for Gospel Studies* (Harrisburg, PA: Trinity Press International, 2002), 60. Also see L. Gaston, "The Messiah of Israel As Teacher of the Gentiles," *Int* 29 (1975): 24–40.

4 W. F. Albright and C. S. Mann agree that the essence of the first Gospel fits the author of Matthew's Gospel as Matthew, the tax collector and the Levite. See Albright and Mann, *Matthew: A New Translation with Introduction and Commentary* (New York: Doubleday, 1971), clxxxiii–clxxxiv.

5 F. C. Baur, *Lectures on New Testament Theology*, trans. R. F. Brown, ed. P. C. Hodgson (Oxford: Oxford University Press, 2016), 77.

who had been involved in the composition of such basic text.[6] It is certainly plausible to accept that the first canonical Gospel was written by the apostle Matthew, who once was the tax collector and became a disciple of Jesus.

Date, Purpose, and Place of Writing

The internal evidence indicates that Matthew's Gospel could have been written prior to the destruction of the Jewish Temple in 70 CE. Jesus, in Matthew's Gospel, approves the payment of the Temple tax (Mt 17:24–27). Jesus tells Peter to go to the sea and to catch a fish. Upon catching it and opening its mouth, Peter will find a shekel, which he will give to the tax collectors. This miraculous saying of Jesus is found only in Matthew's Gospel and suggests that the Jewish Temple was still in existence when the Gospel was written. After its destruction, the Temple tax was shifted to the temple of Jupiter Capitolinus in Rome as mentioned by Josephus.[7]

An additional piece of evidence is that at the cleansing of the Temple, Jesus refers to the situation of the Temple in the present tense: "but you are making it a den of robbers" (Mt 21:13b; cf. Jer 7:11). But both Mark and Luke put it in the past tense: "but you have made it a den of robbers" (Mk 11:17; Lk 19:46).

Matthew talks about the rending of the Temple curtain at the time of Jesus's death, followed by the earthquake, the splitting of the rock, and the resurrection of the saints, including their entrance to the holy city and their appearance to many (Mt 27:51–53; cf. Mk 15:38). Matthew begins the series of events following Jesus's death with a conjunction and a demonstrative particle ("And behold").[8] Again, Matthew shows an awareness of the existence of the Temple

---

6 Baur, 77.

7 Josephus, *J.W.* 7.6.6. Josephus (37–100 CE) was a Jewish historian. His major works included *Jewish Wars, Antiquities of the Jews,* and *Against Apion.* For the complete works of Josephus, see *The Works of Josephus: Complete and Unabridged,* trans. W. Whiston, updated ed. (Nashville: Thomas Nelson Publishers, 1998).

8 See M. de Jonge, "Matthew 27:51 in Early Christian Exegesis," *HTR* 79 (1986): 67–79.

by alluding to the rending of the Temple curtain but not to destruction of the Temple building itself.

Patristic evidence suggests that Matthew could have been written prior to 60 CE. Clement of Alexandria writes that "Matthew had first preached to Hebrews, and when he was on the point of going to others he transmitted in writing in his native language the gospel according to himself, and thus supplied by writing the lack of his own presence to those from whom he was sent."[9] The testimony of Clement suggests that Matthew wrote his Gospel before he left for other nations. Matthew's journey to other nations would have happened before the destruction of Jerusalem, particularly during the time of the apostle Paul's first visit to Jerusalem after his conversion. Paul's conversion probably took place around 34 CE. Then Paul went to Jerusalem after three years. In his letter to the Galatians, Paul says, "Then after three years I did go up to Jerusalem to visit Cephas and stayed with him fifteen days; but I did not see any other apostle except James the Lord's brother" (Gal 1:18–19). I take the position that most of the apostles, including Matthew, left Jerusalem prior to Paul's arrival in 37 CE. In that case, Matthew may have composed the Gospel around 36 CE before he left for other nations.[10]

Irenaeus testified that "Matthew also issued a written gospel among the Hebrews in their own dialect, while Peter and Paul were preaching at Rome, and laying the foundations of the Church."[11] Irenaeus's assertion suggests that Matthew was already in existence when Peter and Paul were preaching in Rome. Both Peter and Paul probably died as martyrs in Rome around 64 CE. According to the Acts of the Apostles,

---

9 Eusebius, *Hist. eccl.* 3.24.6.

10 According to *Pseudo-Abdias*, a Latin manuscript containing accounts of the lives of the apostles, Matthew traveled to Naddaver, Ethiopia, where he had a successful ministry including baptism and church planting; he died there as a martyr. For a discussion on Pseudo-Abdias, see E. Rose, "'*Abdias Scriptor Vitarum Sanctorum Apostolorum*': The Collection of Pseudo Abdias Reconsidered," *RHT* 8 (2003): 227–68.

11 Irenaeus, *Haer.* 3.1.1, in *The Apostolic Fathers with Justin Martyr and Irenaeus*, ed. A. C. Coxe, vol. 1 of *Ante-Nicene Fathers*, ed. A. Roberts and J. Donaldson (Peabody, MA: Hendrickson Publishers, 1999), 414.

at the end of Paul's last missionary journey, he arrives in Rome, where he freely preaches the gospel without any hindrance (Acts 28:30). Scholars like Robert Jewett place Paul's landing in Rome around 61 CE.[12] If Paul arrived in Rome around 60 CE, then Matthew's Gospel may have been written prior to Paul's arrival. Considering both internal and patristic evidence together, the composition of Matthew's Gospel may be dated anywhere between 36 and 60 CE.

Matthew's Gospel is clearly composed for a Jewish audience by making use of Jewish life and Jewish modes of thinking. It is an apologetic work intended to explain that Jesus was the long-awaited Jewish Messiah, while at the same time explaining why Jesus was not accepted by Israel, to whom he was sent. Matthew also includes Jesus's ministry among the Gentiles and Jesus's commissioning of the eleven disciples to a worldwide ministry to all nations. This suggests that Matthew wrote to encourage both Jewish and Gentile Christians in their faith in Jesus as both Messiah and *Emmanuel* ("with us God") and to undertake a worldwide mission to proclaim the gospel of Jesus Christ.

Matthew makes use of Old Testament quotations to describe the life of Jesus as fulfillment of prophecy. He uses the phrase "kingdom of heaven" as opposed to the phrase "kingdom of God" primarily used in the Gospels of Mark and Luke. As a Jew himself, Matthew substitutes "heaven" for "God" because the Jews widely avoided the pronunciation of the divine name. However, on four occasions Matthew uses the phrase "kingdom of God" rather than the more frequent use of "kingdom of heaven" (Mt 12:28; 19:24; 21:31, 43).[13] The Sermon on the Mount recollects the giving of the law on Mount Sinai, whereas in the Gospel of Luke Jesus gives the Sermon on the Plain (Mt 5:1; cf. Lk 6:17). Jesus declares that he has come not to abolish the law or the prophet but to fulfill it (Mt 5:17). The Parable of the Wicked Tenants alludes to Jesus's rejection by his own people

---

12   See R. Jewett, *A Chronology of Paul's Life* (Philadelphia: Fortress Press, 1979), 44.

13   For discussion of Matthew's use of the phrase "kingdom of God," see J. C. Thomas, "The Kingdom of God in the Gospel According to Matthew," *NTS* 39 (1993): 136–46.

and his subsequent exaltation (Mt 21:33–44). All these features point toward a Jewish origin of Matthew's Gospel, which was likely written for a primarily Jewish-Christian audience in order to redefine God's promised salvation in light of the coming of Jesus as the Messiah.

Earlier, Clement of Alexandria remarked that Matthew preached the gospel to Hebrews and wrote his Gospel before he left for other nations. This suggests that Matthew's Gospel may have been written in Judea because of its close affinity with the heart of Judaism. It is possible that a copy of Matthew's Gospel may have gone to Caesarea, near Jerusalem. Jerome asserted that Matthew first composed his Gospel in Hebrew, a copy of which was preserved in the library at Caesarea.[14] It is not clear from Jerome if he thought that the Hebrew Gospel of Matthew was composed in Caesarea;[15] it is more likely that Jerome's remarks point to the location of the Hebrew Gospel of Matthew preserved in the library of Caesarea but not to the composition of Matthew's Gospel there.

Among the Church Fathers, Bishop Ignatius of Antioch was the first one to allude to Matthew's Gospel. In his *Epistle to the Ephesians*, Bishop Ignatius refers to "a star above all other stars" at the manifestation of God in human form (*Ign. Eph.* 19.1–3; cf. Mt 2:2). In his *Epistle to the Smyrnaeans*, Bishop Ignatius alludes to Jesus's virgin birth as "He was truly born of a virgin" (*Ign. Smryn.* 1.1; cf. Mt 1:20–23). Again, in his *Epistle to Polycarp*, Bishop Ignatius alludes to Jesus's words: "Be in all things wise as a serpent, and harmless always as a dove" (*Ign. Pol.* 2.2; cf. Mt 10:16). This suggests that the

---

14 Jerome, *Vir. ill.* 3.1–2: "Matthew, surnamed Levi, first publican, then apostle, composed a gospel of Christ at first published in Judea in Hebrew for the sake of those of the circumcision who believed, but this was afterwards translated into Greek, though by what author is uncertain. Moreover, the Hebrew itself has been preserved until the present day in the library at Caesarea which Pamphilus the martyr so diligently gathered. I have also had the opportunity of having the volume described to me by the Nazarenes of Beroea, a city of Syria, who use it." Saint Jerome, *On Illustrious Men*, trans. T. P. Halton, *The Fathers of the Church*, vol. 100 (Washington, DC: The Catholic University of America Press, 1999), 10.

15 For a view of a Caesarean province for the composition of the Gospel of Matthew, see B. T. Viviano, "Where Was the Gospel According to St. Matthew Written?" *CBQ* 41 (1979): 533–46.

Gospel of Matthew was already known to the church in Antioch and that Bishop Ignatius quoted from it. Early patristic evidence did not place Matthew in Antioch, where he could have composed the Gospel. Given the presence of the apostle Matthew in Judea, and his strong familiarity with Jewish life and customs, Judea is the most plausible location for the earliest form of this Gospel.

Main Themes

The opening words of Matthew's Gospel in Greek read: "An account of the genealogy (Genesis) of Jesus the Messiah, the son of David, the son of Abraham" (Mt 1:1). This statement applies not just to the genealogy section but to the entire Gospel of Matthew.[16] By attributing the title "son of Abraham" to Jesus at the very start of his Gospel, Matthew not only links his Gospel to the Old Testament but also likens it to the first book of Genesis in the Christian tradition. Both Isaac and Jesus are the promised children, both go obediently to their sacrificial deaths, and both are saved miraculously by God (cf. Gn 21–22).[17] For Matthew, Jesus is also the son of David. As the son of David, Jesus fulfills the prophecy of Nathan that he came to establish God's kingdom (cf. 2 Sm 7:12–13).

Matthew's Gospel is an ecclesiastical one. The word *church* (Gk: *ekklēsia*) occurs three times in Matthew's Gospel only. The first occurrence is in the context of Peter's confession at Caesarea Philippi. Jesus says to Peter, "And I tell you, you are Peter, and on this rock I will build my church, and the gates of Hades will not prevail against it" (Mt 16:18). The second occurrence is in the context of disciplining members of the church. Jesus proposes, "If the member refuses to listen to them, tell it to the church; and if the offender refuses to listen even to the church, let such a one be to you a Gentile and a

---

16 Cf. U. Luz, *Matthew 1–7: A Continental Commentary*, trans. W. C. Linss (Minneapolis: Fortress Press, 1989), 103–4.

17 The title "son of Abraham" is used by Matthew as a christological model that encompasses the entire Gospel. See L. A. Huizenga, "Matt 1:1: 'Son of Abraham' as Christological Category," *BT* 30 (2008): 103–13.

tax collector" (Mt 18:17). The third occurrence is in the context of forgiveness. Peter asks Jesus, "Lord, if another member of the church sins against me, how often should I forgive? As many as seven times?" (Mt 18:21). The sporadic references to "church" in Matthew's Gospel suggest that the Gospel as a whole serves as a discipline book for the ministry of the church.

Major themes of Matthew's Gospel are related to the way the Gospel is structured. Each narrative sequence is centered around Jesus's identity as God's promised Messiah.[18] Five segments of teaching materials end with "And Jesus finished these sayings" (Mt 7:28; 11:1; 13:53; 19:1; 26:1). These include six lengthy discourses that are centered around Jesus as the teacher of Israel: the Sermon on the Mount (Mt 5:1–7:28); the Commissioning of the Twelve (Mt 10:1–42); the Kingdom Parables (Mt 13:1–52); the teaching on greatness and forgiveness (Mt 18:1–35); the confrontation with the religious leaders (Mt 23:1–39); and the Olivet discourse (Mt 24:1–25:46). With other materials Matthew contains, I propose the following structure, which illustrates the overarching theme of the messianic identity of Jesus:

1. Prologue: Jesus's birth, upbringing, and commissioning (Mt 1:1–4:25)

2. Book 1: Jesus's teaching and healing (Mt 5:1–9:38)

3. Book 2: Jesus's commissioning the Twelve; Jesus's teaching on the Kingdom of Heaven; and Jesus's encounter with the religious leaders (Mt 10:1–16:28)

4. Book 3: Jesus's transfiguration and Jesus's teaching on various subjects (Mt 17:1–20:34)

5. Book 4: Jesus's entry into Jerusalem and Jesus's prophetic oracles (Mt 21:1–25:46)

---

18 For a discussion on the structure of Matthew's Gospel, see W. Carter, "Kernels and Narrative Blocks: The Structure of Matthew's Gospel," CBQ 54 (1992): 463–81; D. R. Bauer, The Structure of Matthew's Gospel: A Study in Library Design, JSNTSup 31 (Sheffield, UK: The Almond Press, 1988).

6. Book 5: Jesus's journey toward the cross and Jesus's death (Mt 26:1–27:66)

7. Epilogue: Jesus's resurrection and Jesus's commissioning of the eleven disciples (Mt 28:1–20)

Prologue: Jesus's Birth, Upbringing, and Commissioning (Mt 1:1–4:25)

In order to establish Jesus's identity as God's promised Messiah, Matthew begins his Gospel with genealogy, starting with Abraham and continuing on to David and through to Joseph, who was Jesus's legal father through adoption (Mt 1:1–17). From the very beginning Matthew wants to establish Jesus's divine Sonship by his supernatural birth. Jesus was conceived of the Holy Spirit in the womb of the virgin Mary in fulfillment of the prophecy of Isaiah (Mt 1:21–23; cf. Is 7:14).[19] Joseph was instructed by the angel to name the child Jesus, "for he will save his people from their sins" (Mt 1:21). In accordance with the prophecy of Isaiah, Jesus will also be called *Emmanuel*, which means "with us God" (Mt 1:23). Matthew clearly defines the role of Jesus through the birth narrative. Jesus comes in the line of Abraham and of David as God's promised Son and Messiah. Jesus's mission is salvific, and his very presence on earth is the presence of God among people.

After Jesus was born in Bethlehem, wise men (Gk: *magoi*) from the East came searching for the newborn King of the Jews (Mt 2:1–12). Through this narrative, Matthew points out that Jesus's birth in Bethlehem was already foretold by the prophet Micah (Mt 2:6; cf. Mi 4:2). The wise men paid homage to Jesus and offered gifts of gold, frankincense, and myrrh (Mt 2:11; cf. Ps 72:15; Is 60:5–6). Jesus is recognized as the King of the Jews even by these strangers from the East. King Herod wants to kill Jesus, so Jesus and his parents escape to Egypt—the event that fulfills the prophecy of Hosea (Mt 2:15; cf. Hos 11:1). Jesus is called out of Egypt as God's Son. The killing of the

---

19 For a recent discussion on the virgin birth of Jesus and its implications for today, see K. Roberts, *A Complicated Pregnancy: Whether Mary Was a Virgin and Why It Matters* (Minneapolis: Fortress Press, 2017).

infants at the order of Herod is seen as the fulfillment of the prophecy of Jeremiah (Mt 2:18; cf. Jer 31:15). Also, this event recalls Pharaoh's act of killing the Hebrew male children at the time of the birth of Moses (cf. Ex 1:15–22). After the death of Herod, Jesus and his parents return to Galilee and make their home in Nazareth. Jesus will be called a "Nazorean" in fulfillment of the prophecy of the prophets (Mt 2:23; cf. Is 11:1; Zec 3:8; 6:12).

After the birth narrative, Matthew moves on to the public appearance of Jesus. Matthew bypasses Jesus's childhood and focuses on his readiness for the mission of God. Jesus comes to Jordan to be baptized by John the Baptist. Although John's baptism is for repentance for sins, Jesus allows himself to be baptized by John to fulfill God's righteousness (Mt 3:14–15). By accepting the baptism of John, Jesus identifies himself with the needs of sinful humanity and begins to focus on them as a central concern of his ministry. After baptism, Jesus is tempted by the devil in the wilderness for forty days and forty nights by food, miracle, and fame (Mt 4:1–11). By fasting and focusing on the power of the word of God, Jesus overcomes all the temptations and proves himself to be God's Son (cf. Dt 6:13, 16; 8:3; Ps 91:11–12.[20] Through recognition as God's Son in baptism and temptation, Jesus begins to teach and heal God's people. He makes his home in Capernaum by the sea in fulfillment of the prophecy of Isaiah (Mt 4:12–16; cf. Is 9:1–2).

Book 1: Jesus's Teaching and Healing (Mt 5:1–9:38)

Matthew presents Jesus as a teacher. The core of Jesus's teaching is found in chapters 5 through 7, which are generally called the Sermon on the Mount. Jesus taught both the people and the disciples (Mt 5:1–2). Formally, his words sound more like the prophetic oracles that proceed from his mouth, except Jesus speaks without invoking the name of the Lord God (cf. Is 45:1–8; Jer 6:16–30; Ez 30:10–19). For Matthew, Jesus is the very presence of God. Whatever Jesus

---

20 For Matthew's use of Psalm 91, see J. S. Subramanian, *The Synoptic Gospels and the Psalms as Prophecy*, LNTS 351 (London: T. & T. Clark, 2007), 92–97.

speaks, it comes from God. Matthew first presents the Beatitudes in an eschatological context (Mt 5:3–11). Those who are poor in spirit and those who are persecuted will inherit the Kingdom of Heaven (Mt 5:3, 10). Those who mourn, those who are meek, those who hunger and thirst for righteousness, those who are merciful, those who are pure in heart, those who are peacemakers, and those who are falsely accused will inherit the full blessings of the Kingdom of Heaven in the age to come (Mt 5:5–11). Jesus's teaching represents the order of latitude of the Kingdom of Heaven, which is already here in the ministry of Jesus. But the full blessings of the life of the Kingdom still lie in the future (cf. Mt 24:14).

Matthew cautions the audience and religious leaders to clear the misconception that Jesus came to do away with the law of Moses and the prophetic words. To do this, Matthew draws attention to what Jesus said on the mountain: "Do not think that I have come to abolish the law or the prophets; I have come not to abolish but to fulfill" (Mt 5:17). The six antitheses that set the law of Moses in contrast to the authoritative teaching of Jesus are in fact no antitheses (Mt 5:21–48). The law of Moses is quoted and then interpreted in a new context. For instance, Jesus first quotes the law of Moses and then sets it in the new context of the world of the Kingdom with his own interpretation. Jesus says, "You have heard that it was said to those of ancient times, 'You shall not murder'; and 'whoever murders shall be liable to judgment'" (Mt 5:21; cf. Ex 20:13; Dt 5:17). Then Jesus goes on to interpret it in a new context by saying, "But I say to you that if you are angry with a brother or sister, you will be liable to judgment; and if you insult a brother or sister, you will be liable to the council; and if you say, 'You fool,' you will be liable to the hell of fire" (Mt 5:22). Jesus is not opposed to the law of Moses nor is he opposed to the religious leaders. He invites everyone to see the law of Moses in a new context, especially in his authoritative teaching, which represents the very will of God.[21] Subsequently, Jesus's

---

21 For a good discussion on the scribal authority of Jesus, see S. Westerholm, *Jesus and Scribal Authority*, ConBNT 10 (Lund, Sweden: C. W. K. Gleerup, 1978).

teaching on prayer, worry, judgment, and practicing the will of God stems from Jesus's understanding of the law of Moses and the prophets in light of God's will (Mt 6:1–7:27). The prayer Jesus taught (known as the Lord's Prayer, or *Pater Noster* in Latin) is found only in Matthew and Luke (Mt 6:9–13; Lk 11:2–4).[22] Outside those two Gospels, it is found in the *Didache* ("The Teaching of the Twelve Apostles"), a first-century teaching manual of the church.[23] This model prayer is meant for those who follow God's will. Matthew concludes this section on Jesus's teaching with these words: "For he [Jesus] taught them as one having authority, and not as their scribes" (Mt 7:29).

Following the teaching of Jesus, Matthew records nine miracle stories of Jesus. Jesus cures a leper (Mt 8:1–4); heals a centurion's servant (Mt 8:5–13); heals Peter's mother-in-law (Mt 8:14–15); casts out the demons from two demoniacs (Mt 8:28–34); heals a paralyzed man (Mt 9:2–8); raises a little girl from the dead (Mt 9:18–19, 23–26); heals a woman from hemorrhages (Mt 9:20–22); heals two blind men (Mt 9:27–31); and heals a mute demoniac (Mt 9:32–34). The healing of the paralytic man reveals that Jesus not only had authority to heal, but he also had authority to forgive sins on earth (Mt 9:5–6).

Matthew sees the healing ministry of Jesus as additional proof that in his ministry the Kingdom has arrived. Jesus fulfills the prophecy of Isaiah: "This was to fulfill what had been spoken through the prophet Isaiah, 'He took our infirmities and bore our diseases'" (Mt 8:17; cf. Is 53:4). Jesus performed miracles not just for the sake of performing miracles. The miracle stories affirm that Jesus came to fulfill the prophets. Within these stories, the account of the call of

---

22 See J. S. Subramanian, "The Lord's Prayer in Matthew's Gospel," in *Resourcing New Testament Studies: Literary, Historical, and Theological Essays in Honor of David L. Dungan*, ed. A. J. McNicol, D. B. Peabody, and J. S. Subramanian (London: T. & T. Clark, 2009), 107–22.

23 *Did.* 8.2. In the *Didache*, believers are urged to say the Lord's Prayer three times a day (*Did.* 8.3). See *The Apostolic Fathers: Greek Texts and English Translations of Their Writings*, trans. J. B. Lightfoot and J. R. Harmer, ed. and rev. M. W. Holmes, 2nd ed. (Grand Rapids, MI: Baker Book House, 1992), 258–59.

Matthew as the tax collector further explains the ministry of Jesus (Mt 9:9). Jesus as the promised Messiah comes to do God's will and gather the sinners and tax collectors into the Kingdom of Heaven. Jesus says, "Those who are well have no need of a physician, but those who are sick. Go and learn what this means, 'I desire mercy, not sacrifice.' For I have come to call not righteous but sinners" (Mt 9:12b–13; cf. Hos 6:6; Mt 12:7).

Book 2: Jesus's Commissioning the Twelve; Jesus's Teaching on the Kingdom of Heaven; and Jesus's Encounter with the Religious Leaders (Mt 10:1–16:28)

The commissioning of the twelve disciples centers around Jesus's authority. As the promised Messiah, Jesus teaches and heals with authority. In the sending of the Twelve, Jesus delegates his authority to the disciples to heal and cast out demons. Matthew introduces the mission of the Twelve with these words: "Then Jesus summoned his twelve disciples and gave them authority over unclean spirits, to cast them out, and to cure every disease and every sickness" (Mt 10:1). The disciples are also instructed to proclaim the good news about the arrival of the Kingdom of Heaven only to the lost sheep of Israel (Mt 10:5–7; cf. 15:24). The restricted mission of the Twelve only to Israel is puzzling. At this point, Jesus (like John the Baptist) is focusing on calling Israel to repentance. References to the Gentiles are primarily to contrast unexpected faith with the dullness of Israel: Jesus heals a Roman centurion's servant (Mt 8:5–13). Jesus heals a Canaanite woman (Mt 15:21–28). Jesus speaks favorably about the Gentile towns, like Tyre and Sidon, that would have repented if they had received the seeds of power extended to Jewish towns like Chorazin and Bethsaida (Mt 11:20–24). Jesus would inaugurate a worldwide mission after his resurrection (Mt 28:18–20); but, for now, Jesus primarily focuses on the Jewish people and the mission of the Twelve to Israel.

Still, Jesus's mission to the Gentiles is already becoming proleptic in Matthew's Gospel. Matthew sees the healing ministry of Jesus as a sign of mission to the Gentiles. The crowds Jesus healed likely would have included some Gentiles (Mt 9:35). Matthew rightly perceives Jesus as God's promised Messiah, who will "proclaim justice to the Gentiles" and in whose name "the Gentiles will hope" in fulfillment of the prophecy of Isaiah (Mt 12:15–21; cf. Is 42:1–4).

Matthew introduces seven parables to show how the teaching of Jesus reveals the growth of the Kingdom of Heaven: the Parable of the Sower (Mt 13:3–9); the Parable of the Weeds among the Wheat (Mt 13:24–30); the Parable of the Mustard Seed (Mt 13:31–32); the Parable of the Yeast (Mt 13:33); the Parable of the Hidden Treasure (Mt 13:44); the Parable of One Pearl (Mt 13:45–46); and the Parable of the Fish Net (Mt 13:47–50). Jesus taught these parables in fulfillment of the prophetic words of the psalmist (Mt 13:34–35; cf. Ps 78:2).[24] For Matthew, not only the prophets but also David predicted Jesus's messianic ministry (Mt 22:43; cf. Acts 4:25–26).

Matthew continues to emphasize Jesus's messianic ministry. Jesus fed the five thousand with five loaves and two fish (Mt 14:13–21). He healed many sick people at Gennesaret (Mt 14:34–36). Jesus healed a Canaanite woman in the region of Tyre and Sidon (Mt 15:21–28). He fed the four thousand with seven loaves and a few small fish (Mt 15:32–39). The confession of Simon Peter at Caesarea Philippi is a very important passage (Mt 16:13–20). Matthew reveals how the true identity of Jesus was revealed. Jesus is "the Messiah, the Son of the living God" (Mt 16:16). Upon this truth, the true "flock of Jesus" is established, and starting with the disciples' adherence to Jesus's teachings even the gates of Hades will not prevail (Mt 16:16–19).

Matthew begins to show how Jesus will accomplish his messianic ministry. It is not only by teaching, preaching, and healing but also by suffering, death, and resurrection. Matthew reports, "From that time on, Jesus began to show his disciples that he must go to Jerusalem and undergo great suffering at the hands of the elders and chief priests and scribes, and be killed, and on the third day be raised" (Mt 16:21). Although Matthew does not quote any prophecy to show the

---

24 For Matthew's use of Psalm 78, see Subramanian, *Synoptic Gospels and the Psalms*, 99–104.

fulfillment of Jesus's suffering, death, and resurrection, the song of the suffering servant of Isaiah seems to underlie Jesus's rejection, sorrow, suffering, death on the cross, and exaltation (cf. Is 52:13–53:12).[25]

Book 3: Jesus's Transfiguration and Jesus's Teaching on Various Subjects (Mt 17:1–20:34)

In this section, Jesus is shown as God's Son who has authority to teach and heal. The account of the transfiguration of Jesus provides divine confirmation of Jesus as God's Son and gives a preview of his glorification (Mt 17:1–8). The appearance of Moses and Elijah along with Jesus represents Jesus's fulfillment of the law and the prophets (Mt 17:3). The heavenly voice affirms Jesus's divine sonship: "This is my Son, the Beloved; with him I am well pleased; listen to him!" (Mt 17:5; cf. Ps 2:7; Is 42:1). Jesus commands the disciples (Peter, James, and John) not to tell what they saw, what they heard, and what they experienced on the high mountain until after the Son of Man has been raised from the dead (Mt 17:9). It clearly shows that the transfiguration event points to Jesus's resurrection, and the disciples are ordered to keep it secret until his exaltation.[26] The healing of a boy with a demon following Jesus's transfiguration demonstrates his power not only over the demon but the unseen world (Mt 17:14–20). Again, Matthew presents Jesus as one standing in the place of God, who has delegated God's power to Jesus to act on God's behalf.

Jesus's teaching is not confined only to the teaching unit in Matthew's Gospel (cf. Mt 5–7), but it is distributed throughout the Gospel to show that Jesus continues to exercise the authority of God in revealing

---

25 Cf. W. H. Bellinger Jr. and W. R. Farmer, eds., *Jesus and the Suffering Servant: Isaiah 53 and Christian Origins* (Eugene, OR: Wipf and Stock, 2009).

26 The secrecy motif in the synoptic Gospels is usually tied to Mark's Gospel since the time of Wilhelm Wrede. See W. Wrede, *Das Messiasgeheimnis in den Evangelien: Zugleich ein Beitrag zum Verständnis des Markusevangeliums* (Göttingen: Vandenhoeck & Ruprecht, 1901); ET: W. Wrede, *The Messianic Secret*, trans. J. C. G. Greig (Cambridge, UK: James Clarke & Co., 1971). Allan J. McNicol takes a fresh look at the messianic secret in Mark's Gospel in light of Mark's use of Matthew and Luke and Mark's configuration of the messianic secret. See A. J. McNicol, "The Messianic Secret in Mark," in Peabody et al., *One Gospel from Two*, 348–53.

the Kingdom of God through teaching. The various teachings of Jesus on the Temple tax, true greatness, temptations, church administration, forgiveness, divorce, eternal life, and servanthood are all related to the presence of the Kingdom of Heaven (Mt 17:24–20:28). The healing of the two blind men in Jericho also attests to the nature of the Kingdom of Heaven when it is present (Mt 20:29–34). For Matthew, Jesus brings about the presence of the Kingdom of Heaven through his teaching, healing, and his very life. Matthew views Jesus as nothing less than "with us God." The same God who acted powerfully in the history of Israel is now at work in the person of Jesus.

Book 4: Jesus's Entry into Jerusalem and Jesus's Prophetic Oracles (Mt 21:1–25:46)

In this section Matthew reports various activities of Jesus in Jerusalem just before the Passover. Jesus comes to Jerusalem riding on a donkey and a colt in accordance with the fulfillment of the Scriptures (Mt 21:1–11; cf. Ps 118:25–26a; Zec 9:9);[27] he cleanses the Temple in accordance with the prophecy of Jeremiah (Mt 21:12–17; cf. Jer 7:11); he curses the fig tree (Mt 21:18–22); he debates with the chief priests and elders (Mt 21:23–27); he teaches in parables (Mt 21:28–32, 33–46; 22:1–14; 25:1–46). More specifically he sets the Parable of the Wicked Tenants in the context of the Scripture (Mt 21:42; cf. Ps 118:22–23;[28] he addresses the question about paying taxes, the resurrection, the greatest commandment, and the Davidic Sonship of the Messiah (Mt 22:15–22, 23–33, 34–40, 41–46); he explains the Davidic Sonship of the Messiah in light of the Scripture (Mt 22:44; cf. Ps 110:1);[29] and he points out the inconsistency of the scribes and Pharisees (Mt 23:1–36) and laments over Jerusalem (Mt 23:37–39). Then he predicts the destruction of the Temple, the future persecution, the appearance

---

27 For Matthew's use of Psalm 118, see Subramanian, *Synoptic Gospels and the Psalms*, 104–7.

28 For Matthew's use of Psalm 118, see Subramanian, 109–12.

29 For Matthew's use of Psalm 110, see Subramanian, 112–15.

of false messiahs and false prophets, and the coming of the Son of Man; and he talks about the delay of the *parousia* in parables (Mt 24:1–25:46). In this unit the use of Scripture is prominent. In all these, Matthew presents Jesus as the Messiah, the Son of God, who fulfills the Scriptures.

Jesus's predictions, his teaching in the parables, his oracles against the scribes and the Pharisees, and his debate with the Pharisees and Sadducees point to Jesus as the authoritative interpreter of the Kingdom of Heaven, which is already permeating his ministry. In light of the future coming of the Kingdom of Heaven, Jesus prepares his followers to face the present situation with endurance and watchfulness (Mt 24:13; 25:13).

Book 5: Jesus's Journey toward the Cross and Jesus's Death (Mt 26:1–27:66)

In this climactic segment Matthew goes on to describe the passion and death of Jesus as the Messiah. Matthew creatively sets the basic outline and content of Jesus's journey toward the cross and his death, which serves as the foundation text for the subsequent Gospel writers. Matthew gives a summary of what went before and what is going to follow: "When Jesus had finished saying all these things, he said to his disciples, 'You know that after two days the Passover is coming, and the Son of Man will be handed over to be crucified'" (Mt 26:1–2). The anointing of Jesus at Bethany (Mt 26:6–13), the Passover with his disciples (Mt 26:17–30), and Jesus's prayer at Gethsemane (Mt 26:36–46) now prepare Jesus for the road ahead. His anointing by the woman at Bethany anticipates the proclamation of the gospel in the whole world (Gk: *cosmos*): "Truly I tell you, wherever this good news is proclaimed in the whole world, what she has done will be told in remembrance of her" (Mt 26:13). Matthew points out that even the preparation for the burial of Jesus is not a private rite but a public act worthy of proclamation to the entire world. The Passover meal with Jesus's disciples also anticipates the future coming of the Kingdom: "I tell you, I will never again drink of this fruit of the vine until that day when I drink it new with you in my Father's kingdom"

(Mt 26:29). Matthew alludes to Jesus's future coming when God's Kingdom will be fully realized on earth (cf. Mt 8:11). Jesus's prayer at Gethsemane deepens his relationship with God as God's Son. Jesus prayed, "My Father, if it is possible, let this cup pass from me; yet not what I want but what you want" (Mt 26:39). Matthew presents Jesus as God's Son who continues to fulfill the will of God rather than pursue his own desires.

Within this frame of this narrative, Jesus predicts his betrayal, abandonment by his disciples, resurrection, and the denial of Peter (Mt 26:24–25, 31–34). Subsequently, the prediction of his vindication culminates in his own resurrection (Mt 28:7, 9, 16). Matthew describes two trials after Jesus's arrest: one before the High Priest and the other before Pilate (Mt 26:57–67; 27:1–2, 11–26). Matthew illustrates that both trials identify Jesus as the Messiah, the Son of God, and the King of the Jews (Mt 26:63; 27:11). Although Jesus does not deny those titles, he sees himself as the exalted Messiah, the Son of Man (Mt 26:27; cf. Ps 110:1; Dan 7:14). Here at the trial narrative, Matthew hints at the exaltation of Jesus as the glorified Messiah, the Son of Man. As in all the Gospels, Matthew also presents Pilate's affirmation of Jesus's innocence of all charges brought by the chief priests and elders by washing his (Pilate's) hands (Mt 27:24). Matthew shows that Jesus is crucified as the King of the Jews, a title for which the soldiers mock Jesus (Mt 27:29). They put a sign over Jesus's head with the words, "This is Jesus, the King of the Jews" (Mt 27:37).

In his account of the crucifixion, Matthew presents Jesus as the Son of God and the King of Israel. The bystanders, as well as the scribes and elders, mock Jesus as the Son of God (Mt 27:40, 43). The scribes and elders ridicule Jesus by saying, "He is the King of Israel" (Mt 27:42). At "about three o'clock Jesus cried with a loud voice, 'Eli, Eli, lema sabachthani?' that is, 'My God, my God, why have you forsaken me?'" (Mt 27:46; cf. Ps 22:1).[30] Some of the bystanders thought that he was calling for Elijah (Mt 27:47). Probably they were expecting

---

30 For Matthew's use of Psalm 22, see Subramanian, 118–21.

that Elijah would come and rescue Jesus (cf. 1 Kgs 2:1; Mal 4:5-6). The centurion and all those with him said, "Truly this man was God's Son" (Mt 27:54). Matthew associates Jesus's death with the rending of the Temple curtain, which symbolized direct access to God for all people (Mt 27:51a; cf. Ex 26:31–35; Hab 9:1–4; 10:19–27). Matthew uniquely also connects Jesus's death with a series of apocalyptic events, such as an earthquake and the resurrection (Mt 27:51b, 52–54; cf. Ez 37:12; 38:18; Dn 12:2; Jl 2:10; Am 8:9; Is 29:16; Zec 14:5b). Here he associates those accounts of the end-time events with the death of Jesus in order to assert that Jesus's death marks the beginning of the new age (cf. Mt 23:39; 26:29, 64).

Epilogue: Jesus's Resurrection and Jesus's Commissioning of the Eleven Disciples (Mt 28:1–20)

In the epilogue of his Gospel, Matthew presents Jesus's resurrection and his commissioning of the eleven disciples. Matthew links the epilogue with the rest of the Gospel: He mentions the earthquake at Jesus's resurrection, which recalls the earthquake at Jesus's death (Mt 28:2a; cf. Mt 27:56). Matthew tells that the angel announced the supernatural event of Jesus's resurrection to the women, just as he tells that the angel proclaimed the supernatural event of Jesus's birth to Joseph (Mt 28:5–6; cf. Mt 1:20–21). After the resurrection Jesus gives the commission to the eleven disciples at the mountain, just as he gives the sermon on the mountain and is transfigured at the mountain (Mt 28:16; cf. Mt 5:1; 17:1). In Matthew's Gospel women are the first ones to see the risen Jesus. A woman—not the disciples—was the first to recognize Jesus's upcoming death and anoint him with oil in preparation for his burial. Women were also the ones to witness Jesus's crucifixion (Mt 28:9; cf. Mt 26:6–13; 27:55–56). The story of guards who witnessed Jesus's resurrection and who were given bribes to bar them from telling the truth recalls an earlier account of posting the Temple guards at the tomb out of fear of deception (Mt 28:11–15; cf. Mt 27:62–66). The authority with which Jesus teaches, forgives sins, and heals people in his earthly ministry has been given to him explicitly at this resurrection (Mt 28:18; cf. Mt 7:29; 9:2; 21:23). Jesus's final words, "And remember, I am with you always, to the end of the age," recall the abiding presence of Jesus as *Emmanuel* at his birth (Mt 28:20b; cf. Mt 1:23).[31]

The commissioning of the eleven disciples echoes Jesus's sending out the Twelve to the house of Israel (Mt 28:19–20a; cf. Mt 10:6). But after the resurrection Jesus sends his disciples to all nations (Gk: *panta ta ethnē*), and his resurrection presence goes with them.[32] The primary commission of Jesus is to make disciples, just as Jesus made the disciples through invitation (Mt 28:19a; cf. Mt 4:18–22; 9:9; 11:1). Discipleship is accomplished through baptism in the name of Father, Son, and Holy Spirit, and through teaching (Mt 28:19b–20a). Not only the eleven disciples but all the future disciples are assured of Jesus's continuous presence in the ministry of disciple-making.

From the beginning to the end, Matthew presents Jesus as the Messiah, the Son of David, the Son of God, who came to redeem both Jews and Gentiles and sought to gather them in the Kingdom of Heaven. Matthew clearly sees the fulfillment of the law and the prophets in the life and ministry of Jesus. Jesus embodied the very presence of God as *Emmanuel* in every aspect of his ministry among all people. With the arrival of Jesus the Kingdom of Heaven has dawned, the new age is beginning to emerge, and the gospel is being proclaimed to all nations.

Theology of Matthew

Matthew presents one single theology from the beginning to the end; it is guided by the prophecy of Isaiah that God is present in the life and ministry of Jesus. Beginning with his birth, Jesus will be called *Emmanuel* as prophesied by Isaiah (Mt 1:23; cf. Is 7:14; 7:7–9; 8:10;

---

31 For a discussion of the final words of the risen Jesus in Matthew's Gospel, see P. M. McDonald, "'I am with you always, to the end of the age': Presence in the Gospel According to Matthew," *PIBA* 28 (2005): 66–86.

32 Samuel Oyin Abogunrin argues that the phrase "all nations" includes both the Jews and the Gentiles, and Matthew has already used the phrase earlier to include all people (cf. Mt 24:9; 25:32). See S. O. Abogunrin, "St. Matthew: The Gospel for All Nations," in *Resourcing New Testament Studies*, 96–106, esp. 104–6.

17:12–14).[33] God's presence continues through the presence of Jesus when Jesus promised to his disciples prior to his death, "For where two or three are gathered in my name, I am there among them" (Mt 18:20). God's presence will continue through Jesus after his resurrection; Jesus commissioned his disciples and assured them, "And remember, I am with you always, to the end of the age" (Mt 28:20b). Matthew wanted his readers to know that God revealed God's presence in every aspect of Jesus's life and ministry, and God's presence will continue in the preaching of the gospel of Jesus Christ.

Matthew provides a coherent narrative to demonstrate God's presence made available, beginning with the birth of Jesus and continuing through the resurrection and beyond.[34] For Matthew, God embraces both Jews and Gentiles through Jesus. In the process of tracing Jesus's lineage back to Abraham, Matthew includes four Gentile women to show their involvement in God's plan for salvation (Mt 1:3, 5–6). The angel who appeared to Joseph in a dream announced the birth of Jesus, whose very name will determine the course of salvation for God's people. Joseph was told to name his son Jesus (Heb.: *Yeshua*, which means "He saves," Mt 1:21). The wise men from the East not only recognized Jesus as the King of the Jews, but they paid homage to him by offering him gifts of gold, frankincense, and myrrh (Mt 2:2, 11; cf. Is 60:5–6). The story of the killing of the infants in and around Bethlehem draws attention to the suffering of God's people during exile and to the situation where Jesus is born to reveal God's presence (Mt 2:16–18; cf. Jer 31:5).

---

33 The Immanuel oracles of Isaiah may point toward a new leader who will restore the fortune of Israel. See J. Lust, "The Immanuel Figure: A Charismatic Judge-Leader. A Suggestion Towards the Understanding of Is. 7,10-17 (8,23–9.6; 11,1-9)," *ETL* 47 (1971): 464–70.

34 Allan J. McNicol demonstrates how Matthew arranges his Gospel to provide a sequential narrative to present the story of Jesus in five segments: (1) Something is stirring in Israel (Mt 1:1–4:16); (2) Jesus's mission to Israel begins in Galilee (Mt 4:17–11:1); (3) the growing conflict with the religious authorities (Mt 11:2–16:20); (4) the Jerusalem journey and revelation of Jesus as Son of David and Son of God (Mt 16:21–28:15); and (5) epilogue: Matthew's triumphant ending (Mt 28:16–20). See A. J. McNicol, *The Persistence of God's Endangered Promises: The Bible's Unified Story* (London: Bloomsbury T. & T. Clark, 2018), 97–117.

Matthew introduces John the Baptist as the forerunner of Jesus; and as a servant, John came to prepare the way of the Lord (Jesus) in fulfillment of the prophecy of Isaiah (Mt 3:1–3; cf. Is 40:3). At his baptism, Jesus is affirmed as God's Son (Mt 3:17; cf. Mt 4:3, 6; 8:29; 11:27; 16:16; 26:63). For Matthew, Jesus stands in the place of God as God's Son. The temptations of Jesus further affirm Jesus as God's Son (Mt 4:1–11).[35] Matthew sees Galilee of the Gentiles as the main base for the messianic ministry of Jesus in fulfillment of Isaiah's prophecy (Mt 1:12–16; cf. Is 9:1–2). With Jesus's base in Galilee, Matthew reports that Jesus started to proclaim, "Repent, for the kingdom of heaven has come near" (Mt 4:17). The Kingdom of Heaven has arrived in the proclamation of Jesus.[36] Matthew will continue to show how Jesus manifests God's presence in his ministry.

Matthew records Jesus's teaching from the mountain in chapters 5 through 7. Although Matthew presents the teaching of Jesus as unified, he persists in continuing it throughout the Gospel. The Kingdom becomes a present reality for those who follow Jesus's teaching. For Matthew, Jesus shows God's presence by calling people to act in light of God's will. The whole intention of Jesus's teaching can be summed up in these words: "Not everyone who says to me, 'Lord, Lord,' will enter the kingdom of heaven, but only the one who does the will of my Father in heaven" (Mt 7:21). Jesus demands from his followers that God's will should be done with the disposition of the heart. Jesus emphasizes that just as anger is a form of murder and lust a form of adultery, so one's intention of doing God's will is to be a matter of the heart (Mt 5:21–22, 27; cf. Mt 6:6, 17–18). The disciples are called to "do to others," for doing the will of God is absolutely necessary for entrance into God's Kingdom (cf. Mt 7:12). Jesus brought God into the life of the people when he said, "For if

---

35 For a good analysis of the temptation of Jesus, see B. Gerhardsson, *The Testing of God's Son (Matt 4:1-11 & Par): An Analysis of an Early Christian Midrash*, trans. J. Toy (Lund, Sweden: C. W. K. Gleerup, 1966; Eugene, OR: Wipf and Stock, 2009).

36 Cf. W. Carter, "Narrative/Literary Approaches to Matthean Theology: The 'Reign of the Heavens' as an Example (Mt. 4:17–5:12)," *JSNT* 67 (1997): 3–27.

you forgive others their trespasses, your heavenly Father will also forgive you; but if you do not forgive others, neither will your Father forgive your trespasses" (Mt 6:14–15; cf. Mt 6:12). What Matthew is trying to point out is that Jesus already knew the mind of God and showed how God acts in human history. For Matthew, Jesus came to reveal how God would create a new community of people who will practice God's will.

Matthew's healing stories witness to the power of God exhibited through Jesus (Mt 8:1–4; 8:5–13; 8:14–17; 8:28–34; 9:2–8; 9:18–19, 23–26; 9:27–31; 9:32–34; 12:9–14; 15:21–28; 20:29–34; cf. Mt 4:23–25; 15:29–31). In all the healing stories, Jesus exhibits the power of God and restores human dignity. When people saw the healings done by Jesus, they began to praise God (Mt 15:30–31). For Matthew, the healing stories testify to God's presence shown in and through Jesus's ministry. Those who were healed by Jesus began to experience God's salvation in fulfillment of the Scripture (Mt 8:17; cf. Is 53:4).[37]

Matthew records fifteen parables of Jesus (Mt 13:1–9, 24–30, 31–32, 33, 44, 45–46, 47–50; 18:10–14, 23–35; 20:1–16; 21:28–32, 33–41; 22:1–14; 25:1–13, 14–30).[38] Jesus speaks through the parables as the one who knows the mind of God. One can miss the Kingdom of Heaven if he or she does not act the way God expects that person to act. For instance, the young maidens do not have enough oil when the bridegroom arrives, so they miss the entrance to the wedding banquet (Mt 25:1–13). A guest is expelled from the wedding banquet because he is not wearing a wedding robe (Mt 22:1–14). The tenants of the vineyard are put to death because they killed the landowner's son (Mt 21:33–41). The parables of Jesus demanded that people be ready to experience God's presence lest they miss the joy of the

---

37 For a discussion of the significance of the healing miracle stories in Matthew's Gospel, see J. P. Heil, "Significant Aspects of the Healing Miracles in Matthew," *CBQ* 41 (1978): 274–87.

38 Jesus's parables are more like similitudes, which compare the Kingdom of Heaven to a story. For an analysis of the interpretation of Jesus's parables, see C. L. Blomberg, "Interpreting the Parables of Jesus: Where Are We and Where Do We Go from Here?" *CBQ* 53 (1991): 50–78.

presence of God. Therefore, Jesus spoke in parables in fulfillment of the Scripture to reveal God's presence and to invite people to God's Kingdom (Mt 13:34–35; cf. Ps 78:2).

Matthew also provides other narratives to affirm how Jesus exhibited God's presence. Jesus corrected the view of the Sadducees on the question of resurrection in light of the Scriptures and the power of God (Mt 22:23–33; Ex 3:6). Jesus pointed out the hypocrisy of the scribes and the Pharisees. Matthew does not seem to present Jesus as being totally hostile to the scribes and Pharisees, because Matthew has only Jesus point out their hypocrisy (Mt 23:1–36). In the Kingdom of Heaven, in the presence of God, there should not be any hypocrisy. On the same level, Jesus also attacked the disciples when they prevented children from coming to him to be blessed. Again, Jesus sees everyone, whether the disciples or the scribes or the Pharisees, in light of God's presence. He tells the disciples, "Let the little children come to me, and do not stop them; for it is to such as these that the kingdom of heaven belongs" (Mt 19:14).

According to Matthew, Jesus also taught the disciples the true meaning of greatness. In God's presence everyone should serve one another. And Jesus set himself as an example to be followed: "just as the Son of Man came not to be served but to serve, and to give his life a ransom for many" (Mt 20:28). From the narratives of Peter's confession, Jesus's transfiguration, and Jesus's entry into Jerusalem, he emerges as God's Son and the Messiah (Mt 16:13–20; 17:1–8; 21:1–11). As God's Son, Jesus is able to predict the destruction of Jerusalem (Mt 24:1–31) and also his own death and vindication (Mt 16:21–24). As God's Messiah, Jesus cleanses the Temple and predicts his future victorious coming (Mt 21:12–13).

In his trial narrative, Matthew again presents Jesus as God's Son, the Messiah, the King of the Jews, and Jesus's future coming as the Son of Man. The high priest questions Jesus as to whether he is the Messiah, the Son of God (Mt 26:63). Jesus's guarded affirmation of the high priest's questioning indicates that he is indeed God's Son and the Messiah only if it is understood properly (Mt 26:64). Matthew even depicts Jesus predicting his glorious coming as the Son of Man in accord with scriptural prophecy (Mt 26:64; cf. Ps 110:1; Dan 7:13–14). Pilate questions Jesus as to whether he is the King of the Jews, and Jesus's affirmation of Pilate's questioning shows that he is indeed the King of the Jews (Mt 27:11; cf. Mt 2:2). Matthew's use of Psalm 22:1 at Jesus's cry from the cross shows that Jesus died in accordance with the Scriptures (Mt 27:46). Even in his death, Jesus is recognized as the Son of God by the centurion and those who witness his death (Mt 27:54). Among all the Gospel writers, Matthew alone records both the rending of the Temple curtain and the resurrection of the saints at the time of Jesus's death (Mt 27:51–53).[39] This shows that God's presence is made available even to the dead, who are brought back to life. In Matthew's Gospel, the risen Jesus first appears to women and then to the eleven disciples (Mt 28:1–10, 16–17). In response to Jesus's appearance, both the women and the eleven worship Jesus (Mt 28:9, 17). It is an act of encountering God's presence through the risen Jesus. The abiding presence of God continues through the risen Jesus in disciple-making, baptism, and teaching.[40] For Matthew, Jesus is *Emmanuel* at birth, *Emmanuel* in ministry, *Emmanuel* at death, *Emmanuel* at resurrection, and *Emmanuel* in eternity.

Matthew's theology is based on Jesus as *Emmanuel*. From beginning to end, the concept of Jesus as "with us God" becomes a theological structure for the entire Gospel of Matthew. Jesus revealed God's presence in every aspect of his life and ministry, and he would continue to reveal God's presence through the ongoing ministry of

---

39 For an examination of the resurrection of the saints in Matthew's Gospel, see D. Senior, "The Death of Jesus and the Resurrection of the Holy Ones," *CBQ* 38 (1996): 312–20; T. Wardle, "Resurrection and the Holy City: Matthew's Use of Isaiah in 27:51-53," *CBQ* 78 (2016): 666–81.

40 Matthew brings together both the birth and the resurrection of Jesus through the prophetic words of Isaiah and Jesus's own words of assurance as *Emmanuel* (Mt 1:23; 28:20b; cf. Is 7:14). Commenting on the resurrection of Jesus in Matthew's Gospel, Raymond E. Brown says, "The resurrection is for Matthew evidence not only that God was with Jesus who conquered death, but also that in Jesus God's abiding presence is with all those who are baptized in the name of the Father, and of the Son, and of the Holy Spirit and who observe all that Jesus has commanded, as taught by the disciples." R. E. Brown, "The Resurrection in Matthew," *Worship* 64 (1990): 170.

the disciples. Matthew has not only linked the affirmation of God's presence with the people in the incarnation of Jesus, he has also connected the mission of the disciples backward to the incarnation and forward to the ongoing presence of God through the risen Jesus with the community of God's people.

John Wesley's Explanatory Notes on Matthew

John Wesley was a logical thinker and expressed himself clearly, concisely, practically, and forcefully in writing. John Wesley's *Explanatory Notes upon the New Testament* (1754) is enlightening as it engages in historical and textual studies of the Scripture.[41] Wesley's sermons and his *Explanatory Notes upon the New Testament* became the doctrinal standards for The United Methodist Church.[42] In his preface dated January 4, 1754, Wesley laid out his task to make the New Testament understandable to the common people: "For many years, I have had a desire of setting down and laying together, what has occurred to my mind, either in reading, thinking, or conversation, which might assist serious persons, who have not the advantage of learning, in understanding the New Testament."[43] Also in his preface to *Explanatory Notes upon the New Testament*, Wesley draws attention to four works upon which he is dependent: Johann Albrecht Bengel's *Gnomon Novi Testamenti*; Philip Doddridge's *The Family Expositor*;

---

41 Robin Scroggs discusses the significance of John Wesley's *Explanatory Notes upon the New Testament* in relation to translation and commentary on the New Testament and articulates John Wesley's biblical scholarship for Christology and anthropology. See R. Scroggs, "John Wesley as Bible Scholar," *JBR* 28 (1960): 415–22. See also T. C. Oden, *John Wesley's Scriptural Christianity: A Plain Expression of His Teaching on Christian Doctrine* (Grand Rapids, MI: Zondervan, 1994).

42 *The Book of Discipline of The United Methodist Church* (Nashville: The United Methodist Publishing House, 2016), 104.

43 John Wesley, *Wesley's Notes on the New Testament* (Oxford: Benediction Classics, 2010), 1. Frank Baker provides a brief history of John Wesley's *Explanatory Notes upon the New Testament*. See F. Baker, "John Wesley, Biblical Commentator," *BJRL* 71 (1989): 109–20. Also see T. L. Smith, "Notes on the Exegesis of John Wesley's *Explanatory Notes upon the New Testament*," *WThJ* 16 (1981): 107–13.

John Guyse's *An Exposition of the New Testament*; and John Heylyn's
Theological Lectures at Westminster Abbey.[44]

John Wesley wrote *Explanatory Notes upon the New Testament*
in canonical order. He thought that Matthew's Gospel was written
first, followed by Mark's Gospel, Luke's Gospel, and John's Gospel.[45]
Wesley believed that Matthew wrote his Gospel in Greek, not in
Hebrew.[46] His notes on Matthew's Gospel are elaborative, almost a
verse-by-verse explanation. He provides his own translation in English
translated from the Greek New Testament. His explanations of only
major texts of Matthew's Gospel are provided here for the teaching and
preaching ministries of the church. Wesley divides Matthew's Gospel
into six sections: (1) The birth of Christ, and what presently followed
it (Mt 1:1–2:23); (2) the introduction (Mt 3:1–4:11); (3) the actions
and words by which Jesus proved he was the Christ (Mt 4:12–16:12);
(4) predictions of Jesus's death and resurrection (Mt 16:13–20:34);

---

44 Wesley, *Wesley's Notes on the New Testament*, 2–3. Johann Albrecht Bengel
(1687–1752) was a Lutheran clergyman and Bible scholar and was educated at the
University of Tübingen. He published *The Greek Text of the New Testament* (1734)
and exegetical commentary known as *Gnomon Novi Testamenti* or *Exegetical Anno-
tations on the New Testament* (1742). Philip Doddridge (1702–1751) was an English
Congregational minister, Bible scholar, and hymn writer. His well-known works
include *The Rise and Progress of Religion in the Soul* (1745); *The Family Expositor*,
6 vols. (1739–1756); *Life of Colonel Gardiner* (1747); and a *Course of Lectures on
Pneumatology, Ethics and Divinity* (1763). John Guyse (1680–1761) was an English
minister and Bible scholar. His publications include *Jesus Christ God-man, Several
Sermons* (1719); *The Holy Spirit a Divine Person, Several Sermons* (1721); *Christ the
Son of God* (1729); *A Present Remembrance of God* (1730); and *An Exposition of
the New Testament in the Form of a Paraphrase*, 3 vols. (1739–1752). John Heylyn
(1685–1759) was an Anglican clergy of the Church of England. His published works
include *Theological Lectures at Westminster-Abbey. With an Interpretation of the
New Testament Part 1. Containing the Four Gospels* (1749); and *An Interpretation
of the New Testament Part 2. Containing the Acts of the Apostles and the Several
Epistles* (1761).

45 John Wesley would have probably been influenced by Henry Owen (1716–1795), an
Anglican clergyman in the Church of England, who maintained that Matthew's Gospel was the first written Gospel for the Jewish converts in Judea, followed by Mark,
Luke, and John. Probably Owen's view on the priority of the Gospels contributed to
the development of the Matthean priority hypothesis by J. J. Griesbach (1745–1812),
a German biblical text critic. For Henry Owen's discussion of the four Gospels, see
H. Owen, *Observations on the Four Gospels; Tending Chiefly, to Ascertain the Times
of Their Publication; And to Illustrate the Form and Manner of their Composition*
(London: Printed for T. Payne, 1764; repr., ECCO Print Editions, 2018).

46 Wesley, *Wesley's Notes on the New Testament*, 10.

(5) transactions at Jerusalem before Jesus's Passion (Mt 21:1–25:46); and (6) Jesus's Passion and resurrection (Mt 26:1–28:20).[47]

The Birth of Jesus (Mt 1:1–2:23)

Wesley translates the opening words of Matthew's Gospel as "The book of the generation of Jesus Christ," which applies strictly to the genealogy of Jesus (Mt 1:1–17). But he notes that the title may also apply to the whole Gospel if it relates to "the history of a person."[48] He draws attention to the mention of four women in Matthew's genealogy (Tamar, Rahab, Ruth, and the wife of Uriah) that they "were remarkable in the sacred history."[49] Commenting on the word *messiah*, Wesley emphasizes the three functions of Christ—prophetic, priestly, and kingly—because the prophets, priests, and kings in the Old Testament were ceremonially initiated into those offices (cf. Ex 40:15; 1 Sm 9:16; 1 Kgs 19:16). He goes on to say that we need Christ as our prophet to "enlighten our minds, and teach us the whole will of God"; as our priest to intercede and mediate on our behalf; and as our king "to reign our hearts, and subdue all things to himself."[50] For Wesley, Jesus is given another name, "Emmanuel" (cf. Is 7:14), which signifies Jesus's nature and office because he is "God incarnate, and dwells by his Spirit in the hearts of his people."[51]

Wesley recognizes Jesus's birthplace as Bethlehem of Judea (Mt 2:5), but he does refer to another Bethlehem in the tribe of Zebulon based on the quotation from Micah 5:2.[52] This shows that Wesley consulted the Old Testament to account for two Bethlehems. He identifies the wise men as "Gentile philosophers" from Arabia. He goes on to comment that God does favor with special revelation others who were not of the

---

47 Wesley, 5–8.

48 Wesley, 9.

49 Wesley, 9.

50 Wesley, 10.

51 Wesley, 10.

52 Wesley, 11.

family of Abraham, as God did to Melchizedek, Job, and several others in the Old Testament.[53] Wesley clearly sees how Matthew altered the original text taken from the Old Testament in order to set the event anew in the new context. He explains, "When this and several other quotations from the Old Testament are compared with the original, it plainly appears, the apostles did not always think it necessary exactly to transcribe the passages they cited, but contented themselves with giving the general sense, though with some diversity of language."[54] Wesley seems to be aware of the complexities of the prophetic texts quoted in the Gospel of Matthew and their counterparts in the Old Testament. For instance, Jesus's return to Nazareth and making Nazareth his home are seen by Matthew as fulfillment of the prophets who said, "He will be called a Nazorean" (Mt 2:23b). But there is no Old Testament passage that agrees with the text quoted by Matthew. He comments that Matthew's quotation in Matthew 2:23 does not correspond to the words of any prophets "in express words."[55] For Wesley, Jesus will be called a Nazarene because "he shall be despised and rejected, shall be a mark of public contempt and reproach."[56] He describes this title primarily in relation to Jesus's rejection and Passion.

The Introduction (Mt 3:1–4:11)

Wesley asserts that both John the Baptist and Christ taught the Kingdom of Heaven to the people so they could perceive it correctly. Wesley explains that both phrases, the "Kingdom of Heaven" and the "Kingdom of God," are the same thing, and they mean "not barely a future happy state, in heaven, but a state to be enjoyed on earth: the proper disposition for the glory of heaven, rather than the passion of it."[57] Commenting on the baptism of Jesus, he sees Christ fulfilling all

---

53 Wesley, 11.

54 Wesley, 11.

55 Wesley, 12.

56 Wesley, 12.

57 Wesley, 13.

God's righteous ordinances through baptism (Mt 3:15). He perceives the manifestation of the Trinity in the voice from heaven at Jesus's baptism that said, "This is my Son, the Beloved, with whom I am well pleased" (Mt 3:17). Wesley writes, "And lo, a voice—we have here a glorious manifestation of the ever-blessed Trinity: the Father speaking from heaven, the Son spoken to, the Holy Ghost descending upon him."[58]

Right after baptism, Jesus was tempted in the wilderness (Mt 4:1–11). With God's love, Jesus was completely ready for the temptation. While in the wilderness, he fasted for forty days and forty nights like Moses and Elijah.[59] At the end of the temptation, angels came and waited on Jesus "to supply him with food, and to congratulate his victory."[60] After John's arrest, Jesus began his ministry in Galilee by preaching repentance and the arrival of the Kingdom of Heaven. Wesley sees a connection between John's preaching and Jesus's preaching. Like John the Baptist, Jesus used the same words in preaching, "because the repentance which John taught still was, and ever will be, the necessary preparation for that inward kingdom."[61] Wesley goes on to explain that the gospel Jesus proclaimed would be the proper name of "our religion" as it is "the joyous message" for all those who embrace it.[62]

The Actions and Words of Jesus Christ (Mt 4:12–16:12)

Wesley sees the whole Sermon on the Mount as an "invitation to true holiness and happiness" (Mt 5–7).[63] He comments that no prophets ever used the words "I say to you" when they spoke, except Christ, who was the great Lawgiver and who is able to save and destroy sins.[64] For Wesley, Jesus taught both inward holiness and purity of

---

58 Wesley, 15.

59 Wesley, 15.

60 Wesley, 15.

61 Wesley, 16.

62 Wesley, 16.

63 Wesley, 17.

64 Wesley, 18.

intention. In that context, Wesley sees Jesus's teaching on judging others as "the chief hindrance of holiness" (Mt 7:1–12).[65] For Wesley, Jesus's teaching on prayer contributes "a most perfect and universal form of prayer" (Mt 6:9–13).[66] He recognizes the parables of Jesus as "similes or comparisons."[67]

When Jesus performed the first miracle in Matthew's Gospel by healing a leper, he told the leper not to tell anyone about it (Mt 8:4); Jesus wanted his identity hidden. This secrecy motif is fully developed in Mark's Gospel (cf. Mk 1:45). Wesley gives four reasons why Jesus commanded many others to tell no one of the miracles he had performed on them: (1) to prevent the multitude from flocking to him (cf. Mk 1:45); (2) to fulfill the prophecy of Isaiah 42:1–4 (cf. Mt 12:17–21); (3) to avoid being taken by force and made a king (cf. Jn 6:15); and (4) to stay away from the anger of the chief priests, scribes, and Pharisees (cf. Mt 16:20–21).[68]

Predictions of Jesus's Death and Resurrection (Mt 16:13–20:34)

In the healing story of a boy with a demon, the boy was first brought to the disciples, who could not heal him, and then he was brought to Jesus, who healed the boy (Mt 17:14–20). Other ancient authorities add verse 21, which says, "But this kind does not come out except by prayer and fasting." Wesley shows awareness of the existence of other ancient Greek manuscripts and comments on Matthew 17:21, stating that "fasting" when added to prayer produces a desired result.[69]

Matthew's Gospel alone records Jesus's teaching on disciplining members of the church (Mt 18:15–17). Jesus provides some practical advice on how to avoid offending someone in the church. Commenting on this advice, Wesley finds a threefold rule that will seldom offend

---

65 Wesley, 25.

66 Wesley, 22.

67 Wesley, 39.

68 Wesley, 27.

69 Wesley, 48.

others and that will never offend oneself: (1) go and reprimand that person either in person or by a messenger or in writing; (2) take with you one or two more who may become a witness of what was said; and (3) inform the elders of the church and put forth the whole matter before those who look after you and that person's soul.[70] Wesley goes on to ask, "Can anything be plainer? Christ does here as expressly command all Christians who see a brother do evil, to take this way, not another, and to take these steps, in this order, as he does to honour their father and mother."[71] Wesley suggests that any ecclesiastical judgment should move from private to public hearing to treat a member of the same religious community with love and respect. The Parable of the Unforgiving Servant further reinforces the act of forgiveness in light of the master's generosity (Mt 18:23–34). Wesley comments on the pardon of the Lord that "our Lord intimates the vast number and weight of our offenses against God and our utter incapacity of making him any satisfaction."[72] He goes on to say that our pardon can be retracted if we do not forgive everyone of their trespasses (cf. Mt 18:34).[73]

Transactions at Jerusalem before Jesus's Passion (Mt 21:1–25:46)

When Jesus entered Jerusalem the crowds said, "This is the prophet Jesus from Nazareth in Galilee" (Mt 21:12). Wesley comments that the crowds failed to perceive Jesus as the Messiah because they saw him as a prophet from Nazareth.[74] He goes on to say that "he [Jesus] was not of Nazareth, but Bethlehem," the birthplace of the Messiah.[75] Matthew records a lengthy teaching of Jesus on hypocrisy (Mt 23:1–36). Wesley outlines the signs of hypocrisy that keep one from attaining true Christianity:

---

70 Wesley, 50.

71 Wesley, 50.

72 Wesley, 50.

73 Wesley, 51.

74 Wesley, 55.

75 Wesley, 55.

1. Punctuality in attending public and private prayer

2. Zeal to make proselytes to our opinion or communion, though they have less of the spirit of religion than before

3. A superstitious reverence for consecrated places or things, without any for Him to whom they are consecrated

4. A scrupulous exactness in little observances, though with the neglect of justice, mercy, and faith

5. A nice cautiousness to cleanse the outward behavior, but without any regard for inward purity

6. A specious face of virtue and piety, covering the deepest hypoc-risy and villainy

7. A professed veneration for all good men, except those among whom they live.[76]

For Wesley, true Christianity lies not on superficial credentials but on authentic practice of justice, mercy, faith, and inward piety.

When Jesus predicts the destruction of Jerusalem and of the Temple (Mt 24:1–28), Wesley draws attention to the writings of Josephus, who also wrote about the fall of Jerusalem and the Temple. Wesley writes: "Of the city and temple. Josephus's History of the Jewish War is the best commentary on this chapter. It is a wonderful instance of God's providence, that he, an eye witness, and one who lived and died a Jew, should, especially in so extraordinary a manner, be preserved, to transmit to us a collection of important facts, which so exactly illustrate this glorious prophecy, in almost every circumstance."[77] Here Wesley alludes to Josephus's writings to show the fulfillment of Jesus's prophecy concerning Jerusalem and the Temple.

Commenting on the last public discourse of Jesus, Wesley sees the question answered in the Parable of the Ten Bridesmaids, the Parable of the Talents, and the Parable of the Judgment of the People (Mt 25:1–46):

---

76   Wesley, 60.

77   Wesley, 62.

"But what will become of those who do no harm?"[78] For Wesley, "doing no harm" means "doing good to all people."[79] Commenting on words of the King—"Truly I tell you, just as you did it to one of the least of these who are members of my family, you did it to me" (Mt 25:40)—Wesley says, "What encouragement is here to assist the household of faith? But let us likewise remember to do good to all men."[80] He consistently emphasizes the need for doing good to everyone.

Jesus's Passion and Resurrection (Mt 26:1–28:20)

Wesley calls the Passover "the Lord's Passover"; Christ substitutes Holy Communion for the Passover (Mt 26:26–29).[81] The bread that Jesus broke symbolizes Christ's body, and the cup is the sign of Christ's blood. For Wesley, the new covenant is confirmed by Christ's blood, which is shed for many since the time of Adam.[82]

The death of Judas is found only in Matthew's Gospel (Mt 27:3–10; cf. Acts 1:15–20). Judas is given thirty pieces of silver to betray Jesus (Mt 26:15). After Jesus is arrested and brought before Pilate for questioning, Judas throws down the pieces of silver in the Temple before he takes his own life (Mt 27:5). The chief priests then use the money to buy the potter's field to bury foreigners (Mt 27:6–8). The act of buying the potter's field with the pieces of silver is seen as a fulfillment of the prophecy of Jeremiah (Mt 27:9). But what is quoted in Matthew is not from the prophet Jeremiah but from the prophet Zechariah (Mt 27:9; cf. Zec 11:13), a discrepancy recognized by Wesley.[83] It shows that Wesley probably checked the Hebrew text to correctly identify the quotation. He was very much conversant with the Greek text of the New Testament and its counterparts in the Hebrew Bible.

---

78 Wesley, 64–66.

79 Wesley, 66.

80 Wesley, 66.

81 Wesley, 68.

82 Wesley, 68.

83 Wesley, 70.

Commenting on Jesus's cry from the cross, "My God, my God, why have you forsaken me?" Wesley writes that Jesus expressed trust in God, and at the same he took on the powers of darkness and the wrath due to the sins of humanity (Mt 27:6; cf. Ps 22:1).[84] Among all the Gospel writers, Matthew alone mentions the rending of the Temple curtain and the resurrection of the saints at the time of Jesus's death (Mt 27:51–53). Wesley comments on the significance of the rending of the Temple curtain: "God thereby signifying the speedy removal of the veil of the Jewish ceremonies the casting down the partition wall, so that the Jews and Gentiles were now admitted to equal privileges, and the opening a way through the veil of his flesh for all believers into the most holy place."[85] On the resurrection of the saints (Mt 27:52–53), Wesley identifies the saints as "Simeon, Zacharias, John the Baptist, and others who had believed in Christ and were known to many in Jerusalem."[86] The resurrection of the saints, Wesley writes, is "God hereby signifying, that Christ had conquered death, and would raise all his saints in due season."[87]

Wesley focuses on the commissioning of the disciples by the risen Jesus. Wesley identifies the mountain from where Jesus gave the commission as "Mount Tabor" (Mt 28:6; cf. Mt 17:1).[88] In Matthew 28:19–20 Jesus commands his disciples to baptize and teach, which for Wesley are the two great branches of discipleship.[89] Wesley goes on to comment that baptism and teaching are to be determined by the context: adults are taught and then baptized, whereas children are baptized and then taught.[90]

Wesley's explanatory notes on Matthew's Gospel are very much

---

84 Wesley, 72.

85 Wesley, 72.

86 Wesley, 72.

87 Wesley, 73.

88 Wesley, 74.

89 Wesley, 74.

90 Wesley, 74.

historical, textual, and contextual. Wesley provided explanation on Matthew's Gospel in the first-century context and clearly saw the relevance of the ancient Christian writings in the contemporary situation. He never imposed his doctrinal beliefs to determine the interpretation of Matthew's Gospel. But he set out to explore the conceptual meaning of the Gospel in its original context. This procedure came to undergird Wesley's doctrinal standards. Wesley was a faithful exegete of the biblical texts, and his quest for discovering the message of the original text of Matthew's Gospel continues to dominate much of modern biblical scholarship.

Teaching and Preaching from Matthew

Teaching

In Matthew's Gospel Jesus commissioned his disciples to make disciples, baptize, and teach (Mt 28:16–20). Teaching primarily has to do with explanations and exhortations, whereas preaching is related to announcing the gospel of Jesus Christ. Teaching is intended for believers to be nourished by the word of God. Preaching focuses on the general mass, including the believers. For instance, Jesus preached the Parable of the Sower to the crowd and to the disciples (Mt 13:1–9). He also preached the sermon both to the crowd and the disciples (Mt 5:1–2), but he privately explained the meaning of the parable to the disciples (Mt 13:18–23).

Sometimes there exists a thin line between teaching and preaching. One could teach while preaching and vice versa. Even in the Gospels both teaching and preaching are spoken of interchangeably. For instance, Matthew reports, "Jesus went throughout Galilee teaching in their synagogues and proclaiming the good news of the kingdom and curing every disease and every sickness among the people" (Mt 4:23). In the same context Mark records, "And he went throughout Galilee, proclaiming the message in their synagogues and casting out demons" (Mk 1:39); and Luke mentions, "So he continued proclaiming the message in the synagogues of Judea" (Lk 4:44). Matthew perceives the ministry of Jesus as that of teaching and preaching in the synagogues, whereas Mark and Luke see it as one of primarily preaching in the synagogues. This suggests that Jesus could teach and preach at the same time in the synagogues.

The author of the Acts of Apostles also refers to the art of teaching and preaching simultaneously. When Peter and John were brought before the council, the religious leaders were "annoyed because they were teaching the people and proclaiming that in Jesus there is the resurrection of the dead" (Acts 4:2). The author of Acts describes another time of teaching and preaching simultaneously: "But Paul and Barnabas remained in Antioch, and there, with many others, they taught and proclaimed the word of the Lord" (Acts 15:35). Paul's missionary work in Rome included both preaching and teaching: Paul "lived there two whole years at his own expense and welcomed all who came to him, proclaiming the kingdom of God and teaching about the Lord Jesus Christ with all boldness and without hindrance" (Acts 28:30–31). From the New Testament point of view, teaching and preaching may go together. Teachers take time to explain the text, and preachers proclaim the message of the text.

The following elements need to be taken into account in teaching a particular passage: (1) Set the passage in context, especially in the context of the Gospel writer who mediated the text to the community. (2) Look for any references or allusions to the Old Testament. The Gospel writers often draw from the Old Testament to relate to the life of Jesus. (3) Draw parallels with other Gospels if the passage is mentioned in more than one Gospel. (4) Discover what the author is trying to communicate through the narrative. (5) Emphasize the central message of the passage as it can be used to edify the believing community. (6) Spend more time consulting study materials to adequately explain the text.[91]

The temptation of Jesus is explained here as an example (Mt 4:1–11).

---

91 For example, W. R. Farmer, *The Gospel of Jesus: The Pastoral Relevance of the Synoptic Problem* (Louisville: Westminster John Knox Press, 1994); *The New Interpreter's Study Bible: New Standard Version with the Apocrypha*, ed. W. J. Harrelson (Nashville: Abingdon Press, 2003); *The New Interpreter's Bible Commentary*, ed. L. E. Keck, 10 vols. (Nashville: Abingdon Press, 2015); *The HarperCollins Study*

The temptation pericope provides an insight into Jesus's role as the messianic Son of God. The testing of God's Son is also paradigmatic, supplying the church with a model for its conduct. The immediate background for the temptation story is Jesus's baptism (Mt 3:1–17). After Jesus is affirmed as God's beloved Son, he is led by the Spirit into the wilderness to be tempted by the devil (Mt 4:1). The setting for the temptation is the wilderness, where food is not to be found, and which is also regarded as the special dwelling place of demons (cf. Lk 8:29). Jesus's encounter with the devil takes place not on a neutral field but on the devil's own turf. Thus, Jesus is the one who enters the strongman's house, binds him, then plunders his goods (cf. Mt 12:29). The temptation is the first battle in Jesus's effort to make God's Kingdom effective among the people. Jesus's confrontation with the devil is in keeping with Matthew's attempt to reveal the true identity of Jesus as God's Son.

Matthew draws attention to the point that a period of fasting for forty days and forty nights occurs prior to the three temptations, which he enumerates (Mt 4:2). The background for such a lengthy fast is found in the experiences of Moses and Elijah (cf. Ex 34:28; 1 Kgs 19:8). These two great figures appear with Jesus at the transfiguration (cf. Mt 17:3). After a lengthy fast, the tempter comes to test Jesus to determine if he is the Son of God (Mt 4:3). Jesus's Sonship is not to be questioned, and the temptation is not to prove his Sonship by performing a miracle. Jesus is already God's Son and has been since the time of his birth (cf. Mt 1:18). Jesus is tested concerning the powers associated with that role. The tempter asks Jesus to display his power as God's Son by turning the stones into loaves of bread to satisfy his hunger (Mt 4:3). Jesus does perform miracles twice to satisfy the hungry crowd (Mt 14:13–21; 15:32–39). However, it would be wrong for Jesus to carry out the devil's proposal, which would make Jesus doubt God's ability to provide for God's Son. That is why Jesus appeals to Scripture in times of crisis so that he could follow the will of God, not the direction of the devil (Mt 4:4; cf. Dt 8:3). To

Bible: Fully Revised and Updated, ed. H. W. Attridge (San Francisco: HarperOne, 2006).

perform a miracle at the direction of the devil would show that Jesus has ceased to trust God and now doubts God in the hour of crisis. Jesus refuses to yield to the temptation of the devil and surrenders his will to the word of God.

Having failed in his first temptation to get Jesus to doubt God, the devil next takes him into the holy city of Jerusalem and places him on the pinnacle of the Temple (Mt 4:5). Now the devil quotes Scripture to persuade Jesus to cast himself down (Mt 4:6; cf. Ps 91:11–12). God does promise to intervene through God's angels to protect those who have faith in God's power (Ps 91:11–12; *Wis* 2:18). Again, Jesus's response comes from Scripture (Mt 4:7; cf. Dt 6:16). The verse in Deuteronomy refers to the episode where the people of Israel tested God in Massah by questioning God's presence among them (Ex 17:1–17). Jesus is tested by the devil to see whether he will question God's presence as did Israel. To leap from the pinnacle of the Temple is to doubt God's presence. So Jesus refuses to yield to the temptation of the devil and affirms his total confidence in God's presence by not undertaking reckless ventures even in the name of divine promises of protection.

Having failed to persuade Jesus to either doubt or test God, the devil next takes him to a very high mountain to induce him to forsake God (Mt 4:8–9). In exchange for the world's glorious kingdoms, the devil demands that Jesus must bow down and worship him. Again, Jesus appeals to the Scripture by showing true allegiance to God (Mt 4:10; cf. Dt 6:13). By refusing to worship the devil, Jesus demonstrates his faith in and obedience to God. In all three temptations Jesus demonstrates that his ultimate goal as God's Son is not to test God but to do and obey God's will.[92] Matthew concludes the temptation account with a ministry by the angels (Mt 4:11; cf. 1 Kgs 19:5–7).

The purpose of the temptation of Jesus in Matthew's Gospel is to show that Jesus is obedient to God's will as revealed in the Scriptures

---

92 Cf. McNicol, *The Persistence of God's Endangered Promises*, 100.

(Dt 6:13, 16; 8:3).[93] For Matthew, Jesus serves as a role model in fulfilling the law and the prophets (cf. Mt 5:17). By placing the story of Jesus's temptation in the wilderness, Matthew reinforces his community's faith in Jesus as the Son of God, who sets a concrete example of trusting God in times of crisis. Like Jesus, the Christian community is invited to use Scriptures, stand against all trials it encounters, and remain faithful to God (cf. Mt 26:9–14).

Preaching

Preaching should build upon teaching. This means that the text chosen should be set in the context of the Gospel writer. Only after a thorough examination of the text in its original context should one proceed to recontextualize the text in preaching. In this book the text chosen for teaching is also used for preaching. On the one hand, the preacher dwells on the message of the text in the context of Matthew's Gospel. On the other hand, the preacher has to deal with the question of how relevant the text assigned is for today. Preachers move between the ancient context and the contemporary situation to make the message relevant and meaningful for today's audience.

The following elements need to be taken into account while preaching from a Gospel text: (1) Set the text in context. (2) Assign a title or theme for the text preached. (3) Have a simple outline of the text. (4) Emphasize the gospel message that comes out of the text. (5) Use both ancient and contemporary illustrations. (6) Have others share their testimony about what God is doing in their lives. (7) Choose appropriate music that will go with the title or the theme. (8) Include a challenge that will motivate the hearers to respond and practice the gospel preached. (9) Include quotes from John Wesley or his exposition of the text. (10) Use the arts. Art gives a way of connecting with God that goes beyond words. It helps people open up their lives to see beauty and give them a feeling of awe. Robin Jensen sums up the

---

93 For a discussion of the use of Deuteronomy in the temptation story, see M. Morris, "Deuteronomy in the Matthean and Lucan Temptation in Light of Early Jewish Anti-demonic Tradition," *CBQ* 78 (2016): 290–301.

significance of the arts in ministry this way: "Art, if it is to have any use for the church, must be vital and dynamic, relevant to the lives we now live. It can affect us and even change us by addressing us at intellectual, emotional, ethical, and spiritual levels. Art can delight our eyes and inspire devotion. Art can deepen our understanding and enrich our worship. It can soothe, delight, and set us on fire."[94]

Both contemporary and ancient arts could be used in preaching to illustrate the message of the text. A simple outline of the text of the temptation of Jesus for preaching may look like this: (1) introduction; (2) setting the temptation of Jesus in context; (3) three temptations of Jesus; (4) temptations today; (5) means to overcome temptations; (6) God's promised deliverance through Jesus Christ; and (7) putting God's promises into practice.

The same text is used for preaching so that preachers can see how preaching can be built upon teaching. It could be titled "Temptation Then and Temptation Now" (Mt 4:1–11). In the context of Matthew's Gospel, Jesus is tested by the devil because he is the Son of God. Jesus is tempted to display the powers connected with being God's Son. After all, who could doubt that God ought to be taking care of God's Son? Jesus ought to have everything he wants. But it turns out that Jesus appealed to Scripture for sustenance. This shows that Jesus came to fulfill the law and the prophets, not to abolish them. Jesus stood firmly on the truth of the word of God. Jesus also chose not to exercise divine privilege or practice miracles to satisfy his own needs. Jesus did not force God to act at the demands of the devil. Jesus would wait on God patiently to discern God's will for his ministry. In Gethsemane Jesus prayed, "My Father, if it is possible, let this cup pass from me; yet not what I want but what you want" (Mt 26:39).

The church that is made up of the people of God is constantly confronted with the temptation to ask God to act in a spectacular way. If you are the daughters and the sons of God, if you are the body of Christ, and if you are the saints in Christ, why not display miraculous

---

94 R. M. Jensen, *The Substance of Things Seen: Art, Faith, and the Christian Community* (Grand Rapids, MI: Wm. B. Eerdmans, 2004), 100.

powers to get attention? Jesus made it clear: God is not someone to be tempted. Rather, the church is God's instrument, God's servant, and God's steward. God wants the church to be the presence, the sign, and the servant of God's will.[95] The church is called to witness to God's power by doing God's will even if God seems to be silent in some situations we face. The prophet Habakkuk expresses his trust in God when everything else fails: "Though the fig tree does not blossom, and no fruit is on the vines; though the produce of the olive fails, and the fields yield no food; though the flock is cut off from the fold, and there is no herd in the stalls, yet I will rejoice in the LORD; I will exult in the God of my salvation" (Hab 3:17–18).

The temptation of Jesus defined his identity as God's Son who chose to trust and follow the will of God rather than the direction of the devil. Likewise, the church receives its identity through baptism, and it is called and sent into the world to witness to the gospel of Jesus Christ. The challenge is that the church can be motivated to demonstrate the available means of divine deliverance in practice. Testimony of the people will be very powerful. Persons may be invited to share in public worship how God helped them overcome temptations and how they used the word of God to fight against all temptations. Those who face temptations in various ways may be invited to follow the example of Jesus and offer hope to those who have yielded to temptations in the world. Other elements, such as illustrations, arts, and John Wesley's thoughts may be integrated into preaching at this point.

The following texts could be used for both teaching and preaching:

1. Mt 5:1–12 (The Beatitudes)

2. Mt 13:24–30 (The Parable of the Weeds among the Wheat)

3. Mt 15:32–39 (The feeding of the four thousand)

4. Mt 20:20–28 (The request of the mother of James and John)

5. Mt 26:6–13 (The anointing at Bethany)

---

95 Cf. C. U. Wolf, "The Continuing Temptation of Christ in the Church: Searching and Preaching on Matthew 4:1-11," *Int* 20 (1966): 297.

Summary

1. The Gospel of Matthew bridges the gap between the Old and the New Testaments. For Matthew, Jesus is the promised Messiah of the Jewish Scriptures. Jesus came not only to save Israel but also the Gentiles. Jesus began his ministry with Israel and expanded to include the Gentiles as future recipients of the Kingdom of Heaven.

2. Matthew, the tax collector, was the author of the first canonical Gospel. It was likely written in the Hebrew language, from which the Greek text of the Gospel emerged. It was probably written around 36 CE in Judea before Matthew went to other nations to proclaim the gospel. It is also probable that Matthew's Gospel was written prior to Paul's arrival in Rome in 60 CE. It was primarily written for the Jewish Christians but was also intended for Gentile believers. In short, Matthew wrote the Gospel to strengthen the faith of Jewish as well as Gentile Christians and encourage them to take the gospel of Jesus Christ to all nations.

3. Matthew discusses the messianic identity of Jesus under seven segments. For Matthew, the promised Messiah is none other than Jesus who is revealed as *Emmanuel* from birth to ascension.

4. Matthew's theology is guided by his conviction that Jesus is *Emmanuel*, who brought the very presence of God through his life and ministry. God's presence will continue to be made available in the preaching of the gospel of Jesus Christ.

5. John Wesley, Bible scholar and founder of Methodism, sought to explain the New Testament to ordinary people in order to make the Scripture clearer and more meaningful in daily life. His exposition of the Gospel of Matthew has implications for textual, contextual, historical, doctrinal, and theological studies.

6. Matthew's Gospel as a whole provides ample opportunities for teaching and preaching in the ministry of the church. Explaining the text in its original context and exposing the message in a contemporary situation constitute the tasks of both teachers and

preachers of the gospel of Jesus Christ. Utilizing contemporary stories, experiences, and art enhance the teaching and preaching ministries of the church.

For Discussion

1. Matthew introduces fourteen quotations from the Old Testament to connect Jesus's life and ministry with scriptural fulfillment (Mt 1:22–23 // Is 7:14; Mt 2:5b–6 // 2 Sm 3:2; Mic 5:2; Mt 2:15b // Hos 11:1; Mt 2:17–18 // Jer 31:15; Mt 2:23b // cf. Is 11:1, Jgs 13:5–7, Zec 3:8, 6:12; Mt 3:3 // Is 40:3; Mt 4:14–16 // Is 9:1–2; Mt 8:17 // Is 53:4; Mt 12:17–21 // Is 42:1–4; Mt 13:14–15 // Is 6:9–10; Mt 13:35 // Ps 78:2; Mt 21:4–5 // Is 62:11, Zec 9:9; Mt 26:56 // no parallel text; Mt 27:9–10 // Zec 11:13). Discuss how Jesus fulfilled each of the Old Testament prophetic quotations. Can you identify more Old Testament prophecies fulfilled in the life and ministry of Jesus Christ?

2. Read the Gospel of Matthew. Can you produce an artistic piece that represents the entire Gospel in its historical/ancient context? Can you also draw one contemporary piece of art that reflects the Gospel of Matthew in today's context?

3. How does Matthew relate the birth of Jesus to his resurrection? Can Christmas and Easter be celebrated together as one event? Share your ideas in the group.

4. Read one healing story of Jesus from Matthew's Gospel. How can the healing ministry be administrated to people in today's context?

5. Read Matthew 18:15–17. How does John Wesley interpret this passage with regard to issues faced within the church? What process does Wesley suggest to resolve any ecclesiastical trials? Discuss an issue that currently affects the church, and bring Wesley into the conversation.

3

The Gospel According to
Mark

Introduction

A fter their departure [Peter and Paul], Mark, the disciple and interpreter of Peter, did also hand down to us in writing what had been preached by Peter."[1] Thus writes Irenaeus about Mark's Gospel. Although Mark was not one of Jesus's disciples, he was identified as the interpreter of Peter, who was one of the chief disciples.

In the canonical order, Mark's Gospel comes between Matthew's and Luke's. Since the time of Origen, Mark is always placed after Matthew and before Luke.[2] But that order may not be the sequential order of composition.[3] Augustine maintained that Mark followed Matthew closely: "Mark follows him [Matthew] closely, and looks like his attendant and epitomizer. For in his narrative he gives nothing in concert with John apart from the others: by himself separately, he has little to record; in conjunction with Luke, as distinguished from the rest, he has still less; but in concord with Matthew, he has a very large number of passages."[4] Augustine's view of

---

1 Irenaeus, *Haer.* 3.1., in *The Apostolic Fathers with Justin Martyr and Irenaeus*, ed. A. C. Coxe, vol. 1 of *Ante-Nicene Fathers*, ed. A. Roberts and J. Donaldson (Peabody, MA: Hendrickson Publishers, 1999), 414.

2 Cf. Eusebius, *Hist. eccl.* 6.25.3–6.

3 See D. B. Peabody et al., *One Gospel from Two: Mark's Use of Matthew and Luke. A Demonstration by the Research Team of the International Institute for Gospel Studies* (Harrisburg, PA: Trinity Press International, 2002), 51–52.

4 Augustine, *Cons.* 1.2.4, in Augustine, *The Harmony of the Gospels*, trans. S. D. F. Salmond, ed. M. B. Riddle, vol. 6 of *Nicene and Post-Nicene Fathers*, ed. P. Schaff (Peabody, MA: Hendrickson Publishers, 1995), 78.

Mark's Gospel as a summary appears to affirm its brevity.[5] A careful study of Mark's Gospel reveals that Mark left out the birth of Jesus and much of his teaching, even though Mark refers to Jesus as teaching regularly (cf. Mk 4:1; 6:2; 8:31; 9:31; 10:1; 12:35; 14:49). Mark's Gospel begins and ends abruptly. It begins not with the birth of Jesus but with the appearance of John the Baptist (Mk 1:1–8); and it ends not with the commissioning of the disciples but with women fleeing from the tomb (Mk 16:1–8). In comparison to Matthew and Luke, Mark chose to introduce a shorter version of the gospel of Jesus Christ.

Authorship

Mark's Gospel never mentions Mark's name anywhere. Some have argued that the story of a "young man" (Gk: *neaniskos*) running naked at the Garden of Gethsemane may point to the author of Mark, but this remains only a guess (Mk 14:51–52).[6] This story is attested neither in Matthew nor in Luke. The second Gospel also mentions a "young man" at the tomb, but here he is "dressed in a white robe" (Mk 16:5). However, the author of the second Gospel chose not to name this young man.

The early Church Fathers identified the author of the second Gospel as John Mark, who is mentioned in Acts 12:12. According to the Acts of the Apostles, Peter knew the mother of John Mark. After the miraculous escape from prison, Peter went to the house of Mary, who is the mother of John, whose other name is Mark (Acts 12:12–17). Accordingly, Mark lived in Jerusalem with his mother Mary, who was a widow. Mark was also a cousin of Barnabas, a missionary companion

---

5 For a detailed discussion of the Augustinian hypothesis (Matthew was reworked by Mark, Luke, and John), see D. B. Peabody, "Augustine and Augustinian Hypothesis: A Reexamination of Augustine's Thought in *De consensu evangelistarum*," in W. R. Farmer, ed., *New Synoptic Studies: The Cambridge Gospel Conference and Beyond* (Macon, GA: Mercer University Press, 1983), 37–66.

6 For a discussion of a mysterious young man running naked in the context of "following" in Mark's Gospel, see S. B. Hatton, "Mark's Naked Disciple: The Semiotics and Comedy of Following," *Neot* 35 (2001): 35–48.

of Paul (Col 4:10), and accompanied both Paul and Barnabas on their first missionary journey (Acts 13:5). However, when a second missionary journey was suggested by Paul, and Barnabas wanted to take John Mark with them, Paul objected. It seems that John Mark had deserted them in Pamphylia and did not finish the journey. Because of Paul's refusal to take John Mark, Barnabas parted company with Paul, taking Mark to Cyprus, while Paul took Silas to Syria and Cilicia (Acts 15:36–41).

Nevertheless, Mark occupies a favorable place in Paul's letters. Paul calls Mark a "fellow worker" (Phlm 1:24) and sends greetings to the church at Colossae from Mark (Col 4:10). In later imprisonment Paul urges Timothy to bring Mark with him and regards him as "useful" in his ministry (2 Tm 4:11). Later tradition has Mark joining the apostle Peter when Peter came to Rome.[7] Peter sends greetings to Christians in five Roman provinces of Asia Minor on behalf of Mark, whom Peter calls "my son" (1 Pt 5:13). Referring to the testimony given by Clement of Alexandria, Eusebius writes,

> But a great light of religion shone on the minds of the hearers of Peter, so that they were not satisfied with a single hearing or with the unwritten teaching of the divine proclamation, but with every kind of exhortation besought Mark, whose Gospel is extant, seeing that he was Peter's follower, to leave them a written statement of the teaching given them verbally, nor did they cease until they had persuaded him, and so became the cause of the Scripture called the Gospel according to Mark.[8]

The early church tradition places Mark with Peter as his companion and identifies Mark as the author of the second canonical Gospel. Since then, because of its association with Peter's preaching, the Gospel of Mark was deemed an authoritative document.

---

7   Cf. Eusebius, *Hist. eccl.* 6.25.5: "Secondly, that according to Mark, who wrote it in accordance with Peter's instructions, whom also Peter acknowledged as his son in the catholic epistle, speaking in these terms: 'She that is in Babylon, elect together with you, saluteth you; and so doth Mark my son.'"

8   Eusebius, 2.15.1.

Date, Purpose, and Place of Writing

Compared with Matthew and Luke, Mark's Gospel does not have many important accounts of what took place in Jesus's life. For example, Mark does not have the birth story of Jesus or the Sermon on the Mount. On the other hand, much of Luke's famous travel account of Jesus going to Jerusalem is omitted in Mark, as are the parables of the Good Samaritan and the Lost Son. Instead, Mark begins his Gospel with an epithet: "The beginning of the good news of Jesus Christ, the Son of God" (Mk 1:1). It shows that Mark is going to narrate the story of Jesus beginning with his public proclamation (Mk 1:14). Mark includes an account of the ministry of John the Baptist (Mk 1:2–8). He alludes to Jesus's baptism (Mk 1:9–12). He mentions an abbreviated version of Jesus's temptation (Mk 1:12–13; cf. Mt 4:1–2, 11). Then he moves on to focus on Jesus's Galilean ministry (Mk 1:14–10:52). Mark devotes the last few sections of his account to Jesus's ministry in Jerusalem and his arrest, death, and resurrection (Mk 11:1–16:8). Mark's briefer account of the life of Jesus gives the appearance of an edited summary of both Matthew and Luke.

A feature of Mark is the translation of certain Aramaic words, presumably for Gentile readers. Matthew and Luke do not emphasize this as much. Mark mentions the nickname "Boanerges" (Sons of Thunder) given to James and John, the sons of Zebedee (Mk 3:17; cf. Mt 10:2; Lk 6:14). In the healing story of Jairus's daughter, Jesus takes the little girl by the hand and says to her, "Talitha cum," which is translated as "Little girl, get up!" (Mk 5:41; cf. Mt 9:25; Lk 8:54). Mark also stresses the tension between the command to honor one's parents and the command to honor oaths to God and uses the word *corban*, which is translated as "an offering to God" (Mk 7:11–12). In the healing story of a deaf man with a speech impediment, Jesus says to the man, "'Ephphatha,' that is, 'Be opened'" (Mk 7:34). At the Garden of Gethsemane, Jesus prays using the Aramaic word *abba*, which means "father" (Mk 14:36; cf. Mt 26:39; Lk 22:42). Mark mentions that Jesus was brought to the place called Golgotha, which means "the place of a skull" (Mk 15:22; cf. Mt 27:33). Mark records the cry of Jesus from the cross in Aramaic words, "'Eloi, Eloi lema sabachthani?,' which means, 'My God, my God why have you forsaken me?'" (Mk 15:34; cf. a more Hebrew form in Mt 27:46). In all, it appears to show that Mark reworked a Palestinian tradition for a wider Greco-Roman audience.

In what is called the "little apocalypse," Mark 13:1–37 has parallels in Matthew 24:1–36 and Luke 21:1–36; it seems to be an interweaving of the two earlier accounts.[9] Like Matthew and Luke, Mark simply forecasts Jesus's prediction of the destruction of the Temple in the future, suggesting that Mark's Gospel was probably written prior to the destruction of the Temple in 70 CE.[10] Mark was not writing *ex post facto* of the events surrounding the destruction of Jerusalem but was standing in solidarity with Matthew and Luke to present the prophecy of Jesus, which was to fulfill in the near future.

The early church tradition puts the composition of Mark's Gospel during the ministry of Peter. Papias, quoting the testimony of the Presbyter (Elder), associates Mark's Gospel with Peter's preaching: "And the Presbyter used to say this, 'Mark became Peter's interpreter and wrote accurately all that he remembered, not, indeed, in order, of the things said or done by the Lord. . . . For to one thing he gave attention, to leave out nothing of what he had heard and to make no false statements in them.'"[11]

We assume that before Mark joined Peter in Rome, Mark lived in Jerusalem, where he would have become familiar with the Palestinian gospel tradition. When Mark accompanied Paul on his missionary work, Mark would have come across the Lukan gospel tradition, as

---

9 See Peabody et al., *One Gospel from Two*, 264–76.

10 Some scholars date Mark's Gospel prior to 70 CE. See A. Y. Collins, *Mark: A Commentary*, ed. H. W. Attridge (Minneapolis: Fortress Press, 2007), 11–14.

11 Eusebius, *Hist. eccl.* 3.39.15. Jerome also indicates that Mark composed his Gospel in accordance with what he heard from Peter in *Vir. ill.* 8.1: "Mark, the disciple and interpreter of Peter, wrote a short gospel at the request of the brethren at Rome, embodying what he had heard Peter tell." *On Illustrious Men*, trans. T. P. Halton, *The Fathers of the Church*, vol. 100 (Washington, DC: The Catholic University of America Press, 1999), 17.

Luke was also the companion of Paul (cf. Phlm 24; Col 4:14). So, when Mark joined Peter in Rome, Mark probably presupposed some gospel traditions that were in circulation. As C. S. Mann comments, "Acting as Peter's interpreter provided an opportunity to hear an eyewitness at first hand; afterward, in the light of that experience and in comparison with sources already known, he could commit the tradition to writing."[12] Early church tradition claims that Mark went to Egypt with his Gospel: "They [Presbyters] say that this Mark was the first to be sent to preach in Egypt the Gospel which he had also put into writing, and was the first to establish churches in Alexandria itself."[13] The testimony of the primitive presbyters suggests that Mark composed his Gospel in Rome when Peter was alive and then brought it to Alexandria. If Peter died around 64 CE, then Mark could have arrived with his Gospel in Egypt after the martyrdom of Peter. Early church tradition also places Peter in Rome during the reign of Emperor Claudius (10 BCE–54 CE) when Philo of Alexandria (10 BCE–50 CE) came to speak to Peter on his visit to Claudius. Eusebius writes, "Tradition says that [Philo] came to Rome in the time of Claudius to speak to Peter, who was at that time preaching to those there."[14] Based on early church tradition, Mark probably composed his Gospel in consultation with Peter and with available sources anywhere between 50 and 64 CE.

Mark's purpose seems to be kerygmatic in accord with the *kerygma* (preaching) of the apostle Peter. In his speech on the Day of Pentecost, Peter gives only a summary of Jesus's ministry without giving any lengthy discourse on Jesus's teaching (Acts 2:22–24). In light of the imminent catastrophic events that would culminate in the destruction

---

12 C. S. Mann, *Mark: A New Translation with Introduction and Commentary*, AB 27 (New York: Doubleday, 1986), 76.

13 Eusebius, *Hist. eccl.* 2.16.1. Jerome also mentions that Mark went to Egypt with his Gospel in *Vir. ill.* 8.3: "So, taking the *Gospel* which he himself had composed, he went to Egypt, and, first preaching Christ in Alexandria, he formed a church with such great continence in doctrine and life that he constrained all followers of Christ to his example." *On Illustrious Men*, 18.

14 Eusebius, *Hist. eccl.* 2.17.1.

of the Temple, the Markan Jesus has less time to complete his ministry. So Mark omits many lengthy discourses and sets out to write a concise Gospel that will prepare his audience to face the future with watchfulness (Mk 13:33–37).[15]

Early Christian writings unanimously associate Mark with Peter, who was preaching in Rome. If Mark composed his Gospel after listening to the preaching of Peter, Rome would be the place of Mark's writing. Eusebius, drawing from the testimony of the primitive elders mentioned in the books of Clement, writes,

> When Peter had publicly preached the word at Rome, and by the Spirit had proclaimed the Gospel, that those present, who were many, exhorted Mark, as one who had followed him for a long time and remembered what had been spoken, to make a record of what was said; and that he did this, and distributed the Gospel among those who asked him. And that when the matter came to Peter's knowledge he neither strongly forbade it nor urged it forward.[16]

Early church tradition puts the composition of Mark's Gospel in Rome. Mark's use of Latin terms further enhances the theory of Roman origin (Mk 5:9, 15; 6:27; 12:15; 15:3; 15:39, 44, 45). Mark alone refers to Simon of Cyrene as "the father of Alexander and Rufus" (Mk 15:21), which indicates Mark's close knowledge of what happened. But Matthew and Luke simply mention the one who carried Jesus's cross as a "Cyrene named Simon" (Mt 27:32) and as "Simon

---

15 According to the view of the great nineteenth-century Tübingen scholar, Ferdinand Christian Baur, Mark summarized both Matthew and Luke to produce a shorter Gospel. Therefore, Mark cannot be considered as an independent source in order to argue for Markan priority. See Baur, *Lectures on New Testament Theology*, trans. R. F. Brown, ed. P. C. Hodgson (Oxford: Oxford University Press, 2016), 79. See J. Samuel Subramanian, review of *Lectures on New Testament Theology*, by F. C. Baur, *Reading Religion*, December 12, 2016, https://readingreligion.org/books/lectures-new -testament-theology. Other scholars argue for Mark and Q as the earliest independent sources in the study of the source question. See C. M. Tuckett, *The Revival of the Griesbach Hypothesis: An Analysis and Appraisal*, SNTSMS 44 (Cambridge: Cambridge University Press, 1983); J. S. Kloppenborg, *Q, The Earliest Gospel: An Introduction to the Original Stories and Sayings of Jesus* (Louisville: Westminster John Knox Press, 2008).

16 Eusebius, *Hist. eccl.* 6.14.6–7.

of Cyrene" (Lk 23:26). It is likely that both Alexander and Rufus were known to Mark's readers in Rome. In his final greetings in the Letter to the Romans, Paul refers to Rufus as the one "chosen in the Lord" (Rom 16:13). Therefore, it is probable that Mark wrote his Gospel for the Roman audience.

Main Themes

Mark begins his Gospel with the preaching of John the Baptist and continues with Jesus's proclamation of the gospel (Mk 1:1–14). Mark emphasizes the itinerant ministry of Jesus with these words: "Jesus came to Galilee, proclaiming the good news of God" (Mk 1:14). The first words uttered by Jesus in Mark's Gospel are: "The time is fulfilled, and the kingdom of God has come near; repent, and believe in the good news" (Mk 1:15). After that, Mark keeps Jesus moving from one place to another in order to highlight Jesus's itinerancy (cf. Mk 1:21, 29, 35; 2:1, 13; 3:1, 7, 13; 5:1, 21; 6:1, 54; 7:24; 9:33; 10:1, 46; 11:1, 27; 13:1).

Mark is not interested in engaging in lengthy discourses and narratives. Only Matthew and Luke have the birth story and most of Jesus's teachings. Although the common source of Mark is found in Matthew and Luke, Mark has a special source that is not attested either in Matthew or in Luke. We see this in that only Mark has these two miracle stories—the healing of the deaf and dumb man (Mk 7:31–37) and the healing of the blind man at Bethsaida (Mk 8:22–26)—and the Parable of the Sprouting Seed (Mk 4:26–29) and Parable of the Doorkeeper (Mk 13:34–37). Based on the materials Mark has, his entire Gospel may be divided into two major sections to highlight the ministry of Jesus: (1) Jesus's ministry near the Sea of Galilee (Mk 1:16–8:21); and (2) Jesus's ministry from Galilee to Jerusalem (Mk 8:22–16:8).[17]

Main themes of Mark's Gospel are related to the way the Gospel

---

17 Mann provides a detailed outline of Mark that is very easy to follow. Mann, *Mark*, 177–90.

is structured.[18] Each narrative sequence is centered around Jesus as the bearer of the good news in and beyond Galilee. Mark focuses on the events surrounding the ministry of Jesus, who comes to proclaim the good news of the kingdom of God as God's special messenger. The following structure summarizes the overarching theme of the proclamation of Jesus as God's envoy:

1. Prologue: The ministry of John the Baptist and the introduction of Jesus (Mk 1:1–15)

2. Book 1: Beginning of Jesus's ministry (Mk 1:16–6:6a)

3. Book 2: Jesus's teaching and healing (Mk 6:6b–8:26)

4. Book 3: Peter's declaration about Jesus, Jesus's predictions about his death and resurrection, and Jesus's transfiguration (Mk 8:27–9:50)

5. Book 4: Jesus's ministry near and in Jerusalem (Mk 10:1–13:37)

6. Book 5: Jesus's suffering and crucifixion (Mk 14:1–15:47)

7. Epilogue: Jesus's resurrection and commissioning (Mk 16:1 8, 9 20)

Prologue: The Ministry of John the Baptist and the Introduction of Jesus (Mk 1:1–15)

The prologue of Mark's Gospel explicates the ministry of Jesus in light of the entire Gospel.[19] John the Baptist is introduced to announce the coming of Jesus (Mk 1:2–8). Jesus is affirmed as God's Son at his baptism (Mk 1:9–11). Jesus is tempted in the wilderness and is ministered to by the angels (Mk 1:12–13). Then Jesus is presented with the ministry of preaching the good news (Mk 1:14–15).

Mark sees the ministry of John the Baptist as fulfilling the prophecy of the Scripture, because Mark quotes the prophet Isaiah as well as

---

18 For a good discussion of the structure of Mark's Gospel and how it relates to its themes, see B. W. Bacon, "The Prologue of Mark: A Study of Sources and Structure," *JBL* 20 (1907): 84–106; S. H. Smith, "A Divine Tragedy: Some Observations on the Dramatic Structure of Mark's Gospel," *NovT* 37 (1995): 209–31; K. W. Larson, "The Structure of Mark's Gospel: Current Proposals," *CBR* 3 (2004): 140–60.

19 Cf. F. J. Matera, "The Prologue as the Interpretive Key to Mark's Gospel," *JSNT* 34 (1988): 3–20.

the prophet Malachi (Mk 1:2–3; cf. Is 40:3; Mal 3:1). The messenger is being sent to prepare the way of the Lord, which is brought by Jesus. Mark makes John the Baptist express his witness to the coming of the Powerful One by declaring himself unfit even to perform the servant's task of untying the sandal of the one who is to come after him (Mk 1:7–8). Mark explicitly states that Jesus was baptized by John the Baptist in the Jordan (Mk 1:9). In this way, Mark shows that Jesus accepts the ministry of John the Baptist, who prepared Jesus's way for his coming. At his baptism Jesus hears a voice from heaven that confirms him as God's Son and messenger (Mk 1:11; cf. Ps 2:7; Is 42:1). Jesus receives the Spirit from above to perform the ministry that lay ahead. The same Spirit consequently drives Jesus to be tempted in the wilderness (Mk 1:12). While the fuller account of Jesus's temptation is found in Matthew 4:1–11 and Luke 4:1–13, Mark makes only a brief reference to Jesus's temptation in the wilderness (Mk 1:12–13). Here Mark alludes to Jesus as the "New Adam" by placing him "with the wild beasts" similarly to the "Old Adam" who was also with the wild beasts (Mk 1:13b; cf. Gn 2:19–20).

Mark's prologue concludes with the arrest of John the Baptist and the preaching of Jesus (Mk 1:14–15). Mark probably learned about the arrest of John the Baptist from his predecessors, Matthew and Luke (Mt 4:12; Lk 3:19–20). After John's arrests Jesus begins to proclaim the gospel of God. For Mark, the good news that Jesus preaches is not just about the message of the Kingdom of God, but it is the whole of Jesus's story, the whole of what he says and does as God's messenger.[20] Each of the segments that Mark lays out in his Gospel attests to the story of Jesus, who is the messenger of the good news of God.

Book 1: Beginning of Jesus's Ministry (Mk 1:16–6:6a)

In this section Mark begins with Jesus calling the four fishermen and ends with Jesus's rejection at Nazareth. Jesus calls Simon and his brother Andrew, and James son of Zebedee and his brother John

---

20 Cf. A. J. McNicol, *The Persistence of God's Endangered Promises: The Bible's Unified Story* (London: Bloomsbury T. & T. Clark, 2018), 160.

(Mk 1:16–20). All four of them leave everything to follow Jesus. Mark mentions the call of Levi son of Alphaeus, who is a tax collector and is noted as Matthew among the list of the twelve apostles (Mk 2:13–17; 3:13–19). In all, Mark specifically speaks of the call of five disciples, and the names of the rest of the disciples are mentioned in the list.

Mark records eight miracle stories of Jesus: the healing of a man with an unclean spirit (Mk 1:21–28), the healing of Simon's mother-in-law with a fever (Mk 1:29–31), the healing of a man with leprosy (Mk 1:40–45), the healing of a paralytic man (Mk 2:1–12), the healing of a man with a withered hand (Mk 3:1–6), the stilling of a storm (Mk 4:35–41), the healing of a woman with a hemorrhage (Mk 5:25–34), and the raising of a little girl from death (Mk 5:22–24, 35–43). In most of the healing stories, Jesus orders the recipients of the miracles not to tell anyone about it.[21] But they all begin to proclaim and spread the word about Jesus. The healing stories serve as a tool to proclaim the one who came to proclaim the good news. The stilling of the storm reveals Jesus's deity, because only God can cause winds to cease (Mk 4:39–41; cf. Ps 107:29). Mark sums up the ministry of Jesus in this way: "And [Jesus] went throughout Galilee, proclaiming the message in their synagogues and casting out demons" (Mk 1:39).

Mark attributes three parables to Jesus: the Parable of the Sower, the Parable of the Growing Seed, and the Parable of the Mustard Seed (Mk 4:1–20, 26–32). The parables serve as a tool for the teaching ministry of Jesus. Not only does Jesus speak in parables to the crowd, but he also explains the meaning of the parables in private to his disciples (Mk 4:34).

Mark emphasizes the healing, teaching, and preaching ministries of Jesus; and he also clarifies some of the misconceptions of Jesus's ministry. This is reflected in Jesus's debate with the Pharisees on the

---

21 The scenario of having Jesus's identity hidden is called "Mark's Messianic Secret." The secret functions as a narrative that shows the message simply could not be hidden. It is Mark's artistic way of keeping Jesus's identity secret until his resurrection. See W. Wrede, *The Messianic Secret*, trans. J. C. G. Greig (Cambridge, UK: James Clarke & Co., 1971); H. Räisänen, *The "Messianic Secret" in Mark's Gospel* (London: T. & T. Clark, 2000).

question of fasting and of working on the Sabbath (Mk 2:18–27) and with the scribes on the question of Jesus's authority over the demons (Mk 3:22–30). Mark identifies Jesus as the bridegroom (Mk 2:20), the Lord of the Sabbath (Mk 2:28), and the possessor of the Holy Spirit (Mk 3:28–30). Although Jesus is rejected in Nazareth, his hometown, people still recognize his extraordinary power. Mark tells that people testified about Jesus this way: "Where did this man get all this? What is this wisdom that has been given to him? What deeds of power are being done by his hands!" (Mk 6:2b). Mark depicts Jesus continuing to heal the sick, even while Mark hints at the future by describing Jesus's amazement at the people's unbelief (Mk 6:5–6a).

Book 2: Jesus's Teaching and Healing (Mk 6:6b–8:26)

In this division Mark focuses on Jesus's teaching and healing. Mark begins this section with these words: "Then [Jesus] went about among the villages teaching" (Mk 6:6b). Jesus sends out the Twelve to preach the message of repentance, cast out demons, anoint the sick with oil, and cure them (Mk 6:7–13). The ministry of the disciples embodies Jesus's ministry, and the feeding of the five thousand is set in the context of Jesus's teaching. Mark again highlights the teaching ministry of Jesus with these words: "As [Jesus] went ashore, he saw a great crowd; and he had compassion for them, because they were like sheep without a shepherd; and he began to teach them many things" (Mk 6:34). Like Matthew, Mark records the feeding of the four thousand in addition to the feeding of the five thousand (Mk 8:1–9; cf. Mt 15:32–39). He records four healing stories in this unit: healing many sick people (Mk 6:53–56), healing the Syrophoenician women's daughter (Mk 7:24–30), healing a deaf man (Mk 7:3–37), and healing a blind man at Bethsaida (Mk 8:22–26). Mark uses the healing stories as a vehicle to proclaim Jesus's ministry and continuously draws attention to the proclamation of the people about Jesus: "Then Jesus ordered them to tell no one; but the more he ordered them, the more zealously they proclaimed it" (Mk 7:36).

Jesus engages the Pharisees and the scribes in teaching the tradition of the elders (Mk 7:1–13). With regard to the washing of the hands before eating, Jesus quotes Isaiah 29:13 to stress the importance of inward purity, which ultimately matters to God (Mk 7:6–8), when he reminds the crowd, "Listen to me, all of you, and understand: there is nothing outside a person that by going in can defile, but the things that come out are what defile" (Mk 7:14b–15). Jesus goes on to explain to his disciples that the only thing that matters to God is a pure heart, not the food (Mk 7:17–23). The Pharisees again come to Jesus and demand a sign from heaven in order to question his ministry (Mk 8:11). Earlier, the disciples also doubt the power of Jesus when they realize they forgot to bring any bread on the boat (Mk 7:14). Jesus then draws attention to the miraculous feeding of the five thousand on one occasion (Mk 7:16–21). Jesus continues to provide signs from heaven through his ministry that the Pharisees and even his disciples fail to comprehend. Jesus even walks on the water to demonstrate yet another sign from heaven that he is indeed God's messenger (Mk 6:47–52). For Mark, everything Jesus does is a sign from heaven, and there is no more sign needed other than the presence of Jesus himself.

Book 3: Peter's Declaration about Jesus, Jesus's Predictions about His Death and Resurrection, and Jesus's Transfiguration (Mk 8:27–9:50)

Here Mark has many things to say about Jesus, who is both the Messiah and the Servant of the Lord. Peter's declaration at Caesarea Philippi affirms that Jesus—not John the Baptist, Elijah, or one of the prophets—is the Messiah (Mk 8:27–30). Mark adds that Jesus ordered Peter not to tell anyone about him (Mk 8:30) because Peter still needs to understand the nature of Jesus's Messiahship. Following Peter's confession Jesus talks about his suffering, death, and resurrection (Mk 8:31); but Peter cannot understand how a Messiah can suffer, so he takes Jesus aside and begins to rebuke him. In turn, Jesus rebukes Peter by saying, "Get behind me, Satan! For you are setting your mind not on divine things but on human things" (Mk 8:33). By doing this, Jesus is set as the Messiah who is to be perceived in relation to divine events. For Mark, divine events include Jesus's suffering, rejection, death, and resurrection. Mark has Jesus using the literary formula "Truly I tell you" to predict the future (Mk 9:1; 13:30; 14:25).[22] The transfiguration of Jesus on a high mountain points to his vindication beyond his death on the cross (Mk 9:2–8). This fact will become important when we examine the ending of Mark's Gospel. For Mark, the disciples—especially Peter, James, and John—would not understand the significance of Jesus's transfiguration until after his resurrection. That is why Jesus "ordered them to tell no one about what they had seen, until after the Son of Man had risen from the dead" (Mk 9:9).

Jesus again teaches his disciples about his betrayal, death, and resurrection. He says to the disciples, "The Son of Man is to be betrayed into human hands, and they will kill him, and three days after being killed, he will rise again" (Mk 9:31). Mark points out that the disciples are not able to understand what Jesus is teaching about his death and resurrection (Mk 9:32), and they will not understand until after Jesus's resurrection.

Jesus's healing of a boy with a spirit illustrates that the disciples could not cast out the evil spirit or bring back the afflicted boy to health. Only Jesus has the divine power to do so (Mk 9:17–27).[23] When the disciples ask why they could not cast out the evil spirit from the boy, Jesus answers, saying, "This kind can come out only through prayer" (Mk 9:29). It shows that the disciples still have much to learn from Jesus. Both Jesus's teaching and his healing ministry continue to elude the comprehension of the disciples.

Jesus's teaching on "greatness" reveals his own ministry of servanthood (Mk 9:33–37). Earlier Jesus talks about his suffering and death (Mk 9:31). Now he teaches that greatness is to be achieved only through humility and service. Jesus says to the disciples, "Whoever wants to be first must be last of all and servant of all" (Mk 9:35). For

---

22 For a discussion of the prophetic sayings of Jesus in Mark and their parallels in Matthew and Luke, see D. B. Peabody, "A Pre-Markan Prophetic Sayings Tradition and the Synoptic Problem," *JBL* 97 (1978): 391–409.

23 For an explication of Jesus's healing of a boy with an unclean spirit in Mark's Gospel, see F. C. Spencer, "Faith on Edge: The Difficult Case of the Spirit-Seized Boy in Mark 9:14-29," *RevExp* 107 (2010): 419–24.

Mark, Jesus embodies the ministry of a servant. Jesus serves others through his preaching, teaching, and healing; and the crowd and the disciples should follow Jesus's example through self-denial and servanthood (cf. Mk 8:34–36). Akin to his concept of servant leadership, Jesus picks up a child, takes the child in his arms, and then says to his disciples, "Whoever welcomes one such child in my name welcomes me, and whoever welcomes me welcomes not me but the one who sent me" (Mk 9:37). Jesus comes like a child and goes unnoticed as a servant—if Jesus is welcomed, God is welcomed. Mark emphasizes Jesus's hidden identity. Just like a child who is not recognized as a person of stature, Jesus is not recognized as God's messenger. But if we do recognize who Jesus is, we will also recognize the God who sent Jesus to teach, heal, suffer, die, and rise from the dead.

Book 4: Jesus's Ministry Near and in Jerusalem (Mk 10:1–13:37)

In this division Mark presents Jesus's ministry on his way to and in Jerusalem. While Jesus and his disciples are on the move toward Jerusalem (Mk 10:7), Jesus engages some Pharisees on the question of divorce (Mk 10:2), where he does acknowledge the then-common interpretation of the Moses's law on divorce. Divorce is permitted according to the law of Moses (Mk 10:4; cf. Dt 24:1–4). However, Jesus acknowledges that because of depravity of the human heart, the marriage bond might be dissolved (Mk 10:5). But he goes on to reiterate the permanence of the marriage bond since the time of God's creation (Mk 10:5–9; cf. Gn 2:24). In his private teaching to the disciples, Jesus seems to reaffirm the permanence of marriage, which is rooted in divine ordinance (Mk 10:10–12).[24]

Mark reports that Jesus not only blesses children, but he also sets them as an example for God's kingdom (Mk 10:13–16). When people bring little children to Jesus, his disciples try to keep the children away (Mk 10:13). But Jesus invites the children to him and says to the disciples, "Let the little children come to me; do not stop them; for it

---

24 For an explanation of Jesus's teaching on divorce in Mark's Gospel, see B. Green, "Jesus's Teachings on Divorce in the Gospel of Mark," *JSNT* 38 (1990): 67–75.

is to such as these that the kingdom of God belongs. Truly I tell you, whoever does not receive the kingdom of God as a little child will never enter it" (Mk 10:14–15). Jesus goes on to declare that no one will be able to enter the Kingdom of God unless he or she receives it as a child. He encourages his followers to be receptive to trusting and embracing the powerlessness. Jesus takes the children up in his arms, lays his hands on them, and blesses them (Mk 10:16), because he sees trust and powerlessness in the children as definitive of the Kingdom of God.

Then Jesus addresses the question of what one should do to inherit eternal life (Mk 10:17–22). He makes it clear that eternal life cannot be attained through riches, but only through self-denial (Mk 10:22). Again, Jesus explains to the disciples in private that those who have given up everything to follow him will receive the reward in this life and eternal life in the age to come (Mk 10:29–30).

Jesus takes his disciples aside and talks about his suffering, death, and resurrection as they travel on the way to Jerusalem (Mk 10:32–34). Here Jesus teaches his disciples about true greatness (Mk 10:35–40). For Jesus, true greatness depends on sacrifice (Mk 10:39), and he sets himself as the example of sacrifice, saying, "For the Son of Man came not be served but to serve, and to give his life a ransom for many" (Mk 10:45).

Before Jesus and his disciples enter Jerusalem, Jesus stops in Jericho to heal Bartimaeus, a blind beggar (Mk 10:46–52). Bartimaeus addresses Jesus with the title "the Son of David" (Mk 10:47–48). He also addresses Jesus with the words, "My teacher" (Mk 10:51), which suggests that Bartimaeus recognizes both the messianic identity of Jesus as the Son of David (cf. 2 Sm 7:12–14) and the authority of Jesus as Teacher.[25] Mark ends the healing story with Bartimaeus following Jesus "on the way" (Gk: *en tē hodō*) to Jerusalem (Mk 10:52).[26] Mark used

---

25 For an interpretation of the healing of blind Bartimaeus as a story of discipleship, see P. J. Achtemeier, "And He Followed Him: Miracles and Discipleship in Mark 10:46–52," *Semeia* 11 (1978): 67–75.

26 Cf. McNicol, *The Persistence of God's Endangered Promises*, 167.

the phrase "on the way" earlier to signify Jesus's journey to Jerusalem (Mk 8:27; 9:33; 10:17, 32), the journey that will end with Jesus's death on the cross. Bartimaeus started following Jesus "on the way." To follow "on the way" is to go to the way of the cross and to know what Jesus's ministry is all about. For Mark, the cross became the culmination of God's redemptive act in the person of Jesus (cf. Mk 10:33–34).[27]

With Jesus's entry into Jerusalem, Mark focuses on Jesus's ministry there (Mk 11:1–13:37). Jesus is welcomed in the words drawn from Psalm 118:25–26a as the one who brings the Kingdom of David (Mk 11:9a–10).[28] Mark clearly sees Jesus as a Davidic Messiah who comes to restore the destiny of King David (2 Sm 7:12–13). Jesus cleanses the Temple as an act of restoring it as "a house of prayer" (Mk 11:17; cf. Jer 7:1–11), thereby linking the cleansing of the Temple with the issue of Jesus's authority. The chief priests, scribes, and elders presume that Jesus speaks against the Temple because he claims authority from "heaven" (Mk 11:27–35). They despise that claim and begin to develop a plot to have him put to death after he tells the Parable of the Wicked Tenants (Mk 12:1–11). Mark uses Psalm 118:22–23 to forecast Jesus's rejection and vindication (Mk 12:10–11).[29] The religious leaders want to arrest Jesus because they think the parable is directed toward them (Mk 12:12). But Jesus continues to debate with the Pharisees, Sadducees, and scribes and silences them. With regard to the payment of taxes, Jesus says, "Give to the emperor the things that are the emperor's, and to God the things that are God's" (Mk 12:17).

With regard to the question of future resurrection, Jesus affirms that God is not the God of the dead but of the living (Mk 12:27). This further suggests that all the departed saints are already living with God and that they will be raised back to life at the general

---

27 It is noteworthy that "The Way" was one of the first, if not the first, names of the Jesus movement (cf. Acts 9:2; 19:9, 23; 22:4; 24:14, 22).

28 For Mark's use of Psalm 118, see J. S. Subramanian, *The Synoptic Gospels and the Psalms and the Psalms as Prophecy,* LNTS 351 (London: T. & T. Clark, 2007), 46–53.

29 For Mark's use of "stone" imagery taken from Psalms 118:22–23, see Subramanian, 53–57.

resurrection (cf. Mk 12:24). In response to the scribes' question of the primacy of the commandments of Moses, Jesus sets the love of God and the love of neighbor as the most important commandment (Mk 12:31; cf. Dt 6:4–5). It is notable that none of this involves worship in the Temple. Again, in response to the scribes' question about the Davidic Sonship of the Messiah, Jesus affirms that the Messiah is not only the Son of David, but also David's Lord (Mk 12:35–37). Here he echoes Psalm 110:1; the successor to David's throne is far greater than David himself.[30]

To complete his ministry in Jerusalem, Jesus takes his disciples to the Mount of Olives and begins to discuss end-time events: the destruction of the Temple, the coming persecution, the coming of false messiahs, and the coming of the Son of Man, who is portrayed in Daniel 7 (Mk 13:1–27). Jesus affirms his words as trustworthy: "Heaven and earth will pass away, but my words will not pass away" (Mk 13:31). He gives his instructions about the imminent end and accompanying signs with an emphasis on "watchfulness." The glorious advent of the Son of Man will only be recognized if the disciples remain vigilant day and night (Mk 13:32–36). So Mark records the final words of Jesus to his disciples and to all: "And what I say to you I say to all: Keep awake" (Mk 13:37).

Book 5: Jesus's Suffering and Crucifixion (Mk 14:1–15:47)

In this section of his Gospel, Mark presents the events that led to Jesus's arrest and then goes on to narrate Jesus's trial, suffering, and crucifixion. First, Mark reports that the chief priests and scribes are looking for a way to arrest Jesus and kill him (Mk 14:1–12). Second, Mark presents a story of a woman who came to anoint Jesus with a costly ointment in Bethany, which is seen as a foreshadowing of Jesus's death (Mk 14:3–9). Third, Mark alludes to Judas's agreement to betray Jesus (Mk 14:10–11). Fourth, Mark introduces Jesus's Passover meal with his disciples in an upper room, where Jesus predicts his betrayal

---

30 For Mark's use of Psalm 110, see Subramanian, 57–64.

and celebrates the breaking of the bread and drinking of the cup in anticipation of his suffering and subsequent vindication (Mk 14:12–25). Fifth, Mark conveys Jesus's prediction of Peter's denial (Mk 14:26–31); and we see that later, Peter does deny Jesus three times in fulfillment of Jesus's prophecy (Mk 14:66–72). Sixth, Mark records Jesus's prayer in Gethsemane before his arrest (Mk 14:32–41). Seventh, Mark mentions the betrayal of Jesus (Mk 14:43–49). In all, Mark describes how "on the way" would look like if anyone seeks to follow Jesus as his disciple. For Mark, discipleship involves suffering. Then, among all four Gospels, Mark alone makes a special mention of a young man who, while following Jesus, wears a linen cloth and then leaves it and runs away so people will not catch hold of him (Mk 14:51–52).

In his account of Jesus's trial before the council, Mark shows Jesus's innocence and Messiahship in an exalted state (Mk 14:53–65). Many false witnesses are brought against Jesus. They testify that Jesus spoke about destroying the Temple and building it again in three days without human hands (Mk 14:57–58). Mark reports that many of their testimonies were proven to be invalid (Mk 14:56, 59). In response to the high priest's question if Jesus is the Messiah, the Son of the Blessed One, Jesus affirms that he is and then goes on to predict his exaltation to the throne of God as the Son of Man and his future return (Mk 14:61–62; cf. Ps 110:1; Dn 7:13–14). The high priest tears his clothes in protest of Jesus's testimony. But that is the testimony that Mark seeks to unveil the messianic identity of Jesus, who is the Messiah, Son of God, and the exalted Son of Man.

In Jesus's trial before Pilate, Mark tells us that Pilate affirmed Jesus as "the King of the Jews" three times (Mk 15:2, 9, 12). Pilate also asserts that Jesus is innocent (Mk 15:14). But Pilate sentences Jesus to be crucified because he wants to satisfy the crowd (Mk 15:15). Consequently, Jesus is crucified with the inscription, "The King of the Jews" (Mk 15:26). Mark then tells that the chief priests and scribes attest that Jesus is the Messiah, the King of Israel (Mk 15:32). On the cross, Jesus utters the words of Psalm 22:1, "My God, my God, why have you forsaken me?," which Mark translates from the Aramaic, "Eloi, Eloi, lema sabachthani?" (Mk 15:34). Jesus's use of the words from Psalm 22 suggests that he experienced both the abandonment of God and God's future vindication (Ps 22:1–2, 4–5, 29–31).[31] In one of the most profound passages in Mark's Gospel, thoughts surrounding abandonment and vindication still cause us difficulty as Mark brings us into the depths of divine reality. He then describes how at Jesus's death the curtain in the Temple tears from top to bottom (Mk 15:38). This symbolizes God's intervention: only God could have torn the curtain from top to bottom, while humans would have torn it bottom to top. By tearing the curtain Mark makes a theological statement. God ends the separation of the holy and the profane—from God's self and humanity—and restores God's intent that we can be united with God through Jesus. The tearing further symbolizes our free access to God through Jesus, the Mediator.

The centurion who witnesses Jesus's death makes a public proclamation by saying, "Truly this man was God's Son!" (Mk 15:39b). Jesus's death is witnessed by women including Mary Magdalene, Mary the mother of James, and Salome, who will also later witness the empty tomb (Mk 15:40–42). In the end, Jesus is given a decent burial by Joseph of Arimathea, who is a member of the council and is waiting for the coming of the Kingdom of God (Mk 15:43–46).

Epilogue: Jesus's Resurrection and Commissioning (Mk 16:1–8, 9–20)

Mark ends his Gospel with a truncated version of Jesus's resurrection (Mk 16:1–8). Three women—Mary Magdalene, Mary the mother of James, and Salome—come to the tomb on the first day of the week to anoint Jesus's body with spices (Mk 16:1–2). As they make their way toward the tomb, they wonder who will roll away the stone (Mk 16:3). But, to their surprise, the stone has already been rolled away (Mk 16:4). They see a young man dressed in white, who tells them that Jesus of Nazareth has been raised (Mk 16:6). The women are given instructions to tell the disciples and Peter to go to Galilee, where the

---

31   For Mark's use of Psalm 22, see Subramanian, 64–69.

resurrected Jesus will meet them (Mk 16:7). But the women flee in terror and amazement, and they do not tell anyone because they are afraid (Mk 16:8). That is where the Gospel ends. One ancient authority has a shorter ending that reads, "And all that had been commanded them they told briefly to those around Peter. And afterward Jesus himself sent out through them, from east to west, the sacred and imperishable proclamation of eternal salvation."[32] The longer ending of Mark has twelve verses (Mk 16:9–20) but is disputed because it is missing from some of the earliest Greek manuscripts.[33]

The longer ending of Mark seems to draw from other canonical Gospels. Jesus's appearance to Mary Magdalene comes from Matthew 28:9–10 and John 20:1–18 (Mk 16:9–11). Jesus's appearance to two disciples is taken from Luke 24:30–31, 36–43 (Mk 16:12–13). His commission to the disciples is derived from Matthew 28:19; Luke 24:47; and John 20:21 (Mk 16:14–18). Jesus's ascension is drawn from Luke 24:51 (Mk 16:19). In the longer ending Jesus assumes the title "Lord" (Mk 16:19–20). Mark's Gospel ends with the disciples proclaiming the good news and continued presence of the risen Lord (Mk 16:20).

Mark begins his Gospel with the good news of Jesus Christ (Mk 1:1) and ends with the disciples who begin to proclaim the good news (as in the longer ending, Mk 16:20). Just as Jesus proclaimed the good news with miracles and authoritative teachings through his life until death and resurrection, the disciples are now sent out to proclaim the good news of Jesus Christ to all the world with the same force.

---

32 The HarperCollins Study Bible, 1951.

33 William R. Farmer did an excellent study on the last twelve verses of Mark's Gospel in relation to both external and internal evidence and noted several possible solutions suggested. He preferred solution number 2, that Mark 16:9–20 represented redactional use of "older material" used by the Evangelist, which was akin to the material kept in the resurrection accounts of the other canonical Gospels. See Farmer, *The Last Twelve Verses of Mark*, SBLMS 25 (Cambridge: Cambridge University Press, 1974). Following in the footsteps of Farmer, David B. Peabody and his research team conclude that the author of Mark 16:9–20 composed a unified narrative taken from the Matthean and Lukan accounts of the resurrection appearance of Jesus. See Peabody et al., "Excurses 15: The Last Twelve Verses of Mark," in *One Gospel from Two*, 328–35. However, it remains unclear whether this was the work of the original author of Mark or whether that ending was lost and the current Mark 16:9–20 was put in place by another author.

Theology of Mark

Mark introduces John the Baptist to prepare for the arrival of Jesus (Mk 1:2–3), who is more powerful than John the Baptist (Mk 1:7). For Mark, Jesus embodies the presence and good news of God (Mk 1:14).[34] Mark's theology is guided by the witness of John the Baptist: "The one who is more powerful than I is coming after me; I am not worthy to stoop down and untie the thong of his sandals. I have baptized you with water; but he will baptize you with the Holy Spirit" (Mk 1:7–8). For Mark, God's presence has arrived in Jesus, who proclaims the Kingship of God by saying, "The time is fulfilled, and the kingdom of God has come near; repent, and believe in the good news" (Mk 1:15). When Jesus called the first four disciples, they all left their vocations and followed him (Mk 1:16–20). These verses show that from the beginning the first four disciples recognized Jesus as the bearer of God's presence, and it was worthy of allegiance. Mark points out that Jesus taught the people with authority (Mk 1:22). Mark tells us that the man with an unclean spirit recognized Jesus as "the Holy One of God" (Mk 1:24).

In the healing story of a paralytic man, Jesus forgives sins as God's representative (Mk 2:5). In response to the scribes' question, "Who can forgive sins but God alone?" (Mk 2:7), Mark draws attention to Jesus's response that "the Son of Man has authority on earth to forgive sins" (Mk 2:10). Mark presents Jesus as the one who stands in the presence of God on earth and pronounces forgiveness of sins. Jesus shows God's presence by embracing all who carry the divine image, even tax collectors and sinners. In response to the scribes' and Pharisees' question, "Why does [Jesus] eat with tax collectors and sinners?" (Mk 2:16a), Jesus says, "Those who are well have no need of a physician, but those who are sick; I have come to call not the righteous but sinners" (Mk 2:17). Mark provides a new understanding of God's presence. God's presence would not exclude tax collectors

---

34 Timothy J. Geddert argues that Mark implicitly presents Jesus as the embodiment of God. See T. J. Geddert, "The Implied YHWH Christology of Mark's Gospel: Mark's Challenge to the Reader to 'Connect the Dots,'" *BBR* 25 (2015): 325–40.

and sinners; rather, it embraces them as demonstrated by Jesus. Mark shows that Jesus possessed the Spirit of God. In Jesus's response to the question by the scribes who accused him of casting out the demons by Beelzebul ("Prince of Demons"), Jesus affirms that he has the Spirit of God, and anyone who does not respect the Spirit of God present in his mission will not be forgiven (Mk 3:22, 28–30).

Mark talks about the hidden Kingdom of God in the teaching of Jesus. When Jesus tells the Parable of the Sower, the disciples do not understand its meaning, so they ask him about it in private (Mk 4:10). Jesus responds that they are given the insight to know "the secret of the kingdom of God" (Mk 4:11–12; cf. Is 6:9–10). In other words, only the disciples will perceive the arrival of the Kingdom of God, which Jesus brought through his ministry. The Parable of the Growing Seed and the Parable of the Mustard Seed witness to the arrival of the Kingdom of God, which is secretly growing in and through the ministry of Jesus (Mk 4:26–29, 30–32).

In the healing story of the Gerasene Demoniac, Mark highlights the status of Jesus as "Lord." When the healed man wants to follow Jesus, Jesus says to him, "Go home to your friends, and tell them how much the Lord has done for you, and what mercy he has shown you" (Mk 5:19). Clearly, Jesus is presented as Lord in the sense that he came to demonstrate the power of God to heal and show mercy. Jesus heals a woman with a hemorrhage (Mk 5:25–34), raises a little girl from the dead (Mk 5:35–43), feeds the five thousand and the four thousand (Mk 6:30–44; 8:1–9), gives authority to the twelve disciples to cast out the demons (Mk 6:7–13), casts out a demon from the daughter of a Syrophoenician woman (Mk 7:24–30), heals a deaf man (Mk 7:31–37), cures a blind man at Bethsaida (Mk 8:22–26), and restores the sight of blind Bartimaeus (Mk 10:46–52).

Mark presents the entry of Jesus into Jerusalem as the entry of the Lord. Jesus sends two of his disciples into the village to bring a colt for him to ride on with this instruction: "If anyone says to you, 'Why are you doing this?' just say this, 'The Lord needs it and will send it back here immediately'" (Mk 11:3). As the one who comes in the name of the Lord, Jesus is welcomed by the crowd (Mk 11:9;

cf. Ps 118:25–26). Jesus cleanses the Temple as he stands in the very place of God. We see this because Jesus quotes the oracle of God (divine utterance) by saying, "Is it not written, 'My house shall be called a house of prayer for all the nations'? But you have made it a den of robbers" (Mk 11:17; cf. Is 56:7; Jer 7:11).[35] Jesus teaches his disciples to watch for the coming of the Lord in the age to come in reference to himself indirectly. Jesus says, "Therefore, keep awake—for you do not know when the master [Lord] of the house will come, in the evening, or at midnight, or at cockcrow, or at dawn, or else he may find you asleep when he comes suddenly. And what I say to you I say to all: Keep awake" (Mk 13:35–37). For Mark, Jesus is already Lord on earth, and he will be the Lord when he comes in glory at the end of time.

Mark attributes the oracle of God to Jesus when Jesus predicts the disillusionment of his disciples. As he leads his disciples to Gethsemane, Jesus says to them, "You will become deserters" (Mk 14:27a). And then Jesus quotes the oracle of God from Zechariah 13:7: "I will strike the shepherd, and the sheep will be scattered" (Mk 14:27b). By placing the oracle of God in Jesus's mouth, Mark emphasizes the role of Jesus as God's representative. Just as God cares for God's people, Jesus cares for his flock (cf. Mk 6:34). In response to the high priest's question as to whether Jesus is the Messiah, the Son of the Blessed One, Jesus not only affirms his status as the Messiah, the Son of God, but also goes on to predict his glorious future coming as the Son of Man (Mk 14:61–62). The high priest tears his clothes, because he takes Jesus's answer as blasphemy (Mk 14:63–64), and is horrified that such a "pathetic figure" like the arrested figure (Jesus) who stands before him would claim to be God's closest associate. Through the high priest's reaction, Mark portrays Jesus as the one who stands in the place of God and who makes such claims that only God can make. We also see this when the astonished Pilate asks Jesus if he is "the King of the Jews" (Mk 15:2). The soldiers mock Jesus as "the King of the Jews" (Mk 15:18), and Jesus is crucified with a sign placed above

---

35 In the Hebrew Bible, divine oracles are uttered by the prophets who are God's representatives (cf. Is 42:5; Jer 49:28b; Ez 29:3; Zec 12:1).

his cross—"the King of the Jews" (Mk 15:26). The chief priests and scribes mocked Jesus as "the King of Israel" (Mk 15:32). Through those mockeries, Mark indicates that this kind of figure is indeed chosen to reign as "King" of God's Kingdom.

The resurrection of Jesus is the culmination of Mark's theology. Jesus's prediction of his vindication becomes a reality at his resurrection (Mk 16:1–8), where Jesus becomes the exalted Lord. Mark concludes his Gospel with the affirmation of Jesus as the Lord. Despite the textual problem, the words at the end of Mark's Gospel are true: "So then the Lord Jesus, after he had spoken to them, was taken up into heaven and sat down at the right hand of God. And they went out and proclaimed the good news everywhere, while the Lord worked with them and confirmed the message by the signs that accompanied it" (Mk 16:19–20).

Throughout Mark's account of the life of Jesus, he presents the good news of Jesus as the good news of God. Jesus comes to embody the very presence of God, whose Kingdom is secretly growing through Jesus's ministry. Jesus teaches with authority, forgives sins, and casts out the demons by the power of God. Jesus dies as "the King of the Jews," and he will come again as "the Son of Man" to reign in glory. During his earthly ministry, Jesus is recognized as Lord and becomes the exalted Lord at his resurrection. In the preaching of the good news by the disciples, Jesus continues to exercise sovereign power as Lord.

John Wesley's Explanatory Notes on Mark

John Wesley divides the Gospel of Mark into three major sections: (1) The beginning of the gospel (Mk 1:1–13); (2) the gospel itself (Mk 1:14–16:14); and (3) the gospel (Mk 16:15–20).[36] Wesley notes that Mark speaks of the beginning of the gospel of Jesus Christ with the ministry of John the Baptist and of the gospel proper in the rest of his book.[37] He categorizes the gospel proper into two major geographical

---

36 John Wesley, *Wesley's Notes on the New Testament* (Oxford: Benediction Classics, 2010), 75–77.

37 Wesley, 78.

segments: Jesus's ministry in Galilee (Mk 1:4–9:50) and Jesus's ministry in Judea (Mk 10:1–16:14).

The Beginning of the Gospel (Mk 1:1–13)

Mark's Gospel begins with a quotation from the Hebrew Bible, which he attributes to the prophet Isaiah (Mk 1:2–3). But the text quoted is a combination of Isaiah 40:3 and Malachi 3:1, which is observed by Wesley, who must have consulted the Septuagint (Greek) text of the Old Testament.[38] John the Baptist preached the baptism of repentance, which serves as both a "sign and means" of repentance.[39] Right after his baptism, Jesus is driven by Satan into the wilderness to be tempted (Mk 1:12–13). Mark provides only a brief summary of Jesus's temptation, whereas both Matthew and Luke have a lengthy account (cf. Mt 4:1–11; Lk 4:1–13). Commenting on the temptation account in Mark's Gospel, John Wesley observes, "St. Mark not only gives us a compendium of St. Matthew's gospel, but likewise several valuable particulars, which the other evangelists have omitted."[40] The particulars Mark includes are (1) use of the word *Satan* instead of "the tempter" (Matthew) or "the devil" (Luke), and (2) the fact that Mark alone mentions that Jesus was with "the wild beasts" in the wilderness (cf. Gn 2:19–20). In order to make such an assertion, Wesley studied not only Genesis 2:19–20, where Adam was with the wild beasts, but the first three Gospels in parallel.

The Gospel Itself (Mk 1:14–16:14)

In many of the healing stories in Mark's Gospel, Jesus tells the healed ones not to publicize their experience. For instance, in the healing of a leper, Jesus told the cleansed leper not to tell anyone about the healing (Mk 1:44), but the cleansed leper proclaimed it anyway (Mk 1:45). Commenting on Jesus's charge to the cleansed leper to keep it secret, Wesley remarks, "But our blessed Lord gives no such charge

38 Wesley, 78.

39 Cf. Wesley, 78.

40 Wesley, 78.

to us. If he has made us clean from our leprosy of sin, we are not commanded to conceal it. On the contrary, it is our duty to publish it abroad, both for the honour of our Benefactor, and that others who are sick of sin may be encouraged to ask and hope for the same benefit."[41] In response to the Pharisees who questioned Jesus's disciples for plucking heads of grain on the Sabbath, Jesus said that the Sabbath is made for people, not people for the Sabbath (Mk 2:23–24, 27). Jesus goes on to say that "the Son of Man is lord even of the sabbath" (Mk 2:28). Wesley notes that Jesus as "the supreme Law giver" has the power to supply his own laws.[42]

Jesus sends out the Twelve to preach and heal (Mk 6:7–12). Mark reports, "They cast out many demons, and anointed with oil many who were sick and cured them" (Mk 6:13). Here Wesley sees the ministry of anointing the sick with oil as an allusion to James 5:13–15, where a specific direction is given. Wesley draws attention to the restoration of health "not by natural efficacy of the oil, but by the supernatural blessing of God."[43] Wesley intends that it is God who effects healing, and the means natural to that end are simply used to receive the healing. One of Jesus's disciples, John, reported to Jesus that he saw someone (not one of Jesus's disciples) casting out demons in Jesus's name (Mk 9:39). Wesley identifies the one who cast out the demons in Jesus's name as a disciple of John the Baptist.[44] But he was not one of the twelve disciples of Jesus. Wesley asks, "And we forbade him, because he followeth not us—How often is the same temper found in us?"[45] Wesley draws attention to the apostle Paul, whom he sets an example for temper: "St. Paul had learnt a better temper, when he rejoiced that Christ was preached, even by those who were his personal enemies."[46]

---

41 Wesley, 79.

42 Wesley, 80.

43 Wesley, 84.

44 Wesley, 88.

45 Wesley, 88.

46 Wesley, 88.

Paul was primarily concerned about preaching the gospel; he was less concerned about who preached the gospel. Wesley goes on to assert, "But to confine religion to them [only] that follow us, is a narrowness of spirit which we should avoid and abhor."[47] Wesley allows for diversity in Christian ministry that would not affect "the essence of religion."[48]

Beginning with chapter 10, Mark reports Jesus's ministry in the region of Judea (Mk 10:1). While Jesus is on the way to Jerusalem, a rich man comes to Jesus and asks, "Good Teacher, what must I do to inherit eternal life?" (Mk 10:17). Jesus asks him to keep the commandments (Mk 10:19). The rich man replies that he has kept the commandments since his youth (Mk 10:20). Jesus says to him that, nevertheless, he lacks one thing (Mk 10:21). Wesley interprets Jesus's words "one thing" as "the love of God."[49] He sees the man's "riches" as a hindrance to the love of God. For Wesley, to give up possessions is to love God.[50] Jesus summarized the entire commandments into two: love God and love neighbor (Mk 12:28–31). Wesley observes that it is Christian duty to keep those two great commandments because it is better than "offering the most noble and costly sacrifices."[51] When Jesus sat opposite the treasury at the Temple, he saw people casting their money in the money receptacles (Mk 12:41). Jesus noted and praised a poor widow who put in two small copper coins in comparison to those who contributed more. She is commended because she gave it out of her livelihood (Mk 12:44). Wesley comments that the poor widow was judged by the "Judge of all."[52] He goes on to say that the smallest gift, which stems from "self-denying love," is the most acceptable gift to Jesus.[53]

---

47 Wesley, 88.

48 Wesley, 88.

49 Wesley, 90.

50 Cf. Wesley, 90.

51 Wesley, 92.

52 Wesley, 93.

53 Wesley, 93.

At the trial before the council, Jesus is accused of destroying the Temple. Some of the false witnesses speak of Jesus and accuse him of saying, "I will destroy this temple that is made with hands, and in three days I will build another, not made with hands" (Mk 14:58). In the synoptic Gospels, Jesus never says directly that he would destroy the Temple. Wesley draws attention to John 2:19, where Jesus says, "Destroy this temple, and in three days I will raise it up."[54] Jesus is speaking of his own body, not of the Temple. By his noting this text, Wesley carefully studied all four Gospels to draw a parallel among them.

The Gospel (Mk 16:15–20)

Wesley treats chapter 16 of Mark's Gospel as one whole unit without dividing into the short (Mk 1:1–8) and long endings (Mk 16:9–20). After the resurrection, Jesus commissions his disciples to preach the good news to all creation (Mk 16:15). Wesley comments that "our Lord speaks without any limitation or restriction."[55] There is no wonder that Wesley saw the world as his parish; he did not want to limit his ministry only to the four walls of the church. He refused to let rigid structures and policies of the church determine for him to whom he should preach the gospel.

The risen Jesus talks about the signs that accompany those who believe (Mk 16:17–18). One of the signs was that if they would drink any deadly thing it would not hurt them (Mk 16:18c). Wesley cautions that "God never calls us to try any such experiments."[56] He indicates that if anyone drinks any deadly poison by their own choice or by intention, God will not come to rescue them.

Wesley's exegetical notes on Mark's Gospel invite the reader to understand it in its original context. He was fully aware of the Greek text (LXX) of the Hebrew Bible, recognized the Scriptures quoted in Mark's Gospel, showed an in-depth study of the four Gospels, and

---

54 Wesley, 95.

55 Wesley, 97.

56 Wesley, 97.

drew parallels between them. Wesley articulated the contemporary meaning of the text.

Teaching and Preaching from Mark

Teaching

Jesus's ministry was governed by healing to a great extent. Mark records the healing of a man with an unclean spirit at the start of Jesus's ministry (Mk 1:21–28) and underscores the importance of Jesus's healing ministry: "And wherever [Jesus] went, into villages or cities or farms, they laid the sick in the marketplaces, and begged him that they might touch even the fringe of his cloak; and all who touched it were healed" (Mk 6:56). The disciples anointed with oil and healed many who were sick (Mk 6:13), and Jesus commissioned the disciples to lay their hands on the sick and to heal them (Mk 16:18a). In the long ending, Mark emphasizes the healing ministry of the disciples.

The healing story of a little girl is good for both teaching and preaching. Teachers need to pay attention to (1) context of the passage; (2) references or allusions to the Old Testament; (3) parallels with other Gospels; (4) the author's message; (5) the meaning of the text; and (6) any additional explanation. This healing story is found in Mark 5:21–24, 35–43 and also in Matthew 9:18–26 and Luke 8:40–56. Only Mark and Luke identify the leader of the synagogue as Jairus; Matthew simply mentions him as a leader of the synagogue. Mark alone notes that the little girl was twelve years of age (Mk 5:42b). The number twelve also corresponds to the twelve years of suffering of the woman with hemorrhages (Mk 5:25; cf. Mt 9:20; Lk 8:43). Differences and similarities between these three texts may be explained without bringing the source question into the study.

Mark's Gospel also includes a healing story that ends with resuscitation to life. A leader of the synagogue named Jairus begs Jesus, saying, "My little daughter is at the point of death. Come and lay your hands on her, so that she may be made well, and live" (Mk 5:23). Note that at the beginning of the story the girl is not dead. It could have turned out to be just another healing story if Jesus went and healed her right away. But Mark is fond of using the so-called sandwich stories, where he begins to narrate one story and then interpolates another story before finishing the first (cf. Mk 3:20–35; 6:7–30; 11:12–23; 14:1–11, 53–72).[57] Here, in the sandwich story, Jesus encounters a large crowd. A woman who has had a hemorrhage for twelve years touches his clothes, and she is instantly healed (Mk 5:25–29). Jesus pauses somewhat, taking time to find out who touched his clothes and was healed (Mk 5:30–31). He tells her, "Daughter, your faith has made you well; go in peace, and be healed of your disease" (Mk 5:34). Mark then returns to the first story. After the delay, Jesus finally gets to the house of the leader of the synagogue to heal his daughter. It is reported to Jesus that before he arrived, the girl died (Mk 5:35). When Jesus enters the house, he says, "Why do you make a commotion and weep? The child is not dead but sleeping" (Mk 5:39). The word *death* was a common metaphor associated with sleep in the biblical tradition (cf. 1 Kgs 2:10; 2 Kgs 14:16; Ps 13:3; Dn 12:2; Jn 11:11–14; Acts 7:60; 1 Cor 15:6; Rv 14:13). The onlookers laugh at Jesus because they think he is simply joking. Mark reiterates that from Jesus's point of view, death is more like sleep or a coma. The little girl was not yet buried in a tomb. But, for the onlookers, the girl is already dead, and there is no way that Jesus can bring her back to life.

But then Jesus speaks these Aramaic words, "Talitha cum" (or "Talitha cumi"), which is interpreted as "Little girl, get up!" (Mk 5:41). By the power of Jesus's touch, and the spoken words, the girl is now able to get up and walk (Mk 5:42). Mark shows his readers that the Lord possessed the power of God to raise the dead. Jesus then orders the parents not to publicize what they have just witnessed (Mk 5:45a), which recalls Jesus's earlier command to keep his healing secret (Mk 1:25, 44; 3:12). Mark portrays that Jesus wants to keep his healing power a secret until his resurrection, when his own power over death is fully revealed (Mk 16:6–7, 15, 20). Mark invites the future disciples

---

57 For a discussion of Mark's technique of sandwiching stories (known as "intercalation"), see J. R. Edwards, "Markan Sandwiches: The Significance of Interpolations in Markan Narratives," *NovT* 31 (1989): 193–216.

to trust the power of Jesus and engage in the healing ministry that lay at the heart of Jesus's ministry.

Preaching

Using the same text for both teaching and preaching helps preachers to incorporate the teaching elements into preaching and make it a moment of teaching. The healing story may be outlined this way: (1) introduction, (2) setting the text in context, (3) healing proper, (4) reclaiming the power of Jesus, and (5) engaging in healing ministry today. The title for preaching could be "Healing Power of Jesus Set Loose."

The healing stories of Jesus remind us of God's power present in Jesus's ministry. The power that went out from Jesus when he healed the woman with the hemorrhage (Mk 5:29–30) is the same power used by Jesus to raise the little girl from the dead (Mk 5:41–42). Jesus took time to come to her house, took her by hand, and raised her back to life. He took Peter, James, and John to witness the healing (Mk 5:37) but otherwise wanted to keep the healing a secret. That seems curious to us, but Jesus was not an ordinary healer. He is the Son of God. He would later be publicly proclaimed as God's Son at his death and resurrection in God's time. The joy Jesus brought to the girl's parents surpassed all understanding. It shows that Jesus feels every pain and that he has power to heal all sickness.

During Jesus's earthly ministry, there are three instances where Jesus brought the dead back to life: the widow's son at Nain (Lk 7:11–17); Jairus's daughter (Mk 5:21–24, 35–43; cf. Mt 9:18–26; Lk 8:40–56); and Lazarus (Jn 11:1–45). In addition, Acts tells us that Peter raised Tabitha (Dorcas) from the dead (Acts 9:36–42), and Paul raised Eutychus (Acts 20:7–12). This shows that, according to the Bible, the early apostles had power to raise the dead. In the context of Mark's Gospel, Jesus demonstrates the power of God in his ministry, and this same power is also available for the ministry of the church.

The church proclaims God's power as demonstrated in the life of Jesus. The raising of the little girl is a sign that celebrates life in the midst of death. It brings hope to the powerless. It brings courage in the face of fear. Wherever the gospel of Jesus Christ is preached, it offers people the potential for new life. Ask your congregation where they need new life. What in their lives needs resurrection? When life comes to a dead end, Jesus brings hope, calls people by name, and gives new life, which brings great joy, just as it did when Jesus gave new life to the little girl.

In Mark, we also see that Jesus's raising the little girl foreshadows his own resurrection, which reminds the church that death is not the end of life. Jesus died, but he rose from the dead; and by commissioning the disciples to proclaim the good news to the whole creation (Mk 16:15), God's power is available to all believers. As the church proclaims the good news, it is called to bring hope and joy to our suffering humanity. The church is called to find ways to demonstrate God's healing in the midst of death and decay. Preachers may share illustrations or stories that changed people's lives to bring to bear the message. Preachers may also invite others to share their testimonies as to how they experienced divine healing in their lives. This presents preachers with the opportunity to talk about how God heals; that is, through medicine, giving the grace to endure, instantaneous healing, the passage of time, and, ultimately, death into life eternal. Preachers may consider holding a healing service, which can involve anointing the sick, whether physically sick or soul sick, with oil.

The following texts can be utilized for both teaching and preaching:

1. Mark 2:1–12 (The healing of a paralytic man)

2. Mark 6:7–13 (The mission of the Twelve)

3. Mark 9:2–8 (The transfiguration of Jesus)

4. Mark 14:3–9 (The anointing of Jesus by a woman at Bethany)

5. Mark 14:22–25 (The institution of the Lord's Supper)

Summary

1. The Gospel of Mark provides a summary of the life of Jesus but focuses primarily on his public proclamation. Mark does not tell the birth narrative, the lengthy sermon of Jesus (mountain or

plain), and other discourses that are found in Matthew and Luke. This could mean that Mark intended his Gospel to be kerygmatic, similar to Peter's speech on the Day of Pentecost.

2. Mark, a missionary companion of Paul and an interpreter of Peter, wrote the Gospel probably anywhere between 50 and 64 CE, where he became accustomed to Peter's preaching in Rome. He was also familiar with the Palestinian tradition. According to well-established tradition, Mark composed his Gospel in consultation with Peter in Rome for the Roman audience to emphasize the public ministry of Jesus.

3. Mark organizes his Gospel under seven segments and emphasizes Jesus's role as God's envoy.

4. Mark's theology emerges from the witness of John the Baptist, but Jesus is more powerful than John. For Mark, Jesus is Lord and the one for whom John the Baptist came to prepare the way. Jesus embodies the very presence of God and continues to reign as Lord.

5. John Wesley carefully studied the Greek text of Mark's Gospel, as well as the Greek text (LXX) of the Old Testament, and sought to understand Mark's Gospel in its original historical context. Wesley articulated the contemporary meaning of the Gospel text in the context of the original author's intention.

6. Mark's Gospel emphasizes the power of Jesus manifest in his ministry. Each narrative invites the church to discover Jesus's power and suggests ways to demonstrate it in the proclamation of the good news. Teachers and preachers are invited to see how Mark displayed the ministry of Jesus and then to articulate the contemporary significance of the good news of Jesus Christ.

For Discussion

1. Mark's Gospel does not include Jesus's birth story. The church draws from both Matthew and Luke in its celebration of Christmas. Given what you have read and learned, compose a short birth narrative that would be consistent with Mark's Gospel.

2. During his earthly ministry, Jesus commissioned the twelve disciples to preach and heal. Mark reports, "So they went out and proclaimed that all should repent. They cast out many demons, and anointed with oil many who were sick and cured them" (Mk 6:12–13). Discuss and propose specific ministries that involve both the proclamation of the gospel to all nations and healing of the sick.

3. Jesus talked about his own return at a later, unspecified time. He said, "Therefore, keep awake—for you do not know when the master of the house will come, in the evening, or at midnight, or at cockcrow, or at dawn, or else he may find you asleep when he comes suddenly. And what I say to you I say to all: Keep awake" (Mk 13:35–37). Every year the church uses the four Sundays of Advent to prepare for the second coming of Jesus. What does it means to be watchful? Talk about the ways the church can use every Sunday to prepare people for the glorious return of Jesus.

4. Many scholars think that Mark ended his Gospel abruptly (Mk 16:1–8). Compose an appropriate ending to the Gospel. Share each of your creative endings in the group.

5. John Wesley insisted that the gospel should be preached to everyone without any limitation or restriction. Are there sometimes ways that the church restricts the gospel from being preached to all? How can you bring John Wesley into the conversation so that the good news is available to everyone? Share your thoughts in the group.

4

The Gospel According to
Luke

Introduction

Of the apostles, therefore, John and Matthew first instill faith into us; whilst of apostolic men, Luke and Mark renew it afterwards. These all start with the same principles of the faith, so far as relates to the one only God the Creator and His Christ, how that He was born of the Virgin, and came to fulfil the law and the prophets."[1] Thus writes Tertullian (155–240), who was an early Christian theologian and polemicist from Carthage in the Roman province of Africa.[2] Tertullian used the Gospel of Luke in defense against Marcion (85–160), a gnostic Christian who possessed a mutilated copy of a fragmentary Gospel of Luke.[3] Tertullian attests that Luke was not an apostle, but an apostolic man who followed the apostle Paul, and therefore his Gospel is authoritative.[4]

---

1   Tertullian, *Marc.* 4.2.18–21, in *Ante-Nicene Fathers*, vol. 3, ed. A. Roberts and J. Donaldson (Peabody, MA: Hendrickson Publishers, 1999), 347.

2   The church in Carthage became a powerful force in North Africa by the end of the second century CE. Tertullian emerged as a leading member of the African church. He is known for his teaching and his defense of Christian beliefs and practices. He is also known for his apologetic writings. Some of his writings include *Adversus Marcionem* ("Against Marcion"), *Adversus Hermogenem* ("Against Hermogenes"), *Adversus Valentinianos* ("Against Valentinus"), and *De resurrectione carnis* ("Concerning the Resurrection of the Flesh"). He is considered the founder of Western Christianity.

3   Marcion's canon consisted of a mutilated Gospel of Luke and ten Letters of Paul. He rejected the authority of the Old Testament and denied Jesus's physical birth. For a comprehensive treatment of Marcion and his theology, see A. von Harnack, *Marcion: The Gospel of the Alien God*, trans. J. E. Steely and L. D. Bierma (Eugene, OR: Wipf and Stock Publishers, 2007); German: A. Harnack, *Marcion: Das Evangelium Vom Fremden Gott*, 1924.

4   Tertullian, *Marc.* 4.2.31–33, in *Ante-Nicene Fathers*, vol. 3, 347–48.

Among the four Gospels, the Gospel of Luke is the only one that is directly connected with another—the Acts of the Apostles (Lk 1:1–4; Acts 1:1–2). Both Luke and Acts are associated with the preface and addressed to someone named Theophilus.[5] The two volumes were probably separated in the second century CE when the Gospel of Luke was placed among the four Gospels and Acts was placed after the Gospel of John.[6] Although both Luke and Acts come from the same author, these two volumes deal with different subjects. The Gospel of Luke focuses on the story of Jesus, beginning with the birth of John the Baptist and ending with Jesus's ascension. The Acts of the Apostles covers the spread of the gospel from Jerusalem to Judea, Samaria, Asia, Europe, and Rome.[7] Acts demonstrates how the proclamation of the gospel in the name of Jesus was carried out in the witness of the church, and it shows how the gospel of Jesus Christ creates the church and changes the world.

Authorship

The third canonical Gospel bears the name of Luke as the author, but nowhere else is Luke's name mentioned. Luke was not one of the disciples of Jesus; however, traditionally, the author of the third Gospel is supposed to be a companion of the apostle of Paul. Paul mentions Luke as "the beloved physician" (Col 4:14), a "fellow worker" (Phlm 1:24), and an associate (2 Tm 4:11).[8] Based on the references to Luke in Paul's letters, it is also generally assumed that the "we" passages

5 For the preface in Luke-Acts in the context of Greco-Roman biography, see V. K. Robbins, "Prefaces in Greco-Roman Biography and Luke-Acts," *PRSt* 6 (1979): 94–108.

6 For a discussion of unity of Luke and Acts, see C. K. Rowe, "Literary Unity and Reception History: Reading Luke-Acts as Luke and Acts," *JSNT* 29 (2007): 449–57.

7 For a historical study of the Acts of the Apostles, see M. Dibelius, *Studies in the Acts of the Apostles*, trans. M. Ling and P. Schubert, ed. H. Greeven (London: SCM Press, 1956; Mifflintown, PA: Sigler Press, 1999). German: M. Dibelius, *Aufsatze zur Apostelgeschichte* (Göttingen: Vandenhoeck und Ruprecht, 1951).

8 Irenaeus attests that Luke was an inseparable companion of Paul in *Haer.* 3.14.1: "But that this Luke was inseparable from Paul, and his fellow-laborer in the gospel, he himself clearly evinces, not as a matter of boasting, but as bound to do so by the truth itself." *The Apostolic Fathers with Justin Martyr and Irenaeus*, ed. A. C. Coxe, vol. 1 of

recorded in Acts include Luke as a travel companion of Paul (Acts 16:10–18; 20:5–15; 21:1–18; 27:1–28:16). For instance, while reporting Paul's journey to Macedonia, the author states, "They went ahead and were waiting for us in Troas; but we sailed from Philippi after the days of Unleavened Bread, and in five days we joined them in Troas, where we stayed for seven days" (Acts 20:5–6). Because the author was writing the travel narrative in the first-person plural, he did not want to identify his own name as the companion of Paul.[9] Paul refers to Luke as his coworker in his letters, so it is probable that Luke traveled with him but chose not to insert his name into Acts' travel narratives. But we can assume that because Luke traveled with Paul, he was very familiar with certain Gentile concerns of the gospel.

The early church tradition is unanimous in identifying Luke as the author of the Gospel. Irenaeus says: "Luke also, the companion of Paul, recorded in a book the Gospel preached by him."[10] In another context Irenaeus mentions Luke's name while quoting from the Gospel: "Luke also, the follower and disciple of the apostles, referring to Zacharias and Elisabeth, from whom, according to promise, John was born, says: 'And they were both righteous before God, walking in all the commandments and ordinances of the Lord blameless'" (cf. Lk 1:6).[11] Eusebius identifies Luke as both the companion of Paul and the author of Luke and Acts:

> Luke, who was by race an Antiochian and a physician by profession, was long a companion of Paul, and had careful conversation with the other Apostles, and in two inspired books left us examples of the medicine for souls which he had gained from them—the Gospel . . .

Ante-Nicene Fathers, ed. A. Roberts and J. Donaldson (Peabody, MA: Hendrickson Publishers, 1999), 437.

9 François Bovon thinks that the author of Luke and Acts could have been a Macedonian man because of his reference to Paul's vision in Macedonia in Acts 16:9–10, where the journey begins with "we." See F. Bovon, Luke 1: A Commentary on the Gospel of Luke 1:1–9:50, trans. C. M. Thomas, ed. H. Koester (Minneapolis: Fortress Press, 2002), 8–9.

10 Irenaeus, Haer. 3.1.1, in Ante-Nicene Fathers, 1:414.

11 Irenaeus, Haer. 3.10.1–2, in Ante-Nicene Fathers, 1:423.

and the Acts of the Apostles which he composed no longer on the evidence of hearing but of his own eyes.[12]

Eusebius also attests to the preface Luke wrote in his Gospel: "Luke himself at the beginning of his treatise prefixed an account of the cause for which he had made his compilation."[13] Jerome, too, refers to Luke as a physician, a companion of Paul, and an author of the Gospel: "Luke, a physician of Antioch, as his writings indicate, was not unskilled in the Greek language. An adherent of the apostle Paul and companion of all his journeying, he wrote a *Gospel.*"[14]

Date, Purpose, and Place of Writing

The prologue to Luke's Gospel suggests that there were already written sources in circulation prior to its composition (Lk 1:1–2). Those written sources, we can presume, were based on the testimony of the eyewitnesses and ministers of the Word. But it remains difficult to conclude that Luke was referring specifically to the written canonical Gospels, such as Matthew, Mark, or even other fragmentary gospel sources. It could be simply that Luke used sources that were also available to other canonical Gospel writers. William Farmer and the research team have taken an approach that Luke used Matthew as a source.[15] It is probable that some of the canonical Gospels were already in circulation and that Luke referred to them as sources. However, one needs to work carefully through the entire Gospel to

---

12 Eusebius, *Hist. eccl.* 3.4.6.

13 Eusebius, *Hist. eccl.* 3.24.15.

14 Jerome, *Vir. ill.* 7.1, in *On Illustrious Men*, trans. T. P. Halton, *The Fathers of the Church*, vol. 100 (Washington, DC: The Catholic University of America Press, 1999), 15. Jerome also attests that Luke wrote both the Gospel and the Acts in *Vir. ill.* 7.5: "He declares this also at the beginning of his work, saying, 'Even as they delivered unto us, who from the beginning were eye-witnesses and ministers of the word.' So he wrote the *Gospel* as he had heard it, but composed the *Acts of the Apostles* as he himself had seen." *On Illustrious Men*, 16.

15 See A. J. McNicol et al., *Beyond the Q Impasse—Luke's Use of Matthew: A Demonstration by the Research Team of the International Institute for Gospel Studies*, preface by William R. Farmer (Valley Forge, PA: Trinity Press International, 1996). Also see M. Goodacre, *The Case Against Q* (Valley Forge, PA: Trinity Press International, 2002).

conclude if Luke did indeed use any of the canonical Gospels. It is a very technical issue.

Luke's favorable portrayal of Rome in his Gospel points to a date prior to the persecution of Christians by Nero (64 CE). The Roman soldiers are favorably addressed by John the Baptist, which is only mentioned in Luke's Gospel (Lk 3:14). The Roman centurion is highly praised for his love of the Jewish people (Lk 7:5). Luke does not report the mocking of Jesus by the governor's soldiers, whereas Matthew and Mark do (Mt 27:27–32; Mk 15:16–20). Luke depicts the Roman centurion at the foot of the cross, declaring Jesus's "innocence" or "righteousness" (Lk 23:47), whereas the centurion, according to Matthew and Mark, confesses Jesus to be "the Son of God" (Mt 27:54; Mk 15:39).

As mentioned previously, the early church identified Luke, the companion of Paul, as the author of both the Gospel and Acts. If Paul met Luke in Antioch, where Paul stayed for a year, then Luke may have known Paul since 46 CE (cf. Acts 11:25–26). However, Luke is not interested in joint authorship of Paul's letters. Perhaps Luke accompanied Paul at times until Paul went to Rome around 61 CE (cf. Acts 28:16). During that time, Luke probably had access to various sources of the Christian movement that were in circulation. It is possible that Luke composed his Gospel between 61 and 64 CE, prior to the destruction of Jerusalem.[16]

Luke is one of the Gospels that states the explicit purpose for writing. Luke says, "I too decided, after investigating everything carefully from the very first, to write an orderly account for you, most excellent Theophilus, so that you may know the truth concerning the things about which you have been instructed" (Lk 1:3–4). If Luke thought that the sources he examined did not set the story in order, he attempted to provide a coherent account of the life of Jesus from

---

16 Joseph B. Tyson dates Luke-Acts around 120–125 CE. This late dating is based on the assumption that Marcion used an early version of Luke's Gospel, which was later expanded to combat Marcion's rejection of the Jewish Scriptures and Jesus's intimate relation with Judaism. As the result of opposing the Marcionite heresy, the present canonical Gospel of Luke emerged in the second century CE. See J. B. Tyson, *Marcion and Luke-Acts: A Defining Struggle* (Columbia: University of South Carolina Press, 2006).

the very beginning. As François Bovon remarks, "The allusion to the orderliness of presentation refers to comprehensive scope, as well as to a chronologically or salvation-historically correct sequence, and also to balanced composition."[17] Luke never says how, however, he reorganized the sources he used to provide an orderly account of the life of Jesus. Probably the way he dealt with the life of Jesus in his Gospel is an indication of how he sought to set the record straight.

As already presumed, church tradition indicates that Luke was a native of Antioch. He was a physician by profession and began to accompany Paul from his second missionary journey until his final imprisonment in Rome. We can also assume that he remained with Paul while others abandoned him (2 Tm 4:11). Since Luke may have accompanied Paul on some of his missionary journeys, he would have become familiar with places like Macedonia, Achaia, Ephesus, Caesarea, and Rome, as well as his hometown, Antioch. Any of those places could be a possible location for the composition of Luke's Gospel.[18] From his association with Paul, Luke understood the universal appeal of the gospel that he intended for all nations.

Main Themes

Luke's preface permeates the entire Gospel. He wanted to write down "an orderly account of the events that have been fulfilled among us" (Lk 1:1). Throughout the Gospel, Luke emphasizes how the plan of God is fulfilled in the life of Jesus in history. Not only Jesus's birth, but also John's birth fulfill the promises of God (cf. Lk 1:24–25). When John the Baptist announces the coming of the Messiah, the readers already knew how God prepared John as the forerunner of Jesus since birth (cf. Lk 3:16–17). For Luke, God's plan of salvation takes place here and now in human history. The birth of John is set in the historical context: "In the days of King Herod of Judea, there was a priest named Zechariah, who belonged to the priestly order

---

17 Bovon, *Luke 1*, 22.

18 Bovon prefers Rome as the place of composition of Luke's Gospel. Cf. Bovon, 8–9.

of Abijah. His wife was a descendant of Aaron, and her name was Elizabeth" (Lk 1:5). The birth of Jesus is also embedded in historical context: "In those days a decree went out from Emperor Augustus that all the world should be registered" (Lk 2:1). Mary and Joseph go to Bethlehem in compliance with the Roman government (cf. Lk 2:5). In every part of the narrative, Luke tries to show how God works in human history to accomplish God's salvation through Jesus.

The divine plan not only encompasses human history but also the promises of God recorded in Scripture. When Jesus goes to the synagogue in Nazareth, he reads from Isaiah 61:1–2 and points to the fulfillment of the Scriptures in his own ministry (Lk 4:21). Luke points out that Jesus fulfilled the Scriptures from the beginning to the end: "[Jesus] said to them, 'These are my words that I spoke to you while I was still with you—that everything written about me in the law of Moses, the prophets, and the psalms must be fulfilled'" (Lk 24:44). After the resurrection Jesus asks the disciples to stay in Jerusalem to wait for the fulfillment of the promise of God, who will send the Holy Spirit to the church for its worldwide ministry (Lk 24:49). For Luke, the story of Jesus is the center of God's plan of salvation and the center of the church's proclamation of the gospel for all humanity. Luke organizes his sources in the following way to show the fulfillment of God's place in the life of Jesus:

1. Prologue (Lk 1:1–4)
2. Book 1: The beginning (Lk 1:5–4:13)
3. Book 2: Jesus's ministry in Galilee (Lk 4:14–9:50)
4. Book 3: Jesus's ministry toward Jerusalem (Lk 9:51–19:27)
5. Book 4: Jesus's ministry in Jerusalem (Lk 19:28–21:38)
6. Book 5: Jesus's arrest, trial, and crucifixion (Lk 22:1–23:56)
7. Epilogue: Jesus's resurrection and ascension (Lk 24:1–52)

Prologue (Lk 1:1–4)

Luke acknowledges the works of his predecessors who have ventured to write an orderly narrative of the life of Jesus (Lk 1:1). But as can be seen from Luke 1:1–2, he does not name those predecessors. It is very difficult to conclude if Luke was referring to the Gospels that were in circulation by the time he set to compose his own account of Jesus's life. Whatever sources Luke used, those sources were based on the testimony of the eyewitnesses and servants of the Word (Lk 1:2).

Luke addresses both his Gospel and Acts to a man called Theophilus (Lk 1:3; Acts 1:1). In the Gospel, Luke addresses Theophilus as "most excellent" (Gk: *kratistos*). In four instances in Acts, Luke uses "most excellent" to address the Roman governor Festus and King Agrippa (Acts 23:26; 24:2; 26:7, 25). Theophilus could be a Roman political figure whom Luke knew. Much like Paul arguing his case before King Agrippa and the governor Festus (Acts 26:2–29), Luke was intending to persuade Theophilus of the truth of the gospel. In Greek the name Theophilus means a "friend of God." If Luke intended his works to be read by anyone other than a historical Theophilus, he probably addressed the future reader by the pseudonym "friend of God." Luke was likely recommending the merits of the gospel of Jesus Christ to an educated reader of the time, thus the genuine term Theophilus as "friend of God."

Book 1: The Beginning (Lk 1:5–4:13)

In this section Luke traces the origin of the gospel narrative by way of the birth of John and the birth of Jesus and provides brief accounts of Jesus's preparation for ministry. Just like Jesus's birth, John's birth is foretold by the angel (Lk 1:13). Luke points out how God prepared John since conception to bear witness to the coming of the Lord. The angel says to Zechariah, "With the spirit and power of Elijah [John] will go before him, to turn the hearts of parents to their children, and the disobedient to the wisdom of the righteous, to make ready a people prepared for the Lord" (Lk 1:17). After John's birth, Zechariah, being filled with the Holy Spirit, prophesies that John will be the one who prepares the way for the Lord. He says, "And you, child, will be called the prophet of the Most High; for you will go before the Lord to prepare his ways, to give knowledge of salvation to his people by the forgiveness of their sins" (Lk 1:76–77). Luke is setting the proper sequence of salvation history.

If John is the forerunner of Jesus, then his birth must precede Jesus's.

The angel Gabriel is sent by God to Nazareth to foretell the birth of Jesus (Lk 1:26–27). He comes to Mary and says, "Do not be afraid, Mary, for you have found favor with God. And now, you will conceive in your womb and bear a son, and you will name him Jesus. He will be great, and will be called the Son of the Most High, and the Lord God will give to him the throne of his ancestor David. He will reign over the house of Jacob forever, and of his kingdom there will be no end" (Lk 1:30–33). Luke points out that Jesus already assumed the title "Son of the Most High" by divine attribution (Lk 1:35). The song of Mary (known as *Magnificat* in Latin) shows how God intends to save God's people through Jesus's birth (Lk 1:46–55). For Luke, the birth of Jesus takes place not by accident, but it has been part of God's plan from the beginning as has God's purpose that Jesus is sent to save humanity.

Luke sets the birth of Jesus in the context of a Roman census decreed by Emperor Augustus and conducted during the governorship of Quirinius (Lk 2:1–2).[19] Luke tries to situate the birth of Jesus in Bethlehem within the context of a Roman census in order to draw attention to the divine plan emerging from the events of history. Jesus's birth is announced to the shepherds by the angel that a Savior was born for them in the city of David (Lk 2:10–11). The song of the angelic choir (known as *Gloria* in Latin) witnesses to the peace that the birth of Jesus brings for all (Lk 2:14). Luke reports that Jesus is presented at the Temple according to the law of Moses (Lk 2:22–24; cf. Ex 13:2; Lv 12:8), and, consequently, Luke shows that Jesus was brought up according to the Jewish customs. The devotion of his family to the

---

19 Outside the Gospel of Luke, there is no historical record of an empire-wide census. Caesar Augustus was a Roman emperor from 27 BCE to 14 CE. According to Luke's Gospel, a local census was conducted during the time of Quirinius as the Roman governor, but secular sources indicate that Quirinius did not become the governor of Syria until 6 CE. Luke declares that Jesus was born under Herod the Great (37 BCE–4 CE). Many scholars think it would be impossible for these events to have taken place at a time when Emperor Augustus, Herod the Great, and Governor Quirinius were all simultaneously in power. Perhaps Quirinius held a lower position earlier but was in the region. The issue still remains something of a puzzle. See J. A. Fitzmyer, *The Gospel According to Luke I–IX: A New Translation with Introduction and Commentary*, AB 28 (New York: Doubleday, 1979), 393.

law and his Davidic heritage indicate that Jesus is fully eligible to claim future kingship. The song of Simeon (known as *Nunc Dimittis* in Latin) further testifies that Jesus will be a light to both Gentiles and Jews (Lk 2:29–32). Simeon and Anna the prophetess speak about Jesus as one who will bring redemption for the people (Lk 2:36–38). Luke places Jesus at the Jewish Temple when he is twelve years old in order to show his dedication to the Temple and his association at a very young age with the teachers of the law (Lk 2:41–52).

Luke situates the ministry of John the Baptist within the time of the Roman rulers and Jewish high priests (Lk 3:1–2). Although John the Baptist baptizes Jesus, he was subservient to Jesus (Lk 3:15–17). At his baptism Jesus receives the Holy Spirit and the heavenly attestation that he is God's Son (Lk 3:22; cf. Ps 2:7; Is 42:1). Luke places the genealogy of Jesus after Jesus's baptism to show his human lineage (Lk 3:23–37), and traces Jesus's ancestral lineage back all the way to the creation of Adam, in order to relate Jesus to all humanity and to affirm the divine Sonship of Jesus like the first Adam (Lk 3:37; cf. Gn 2:7). The story of the temptation of Jesus further affirms that Jesus is tested and proven to be the Son of God (Lk 4:1–13). Jesus overcomes the temptation of the devil by using the Scriptures (cf. Dt 6:13; 8:3) and corrects the devil's misinterpretation of the Scripture (Lk 4:10–11; cf. Dt 6:16; Ps 91:11–12).[20] Luke brings Jesus to the public ministry as the one who is fully prepared to save humanity.

Book 2: Jesus's Ministry in Galilee (Lk 4:14–9:50)

In this unit Luke places Jesus's inaugural ministry in Galilee. Right after his temptation, Jesus appears in public ministry and begins to teach in the synagogues (Lk 4:15). Luke draws attention to Jesus's proclamation at a synagogue in Nazareth by telling us that Jesus read from Isaiah 61:1–2 and spoke about the fulfillment of the Scripture (Lk 4:18–21). From this we can see that Jesus is called by God to proclaim the good news, especially in the year of Jubilee (cf. Lv 25:8–12). Jesus comes

---

20 For Luke's use of Psalm 91, see J. S. Subramanian, *The Synoptic Gospels and the Psalms as Prophecy*, LNTS 351 (London: T. & T. Clark, 2007), 72–75.

to set people free from all kinds of bondage. Freeing people from bondage is the theme of Jesus's first healing, which is the liberation of a man from an unclean spirit (Lk 4:31–35). Here Jesus subdues the clean spirit and sets the man free. Luke reports that Jesus heals many who are sick and casts out demons (Lk 4:40–44). Luke also reports that Jesus continues to proclaim the good news of the Kingdom of God in the synagogues of Judea (Lk 4:43–44).

Right after the call of the first three disciples (Simon Peter, James, and John), Jesus continues to engage in a healing ministry. He cleanses a leper, heals a paralytic man, and restores a man with a withered hand (Lk 5:12–16, 17–26; 6:6–11). Jesus also takes time to address the question asked by the Pharisees and scribes about why his disciples do not fast (Lk 5:33). Jesus answers by alluding to wedding guests who will not fast as long as the bridegroom is with them; rather, they fast only when the bridegroom is taken away from them (Lk 5:34–35). In addition, Jesus permits his disciples to pluck and eat grain on the Sabbath (Lk 6:1), but some Pharisees question if the disciples did it unlawfully since it was the Sabbath (Lk 6:2; cf. Ex 34:21). Jesus then draws attention to the incident when David and his companions entered the Temple and ate the bread of the Presence, which is not lawful for anyone except the priests (Lk 6:3–4; cf. 1 Sm 21:1–6). Luke shows that Jesus has the authority to justify the action of the disciples on the Sabbath because he is the Lord of the Sabbath (Lk 6:5).

Luke continues to highlight Jesus's teaching and healing ministries. Jesus stands on a level place and teaches about blessings, woes, love for enemies, judging others, fruit of the tree, and building a solid foundation (Lk 6:20–49). In the context of teaching, Jesus heals many who are sick. Luke reports, "And all in the crowd were trying to touch [Jesus], for power came out from him and healed all of them" (Lk 6:19). Then Jesus goes on to heal a centurion's servant, raise a widow's son at Nain, forgive a sinful woman, cast out many demons from a Gerasene man, heal a woman from hemorrhages, raise Jairus's daughter, and cast out a demon from a boy (Lk 7:1–10, 11–17, 36–50; 8:26–39, 40–42, 43–48; 49–56; 9:37–43). These healing stories attest that Jesus came to set people free from their infirmities;

consequently, the mission of the disciples echoes the ministry of Jesus. Luke states, "[The twelve] departed and went through the villages, bringing the good news and curing diseases everywhere" (Lk 9:6). Luke even reports that some women accompany Jesus along with the Twelve in the proclamation of the Kingdom of God (Lk 8:1–3).

Luke again reiterates the preaching and healing ministries of Jesus. Luke asserts, "When the crowds found out about it, they followed [Jesus]; and he welcomed them, and spoke to them about the kingdom of God, and healed those who needed to be cured" (Lk 9:11). The feeding of the five thousand shows that Jesus is also concerned about the physical needs of the people (Lk 9:12–17). Luke goes on to disclose the true identity of Jesus. In response to the question of John the Baptist's disciples who ask if Jesus is the expected one, Jesus says, "Go and tell John what you have seen and heard: the blind receive their sight, the lame walk, the lepers are cleansed, the deaf hear, the dead are raised, the poor have good news brought to them. And blessed is anyone who takes no offense at me" (Lk 7:22–23; cf. Dt 18:21–22; Is 26:19; 29:18–19; 35:5–6; 61:1).

For Luke, Jesus is a healer and preacher. Jesus is also the one who has power over nature. After Jesus calms a storm, the disciples say to one another, "Who then is this, that he commands even the winds and the water, and they obey him?" (Lk 8:25b). Then Peter confesses that Jesus is the Messiah of God (Lk 9:20b), and even the demons recognize Jesus as "Son of the Most High God" (Lk 8:28). At Jesus's transfiguration, Jesus is again recognized as God's Son. The voice from heaven says, "This is my Son, my Chosen; listen to him!" (Lk 9:35; cf. Dt 18:15; Ps 2:7; Is 42:1). At the end of time, Jesus will come as the Son of Man (Lk 9:26). Meanwhile, Jesus predicts that he will face suffering and death and eventually vindication (Lk 9:21–22, 44). In all, Luke sets forth through the narratives what he believes to be the true historical identity of Jesus.

Book 3: Jesus's Ministry toward Jerusalem (Lk 9:51–19:27)

In this unit Luke focuses on Jesus's journey toward Jerusalem and on his teaching ministry. Luke begins this segment by remarking,

"When the days drew near for [Jesus] to be taken up, he set his face to go to Jerusalem" (Lk 9:51). For Luke, Jesus's ministry in Galilee is as important as what he does as he travels toward Jerusalem. This is evidenced by the fact that Jesus sends out seventy disciples (some ancient manuscripts mention seventy-two) with these words, "The harvest is plentiful, but the laborers are few; therefore ask the Lord of the harvest to send out laborers into his harvest" (Lk 10:2). Here Jesus is recognized as "the Lord of the harvest." Healing the sick and preaching the Kingdom of God constitute the mission of the seventy (Lk 10:9), and Luke reports that the seventy come back with joy and say to Jesus, "Lord, in your name even the demons submit to us!" (Lk 10:17). Jesus encourages his disciples to rejoice, not because they can cast out the demons, but because their names will be written in heaven (Lk 10:22). Luke also reveals that Jesus rejoices in the Holy Spirit because God has chosen him to reveal God (Lk 10:22).

This unit is full of parables. The Parable of the Good Samaritan (Lk 10:29–37) serves to remind us that even strangers and enemies can be good neighbors; the question "Who is our neighbor" echoes "Am I my brother's keeper?" (Gn 4:9). The Parable of the Rich Fool focuses on life lived in constant awareness of God (Lk 12:13–21). The Parable of the Barren Fig Tree reminds us of God's patience (Lk 13:6–9). The Parables of the Mustard Seed and the Yeast talk about the growth of the Kingdom of God (Lk 13:18–19, 20–21). The Parable of the Great Dinner addresses both the invitation and the outcome of refusing an invitation to enter God's Kingdom (Lk 14:15–24). The Parables of the Lost Sheep, the Lost Coin, and the Lost Son reveal God's love for humanity and the lengths to which God goes to demonstrate that love (Lk 15:1–32). The Parable of the Dishonest Manager emphasizes not so much the manager's dishonesty but his prudence, which is required of discipleship (Lk 16:1–9). The story of the rich man and Lazarus invites everyone to live a life in accordance with the law and the prophets (Lk 16:19–31). The Parable of the Widow and the Unjust Judge highlights the difference between God's justice and mercy and human justice and indifference (Lk 18:1–8). The Parable of the Pharisee and the Tax Collector highlights the contrast between the righteous and the sinner and the verdict given by God (Lk 18:9–14). The Parable of the Ten Minas (pounds) draws attention to active participation in the mission of God here and now until the glorious appearance of God's Kingdom (Lk 19:11–27).

Dispersed between the parables, Luke records extensively Jesus's teachings on various subjects, such as prayer, hypocrisy, worry, watchfulness, faithfulness, cost of discipleship, and the coming of the Kingdom of God (Lk 11:1–13; 12:1–3, 22–34, 35–40, 41–48; 14:25–33; 17:20–37). In light of the approaching Kingdom of God, Jesus teaches his followers to store up treasure in heaven. He says, "Do not be afraid, little flock, for it is your Father's good pleasure to give you the kingdom. Sell your possessions, and give alms. Make purses for yourselves that do not wear out, an unfailing treasure in heaven, where no thief comes near and no moth destroys. For where your treasure is, there your heart will be also" (Lk 12:32–34). On his way to Jerusalem, Jesus also takes time to heal a crippled woman, a man with dropsy, and ten lepers (Lk 13:10–17; 14:1–6; 17:11–19). Jesus commands the rich young ruler to sell all his possessions and give them to the poor and then begin to follow him (Lk 18:22). Jesus sees that it is not just sickness but also riches that prevent people from being set free. His encounter with Zacchaeus even touches on salvation. After Zacchaeus promises that he will make restitution, Jesus says to him, "Today salvation has come to this house, because he too is a son of Abraham. For the Son of Man came to seek out and to save the lost" (Lk 19:9–10). Jesus's teaching, healing, and encounters with people amount to his saving activity. Even before he enters Jerusalem, he has already emerged as a Savior. But it is in Jerusalem where Jesus will fully accomplish his saving activity. Jesus says to the twelve disciples, "See, we are going up to Jerusalem, and everything that is written about the Son of Man by the prophets will be accomplished" (Lk 18:31; cf. Is 53:7–8). Luke concludes this section by narrating the Parable of the Ten Minas (Lk 19:12–27),[21] which alludes to Jesus's rejection in Jerusalem and his future reign as King.

---

21   The Parable of the Ten Minas is a non-Matthean tradition. Luke places this story in the context of Jesus's arrival in Jerusalem, where he will face rejection and subsequent

Book 4: Jesus's Ministry in Jerusalem (Lk 19:28–21:38)

In this crucial unit Luke focuses on Jesus's ministry in Jerusalem. Jesus's arrival in Jerusalem is at first met with great enthusiasm. But it does not end well. Luke reports that the whole multitude praises God by saying, "Blessed is the king who comes in the name of the Lord! Peace in heaven, and glory in the highest heaven!" (Lk 19:38; cf. Ps 118:26; Lk 2:14).[22] Jesus is clearly recognized as the King who comes to reign over all the earth (cf. Zec 9:9–10). Luke draws attention to Jesus's lament over Jerusalem, because Jerusalem does not fully recognize Jesus as an envoy from God (Lk 19:41–44). As a sign of visitation from God, Jesus cleanses the Temple (Lk 19:45–46; cf. Mal 3:1–2; Is 56:7; Jer 7:11). He then predicts that the Temple will be totally destroyed in the future (Lk 21:6), as will all of Jerusalem (Lk 21:20–24). But Jesus also focuses on the future redemption of humanity when the Son of Man will appear with power and great glory (Lk 21:27).

Luke narrates Jesus's teaching in the Temple and his engagement with his adversaries, such as the chief priests, scribes, elders, and Sadducees; although we also learn from John's Gospel that some Jewish leaders were followers of Jesus, namely Nicodemus and Joseph of Arimathea (Jn 19:37–39). When Jesus's opponents question his authority, he draws attention to the ministry of John the Baptist, who was sent from God (Lk 20:1–6) and whom the people believed was a prophet. As the religious leaders could not decide if John the Baptist was of human origin or of divine (Lk 20:7), likewise Jesus will not answer whether his authority comes from God or humanity (Lk 20:8).

Jesus tells the Parable of the Wicked Tenants, alluding to Israel's impending judgment (Lk 20:9–19). The tenants that God installed as leaders over God's people will be destroyed, and the rejected stone will become the cornerstone. The rejected stone is an allusion to Jesus's death and resurrection (Lk 20:16, 17–18; cf. Ps 118:22;

---

death on the cross. See McNicol et al., *Beyond the Q Impasse*, 243–44.

22 For Luke's use of Psalm 118 in the context of Jesus's arrival in Jerusalem, see Subramanian, *Synoptic Gospels and the Psalms*, 78–80.

Is 8:14–15; Dn 2:34–35, 44–45).[23] With regard to the question of paying taxes, Jesus teaches we give both the government what is due—taxes/money—and we give God everything (Lk 20:25). The poor widow's offering at the treasury in the Temple serves as an important teaching to show how one should give to God (Lk 21:1–4). The Sadducees, who did not believe in resurrection, come to Jesus and ask about how marriage on earth will be treated in the afterlife, which they don't believe in anyway (Lk 20:27–33). Jesus answers that there will be resurrection in the future, because God is not the God of the dead but of the living. The resurrected ones will be more like angels and children of God (Lk 20:36–38). Jesus also takes time to teach that the Messiah will be more than David's Son; he is indeed David's Lord (Lk 20:41–44; cf. Ps 110:1).[24]

Luke mentions that Jesus continued to teach in the Temple until the Festival of Unleavened Bread (the Passover). Luke ends this unit with these words: "Every day [Jesus] was teaching in the temple, and at night he would go out and spend the night on the Mount of Olives, as it was called. And all the people would get up early in the morning to listen to him in the temple" (Lk 21:37–38). This seems to indicate that at first for Luke there were many in the holy city who heeded Jesus's teaching.

Book 5: Jesus's Arrest, Trial, and Crucifixion (Lk 22:1–23:56)

In this section Luke shows how Jesus prepares himself and the disciples leading up to his arrest, trial, and crucifixion. First, Luke describes how the chief priests and scribes bribe Judas Iscariot to betray Jesus (Lk 22:1–6). In the meantime Jesus sends Peter and John to prepare a guest room in a house for the celebration of Passover (Lk 22:7–13). Within the context of the Passover, Jesus passes the cup of wine and a loaf of bread in anticipation of his death. When he breaks the

---

23 For Luke's use of Psalm 118 in the context of the Parable of the Wicked Tenants, see Subramanian, 80–82.

24 For Luke's use of Psalm 110 in the context of the question of the Davidic Sonship of the Messiah, see Subramanian, 82–85.

bread, he gives it to the disciples and says, "This is my body, which is given for you. Do this in remembrance of me" (Lk 22:19). Then he passes the cup, saying, "This cup that is poured out for you is the new covenant in my blood" (Lk 22:20b). For Luke, Jesus inaugurates the new covenant through his death on the cross, and these words of institution of the Lord's Supper echo the arrival of the new covenant (cf. Jer 31:31–33). Jesus also talks about his betrayal (Lk 22:21–23). He predicts Peter's denial, which was fulfilled after Jesus's arrest (Lk 22:31–34, 54–62). Jesus takes time to teach his disciples about true greatness (Lk 22:24–26), which he demonstrates by example—acting as a servant. He says, "For who is greater, the one who is at the table or the one who serves? Is it not the one at the table? But I am among you as one who serves" (Lk 22:27).

Immediately after the supper, Luke says that Jesus, along with his disciples, goes to the Mount of Olives so Jesus can pray (Lk 22:39–42). Luke draws attention to the intensity of Jesus's turmoil, such that his sweat becomes like drops of blood: "Then an angel from heaven appeared to him and gave him strength. In his anguish he prayed more earnestly, and his sweat became like great drops of blood falling down on the ground" (Lk 22:43–44).[25] Luke shows that Jesus receives strength from an angel so he can face his impending suffering and death in the midst of his great agony. Then Judas betrays Jesus, who is taken to the house of the high priest (Lk 22:47–54). Jesus

---

25 Luke 22:43–44 poses a textual issue. Some of the ancient manuscripts such as Papyrus 69, Papyrus 73, Codex Sinaiticus 1, Codex Alexandrinus, and Codex Vaticanus do not include the passage. Other manuscripts such as Codex Sinaiticus, Codex Laudianus, Codex Seidelianus I, Codex Seidelianus II, and Codex Campianus also omit the passage. Early Church Fathers from the second century CE such as Hippolytus, Justin Martyr, and Irenaeus quote this passage in their writings, which suggests that Lk 22:43–44 was part of the original manuscript and somehow dropped out in some key manuscripts. For further discussion, see D. E. Anne, "The Text-Tradition of Luke-Acts," *BETS* 7 (1964): 69–82; B. D. Ehrman and M. A. Plunkett, "The Angel and the Agony: The Textual Problem of Luke 22:43–44," *CBQ* 45 (1983): 401–16; B. D. Ehrman, *The Orthodox Corruption of Scripture: The Effect of Early Christological Controversies on the Text of the New Testament* (New York: Oxford University Press, 1993), 187–94; McNicol et al., *Beyond the Q Impasse*, 288; L. H. Blumell, "Luke 22:43–44: An Anti-Docetic Interpretation or an Apologetic Omission," *TC* 19 (2014): 1–35; M. Pope, "The Downward Motion of Jesus's Sweat and the Authenticity of Luke 22:43–44," *CBQ* 79 (2017): 261–81.

is brought before the council and questioned to ascertain whether he is the Messiah (Lk 22:66–67a). Jesus responds that the Son of Man "will be seated at the right hand of the power of God" (Lk 22:69). The religious leaders ask if he is indeed the Son of God (Lk 22:70a). Jesus acknowledges their question, which is taken as an admission that yes, he is the Son of God (Lk 22:70b).

Jesus is then led before Pilate to be questioned. Pilate asks Jesus if he is the King of the Jews (Lk 23:3a). Again, Jesus acknowledges what Pilate says of him (Lk 23:3a). But Pilate finds no basis for fault against Jesus (Lk 23:4). Luke mentions that Jesus is sent to Herod Antipas, who happens to be in Jerusalem, because Jesus came from Galilee, which is under Herod's jurisdiction (Lk 23:6–7). Jesus's ordeal continues as he is questioned by Herod, but here Jesus gives no answer (Lk 23:9). Jesus is again brought back to Pilate, who protests that he does not find Jesus guilty of any charge (Lk 23:13–14). Pilate also states that Herod did not find Jesus guilty of any crimes that deserved a death sentence (Lk 23:15), so Pilate commands that Jesus be flogged and released (Lk 23:14). But the religious leaders insist that Jesus should be crucified, and when Pilate offers the crowd a choice as to whom should be released— Barabbas, a murderer, or Jesus, a life-giver—the crowd chooses Barabbas (Lk 23:18), and Pilate yields (Lk 23:24–25).

Luke alludes to Simon of Cyrene, who is made to carry Jesus's cross (Lk 23:26). Luke also refers to many people, including women who weep and follow Jesus to his execution, at the place called the Skull (Lk 23:27). Jesus turns toward the women and says, "Daughters of Jerusalem, do not weep for me, but weep for yourselves and for your children" (Lk 23:28). Jesus is sympathetic because Jerusalem's destruction is coming (Lk 23:29–31; cf. Is 51:4; Ez 20:47; Hos 10:8).

Luke records three sayings of Jesus from the cross. First, Jesus says, "Father, forgive them; for they do not know what they are doing" (Lk 23:34a).[26] Here Luke emphasizes the theme of forgiveness that runs

---

26 Luke 23:34a poses a textual dilemma. Some of the ancient manuscripts exclude this verse. For further discussion, see McNicol et al., *Beyond the Q Impasse*, 303–4; J. H. Petzer, "Anti-Judaism and the Textual Problem," *Neot* 5 (1992): 199–203; J. A.

throughout his Gospel (cf. Lk 5:20; 6:27; 7:36–50; 11:4; 17:4). Second, one criminal, who is being crucified next to Jesus, declares Jesus's innocence and recognizes him as King (Lk 23:41–42). Jesus turns toward him and says, "Truly I tell you, today you will be with me in Paradise" (Lk 23:43). Third, right after the Temple curtain is torn in two, Jesus cries with a loud voice: "Father, into your hands I commend my spirit" (Lk 23:46; cf. Ps 31:5).[27] Luke emphasizes Jesus's absolute trust in God in the midst of death. The centurion who witnesses Jesus's death says, "Certainly this man was innocent [righteous]" (Lk 23:47). Luke sees the centurion's statement as eyewitness testimony that Jesus was innocent, or righteous, even in death.

Luke refers to Joseph of Arimathea as one who "was waiting expectantly for the kingdom of God" (Lk 23:50–51). Joseph comes, takes Jesus's body, and lays it "in a rock-hewn tomb where no one had ever been laid" (Lk 23:53). The women witness Jesus's burial (Lk 23:55) and go home only to return to the tomb a day after the Sabbath in order to anoint the body with spices and ointments (Lk 23:56).

Epilogue: Jesus's Resurrection and Ascension (Lk 24:1–52)

In this final section, Luke focuses on the climax of Jesus's ministry. The resurrection of Jesus is seen as fulfillment of both Jesus's own predictions and the Scripture's. On Sunday, the women who come to the tomb to anoint the body are surprised to find the stone that had sealed the tomb has been rolled away and the body is gone (Lk 24:1–3). Not surprisingly, the women are terrified to see two men in dazzling clothes who proclaim the resurrection of Jesus (Lk 24:5). These men call attention to what Jesus had predicted about his resurrection while still in Galilee: "Remember how he told you, while he was still in Galilee, that the Son of Man must be handed over to sinners, and

---

Whitlark and M. C. Parsons, "The 'Seven' Last Words: A Numerical Motivation for the Insertion of Luke 23.34a," *NTS* 52 (2006): 188–204; N. Eubank, "A Disconcerting Prayer on the Originality of Luke 23:34a," *JBL* 129 (2010): 521–36.

27 For Luke's use of Psalm 31 in the context of Jesus's death, see Subramanian, *Synoptic Gospels and the Psalms*, 85–89.

be crucified, and on the third day rise again" (Lk 24:6–7; cf. Lk 9:22, 44). For Luke, the resurrection of Jesus took place in accordance with Jesus's earlier word.

Luke describes the resurrection fully through a narrative of Jesus's post-resurrection appearance to two disciples on the road to Emmaus (Lk 24:13–35). In this beautiful unit, one of the disciples is Cleopas, while the other disciple is not named (Lk 24:13, 18). Luke includes a witness to Jesus's resurrection by two disciples who are not part of the Twelve. Jesus interprets the Scriptures, which helps them see how the Scriptures testify to the suffering and vindication of the Messiah. Jesus says to them, "Oh, how foolish you are, and how slow of heart to believe all that the prophets have declared! Was it not necessary that the Messiah should suffer these things and then enter into his glory?" (Lk 24:25–26). Earlier, Jesus himself had predicted that he would suffer in order to fulfill God's scheme of salvation (Lk 9:22, 44–45; 12:50; 13:32–33; 17:25; 18:31–34). Now the two disciples are invited to understand the suffering and glorification of the Messiah in light of Scriptures (cf. Nm 24:17; Dt 18:15; Is 9:6; 50:6; 53:4–5; Zec 9:9; 13:7; Mal 3:1). Luke draws attention to Scripture as a living testimony to the life and ministry of Jesus. Upon reaching a house in Emmaus, Jesus is then revealed to the disciples as the risen Lord in the breaking of the bread (Lk 24:30–31). Luke highlights the effect and significance of the Lord's Supper through which the risen Jesus can be recognized (Lk 24:35; cf. Lk 22:19).

Luke again gives special importance to Scripture as a key witness to understand the life of Jesus. Then when Jesus appears to the eleven disciples, he draws attention to Scripture that bears witness to his suffering and resurrection. He says to them, "These are my words that I spoke to you while I was still with you—that everything written about me in the law of Moses, the prophets, and the psalms must be fulfilled" (Lk 24:44).[28] He further says, "Thus it is written, that

---

28 David Flusser argues that Luke's tripartite division of the Hebrew Bible as the Law, the Prophets, and the Psalms (Lk 24:24) resembles the Qumran text 4QMMT (4Q394), which also refers to the Hebrew Bible as the books of Moses, the Prophets, and David's

the Messiah is to suffer and to rise from the dead on the third day, and that repentance and forgiveness of sins is to be proclaimed in his name to all nations, beginning from Jerusalem. You are witnesses of these things" (Lk 24:46–48). Jesus urges the disciples to stay in Jerusalem until they receive the power from above: "And see, I am sending upon you what my Father promised; so stay here in the city until you have been clothed with power from on high" (Lk 24:49). In many ways this word sets the agenda for Luke's second volume, Acts. Finally, Jesus commissions his disciples to bear witness to the life of the Messiah through the power of the Holy Spirit (Lk 24:48–49).

Luke gives a brief account of Jesus's ascension (Lk 24:50–51). This emphasis on the ascension is unique to Luke. Luke states that Jesus blessed the disciples and then was lifted up into heaven. The ascension account completes Jesus's journey to Jerusalem (cf. Lk 9:51). It also fulfills what was indicated at Jesus's transfiguration: "[Moses and Elijah] appeared in glory and were speaking of his departure, which he was about to accomplish at Jerusalem" (Lk 9:31). The disciples return to Jerusalem and remain in the Temple blessing God (Lk 24:52–53), thus concluding Luke's Gospel where it began—in the Temple (Lk 24:53; cf. Lk 1:8–9). Luke concludes with the disciples in the Temple, where they remain until they receive the Holy Spirit to go to all nations to preach the gospel in Jesus's name (Lk 24:47–49).

Luke has systematically narrated Jesus's life to Theophilus. He has convinced Theophilus that the gospel of Jesus Christ had a divine origin. It was divine necessity that God send Jesus as the Messiah, the Savior to bring salvation to humanity. For Luke, the whole event that constitutes the life of Jesus is God's doing. Divine involvement in human salvation through Jesus lies at the heart of Luke's theology. From birth to ascension, Jesus fulfilled God's plan of salvation. His ministry was affirmed by God and was testified by human witnesses, including Roman authorities. What happened in Jerusalem, however, will not be kept secret. The disciples will publicly proclaim to all

---

Psalms. See D. Flusser, "Wie in den Psalmen über mich geschrieben steht (Lk 24:44)," *Judaica* 48 (1992): 40–42.

nations how God fulfilled God's promises written in the Scriptures about the life, death, and resurrection of Jesus Christ.

Theology of Luke

Luke wrote to Theophilus in order to give an eyewitness account of how God fulfilled God's promises for the salvation of the world through Jesus Christ (Lk 1:1–4). Then he set out to describe how God's plan of salvation worked through the activity of Jesus, not only for Israel, but for all nations. As François Bovon says, "Jesus' activity is the final and conclusive attempt of the benevolent God somehow still to win Israel for himself and, at the same time, to reach the Gentiles. All that the Messiah Jesus does, the Son, Lord, Savior, Teacher, and Physician, is on behalf of the one nation and, at the same time, nations as a whole."[29]

Luke's theology is centered around the events of salvation that have been fulfilled in the ministry of Jesus, and the angels' proclamation to the shepherds at his birth remains an essential component because it was God's plan to send Jesus to save humanity. The angel said to the shepherds, "Do not be afraid; for see—I am bringing you good news of great joy for all the people: to you is born this day in the city of David a Savior, who is the Messiah, the Lord. This will be a sign for you: you will find a child wrapped in bands of cloth and lying in a manger" (Lk 2:10–12). For Luke, the birth of Jesus has universal implications. Jesus will be the Savior not just for Israel, as represented by the shepherds, but for all nations as represented by Theophilus. As Allan J. McNicol remarks, "The house of God's servant David is about to be restored and Israel's redemption is at hand. Not only will glory return to Israel, but in keeping with the word of several of the later prophets this occurrence will bring 'light to the Gentiles'" (Lk 2:32).[30] Luke tells us that Zechariah spoke about

---

29 Bovon, *Luke 1*, 10.

30 A. J. McNicol, *The Persistence of God's Endangered Promises: The Bible's Unified Story* (London: Bloomsbury T. & T. Clark, 2018), 145.

the coming Savior (Lk 1:68–79) and that Mary praised God for the salvation of not just now but all generations (Lk 1:46–55). For Luke, the birth of the Savior took place in accordance with the prophecy in the concrete, everyday events of Roman history (Lk 2:1–2). The son of Simeon affirms the fulfillment of God's salvation for all people through the birth of Jesus: "Master, now you are dismissing your servant in peace, according to your word; for my eyes have seen your salvation, which you have prepared in the presence of all peoples, a light for revelation to the Gentiles and for glory to your people Israel" (Lk 2:29–32).

Luke traces the genealogy of Jesus back to Adam to show that Jesus is the Son of God for all humanity (Lk 3:38). Luke defines the ministry of Jesus as the fulfillment of the prophecy of Isaiah, which is why Jesus came to preach the good news to the poor and set the oppressed free (Lk 4:18–21; cf. Is 61:1–2). Jesus was sent to proclaim the good news to all. When he was prevented from leaving by the crowd of people, he said to them, "I must proclaim the good news of the kingdom of God to the other cities also; for I was sent for this purpose" (Lk 4:43). This also explains why Jesus pronounces the forgiveness of sins of a paralytic man and a sinful woman (Lk 5:19; 7:48). Luke shows how God becomes active through Jesus's ministry in forgiving the sins of humanity. In the raising of the widow's son at Nain, Jesus acts on behalf of God to raise the dead back to life (Lk 7:11–15). Luke reports that people praised God, saying, "'A great prophet has risen among us!' and 'God has looked favorably on his people!'" (Lk 7:16). In the healing story of the Gerasene demoniac, Jesus tells the man, "Return to your home, and declare how much God has done for you" (Lk 8:39a). Luke adds that the man went and talked about Jesus: "So he went away, proclaiming throughout the city how much Jesus had done for him" (Lk 8:39b). Luke emphasizes that God has become present in Jesus through Jesus's redemption of the people. Again, when Jesus healed a boy with a demon, people saw the greatness of God in the ministry of Jesus (Lk 9:43). For Luke, God has visited God's people through Jesus, leaving a trail of healing, forgiveness, and redemption.

Luke mentions the mission of the seventy in addition to the mission of the Twelve (Lk 10:1–12; cf. Lk 9:1–6). The seventy disciples who later may start their own ministry to the Gentiles were specifically sent to proclaim the arrival of the Kingdom of God. Jesus tells them, "Yet know this: the kingdom of God has come near" (Lk 10:11b). Then when the disciples return from their mission, they are overwhelmed at the power they possess. They say to Jesus, "Lord, in your name even the demons submit to us!" (Lk 10:17). Luke seems to attest that the Kingdom of God that Jesus proclaimed even prevails over hostile powers (cf. Lk 11:14–20; 13:16; 22:31–32). Luke has already shown in the temptation narrative that Jesus subdued the devil by the power of the Holy Spirit (Lk 4:1–13).

Luke stresses the importance of Jesus's engagement with people. For Luke, Jesus is constantly urging and pressing people to make decisions in light of God's presence in human history. Jesus tells the Parable of the Good Samaritan in response to a lawyer who wanted to inherit eternal life (Lk 10:25–37), where Jesus taught that the love of God should be shown in one's love for neighbor. The Samaritan shows God's love through acts of mercy (Lk 10:33–35). Jesus tells the lawyer to go do likewise (Lk 10:37b). In the Parable of the Rich Fool, Jesus teaches that God is actively observing human history. Jesus brings the presence of God into the story. It is God who says to the rich man, "You fool! This very night your life is being demanded of you. And the things you have prepared, whose will they be?" (Lk 12:20). Jesus teaches that people should make personal responses and decisions in recognition of God's active involvement in human history (Lk 12:21).

In the Parable of the Great Dinner, Jesus teaches that those who reject the invitation to the coming banquet will not enter the Kingdom of God (Lk 14:15–24). The time to respond is now. The Parables of the Lost Sheep, the Lost Coin, and the Prodigal Son highlight the character of a God who has been actively seeking out and waiting for the people to enter into the joy of God's Kingdom (Lk 15:1–32). Jesus tells the story of the rich man and Lazarus to warn of a life lived in isolation, outside of the law of Moses and the prophets, who bear witness to God's plan of salvation (Lk 16:19–31; cf. Lk 24:26–27, 44–48). The Parable of the Pharisee and the Tax Collector draws attention to what

God has been looking for in the lives of humanity (Lk 18:9–14). God justifies the sinners, not those who seek their own righteousness; thus, Jesus teaches that God has been busy saving sinners and tax collectors. Luke asserts that Jesus's encounter with Zacchaeus, a chief tax collector, has brought salvation to the household (Lk 19:1–10). Jesus came to seek out the lost and make God's salvation available to all, so Jesus says to Zacchaeus, "Today salvation has come to this house, because he too is a son of Abraham. For the Son of Man came to seek out and to save the lost" (Lk 19:9–10).

Luke seals his Gospel with God accomplishing the plan of salvation through an account of Jesus's death on the cross. Luke states, "When the days drew near for him to be taken up, he set his face to go to Jerusalem" (Lk 9:51). Luke reports that Jesus sent a message to Herod, saying, "Listen, I am casting out demons and performing cures today and tomorrow, and on the third day I finish my work. Yet today, tomorrow, and the next day I must be on my way, because it is impossible for a prophet to be killed outside of Jerusalem" (Lk 13:32–33). Jesus weeps over Jerusalem because he is aware of his impending persecution and martyrdom, which was the fate of prophets in the past (Lk 13:34; cf. 2 Chr 24:20–22; Jer 26:20–23).

At the celebration of the Passover meal, Jesus alludes to his death as a sign of the new covenant when he takes the cup and says, "This cup that is poured out for you is the new covenant in my blood" (Lk 22:20; cf. Ex 24:3–8; Lv 17:11). On the Mount of Olives, Jesus prays for God's will to accomplish God's plan: "Father, if you are willing, remove this cup from me; yet, not my will but yours be done" (Lk 22:42). Luke reports that Jesus died on the cross with confidence that he fulfilled God's will. Jesus cries with a loud voice and says, "Father, into your hands I commend my spirit" (Lk 23:46; cf. Ps 31:5).

Luke's account of Jesus's resurrection appearances focuses on the fulfillment of Scripture in the plan of God's salvation. The two men at the tomb tell the women that Jesus has been raised in accordance with his own predictions (Lk 24:6–7; cf. Lk 9:22, 44). When Jesus appears to the two disciples on the road to Emmaus, he explains how the suffering and vindication of the Messiah fulfills Scripture

(Lk 24:25–27). And, again, coming to the eleven disciples, he speaks about the fulfillment of the law of Moses, the prophets, and the psalms in his ministry (Lk 24:44). Now the disciples have a mission to accomplish after Jesus is taken up into heaven. Jesus appoints them to bear witness to the events that happened in fulfillment of the Scriptures (Lk 24:48).

Luke narrates the Gospel of Jesus Christ as the gospel of God's salvation for all humanity. God sent Jesus to be the Savior to accomplish redemption for both Israel and all nations in accordance with Scripture. The events narrated in Luke's Gospel are the events of the divine plan revealed in the life and ministry of Jesus. God worked out salvation in human history through Jesus of Nazareth, such that disciples are now called upon to proclaim the message of salvation in Jesus's name to all nations, beginning in Jerusalem (Lk 24:47).

John Wesley's Explanatory Notes on Luke

John Wesley divides Luke's Gospel into three major sections: (1) the beginning (Lk 1:1–2:40); (2) the middle (Lk 2:41–52); and (3) the course of history (Lk 3:1–24:53).[31] Further, Wesley classifies section 3 into four subdivisions: (a) the introduction (Lk 3:1–4:13); (b) the acceptable year in Galilee (Lk 4:14–9:17); (c) the preparation for Jesus's Passion (Lk 9:18–19:28); and (d) transactions at Jerusalem (Lk 19:29–24:53).

The Beginning (Lk 1:1–2:40)

In the preface of his Gospel, Luke refers to many who have engaged in previous attempts at writing the events (Lk 1:1). Wesley thinks that "many" does not mean Matthew or Mark, which some scholars presuppose today.[32] Since Luke does not explicitly refer to any specific sources by name, it can only be inferred that there were many people who were attempting to recount the events of the life of Jesus.

---

31 John Wesley, *Wesley's Notes on the New Testament* (Oxford: Benediction Classics, 2010), 98–101.

32 Wesley, 102.

For Wesley, Luke writes the narrative in "order of time."[33] First, Luke accounts for Jesus's life in the Gospel. Second, Luke writes about the apostles' accomplishments in the Acts of the Apostles.

Wesley shows familiarity with some Jewish apocryphal writings by alluding to them in his works. When the angel appeared to Zechariah, the angel said, "I am Gabriel. I stand in the presence of God, and I have been sent to speak to you and to bring you this good news" (Lk 1:19). Commenting on the appearance of Gabriel to Zechariah, Wesley alludes to "seven angels" that stand before the presence of God, perhaps echoing Revelation 1:20.[34] The reference to the seven angels comes from the Jewish apocryphal book of *Tobit*, which reads, "I am Raphael, one of the seven angels who stand ready and enter before the glory of the Lord" (*Tb* 12:15).

Wesley attributes a new title to Jesus. For Wesley, Jesus is the Redeemer (cf. Lk 2:14). Commenting on the praise of the heavenly host at Jesus's birth, Wesley remarks, "For with the Redeemer's birth, peace, and all kind of happiness, come down to dwell on earth: yea, the overflowing of Divine good will and favour are now exercised toward men."[35] Anna, a prophet, also saw Jesus as the Redeemer. When Jesus was presented at the Temple, she praised God and spoke about "the child to all who were looking for the redemption of Jerusalem" (Lk 2:38).

The Middle (Lk 2:41–52)

At the age of twelve Jesus was brought to the Temple by his parents for the Passover festival (Lk 2:41). But Jesus did not return with his parents. It took three days for them to find him at the Temple (Lk 2:46). When his parents found him, they told him that they had been searching for him (Lk 2:48). Jesus said to them, "Why were you searching for me? Did you not know that I must be in my Father's

---

33 Wesley, 102.

34 Wesley, 103.

35 Wesley, 106.

house?" (Lk 2:49). Wesley comments, "He does not blame them for losing, but for thinking it needful to seek him: and intimates, that he could not be lost, nor found any where, but doing the will of a higher parent."[36] Here Wesley sees God as parent who creates the family of God. After the incident, Jesus went with his parents to Nazareth, and Luke draws attention to Jesus's growing in divine and human favor: "And Jesus increased in wisdom and in years, and in divine and human favor" (Lk 2:52). Commenting on Jesus's increase in wisdom, Wesley asserts, "It plainly follows, that though a man were pure, even as Christ was pure, still he would have room to increase in holiness, and in consequence thereof to increase in the favour, as well as in the love of God."[37] Wesley suggests that all Christians should grow in holiness just as Jesus did.

The Course of History (Lk 3:1–24:53)

Right after the temptation, Jesus returned to Galilee and began to teach in the synagogues (Lk 4:14–15). When he went to the synagogue in Nazareth, he opened the Scripture and read from Isaiah 61:1–2 (cf. Lk 4:18). Wesley perceives the doctrine of the Trinity (one God in three divine persons as Father, Son, and Holy Spirit) embedded in Jesus's reading, referring to the Spirit and the Lord. Jesus, the Spirit, and the Lord interface in Scripture.[38] Wesley presumes the doctrine of Trinity is integrated in Jesus's reading.

Jesus told the Parable of the Good Samaritan to answer the lawyer's question, "Who is my neighbor?" (Lk 10:29–37). Jesus told the lawyer to become like the Samaritan who showed mercy to the wounded man (Lk 10:37). Commenting on Jesus's words, "Go and do likewise," John Wesley states,

> Let us go and do likewise, regarding every man as our neighbour who needs assistance. Let us renounce that bigotry and party zeal

---

36 Wesley, 107.

37 Wesley, 107.

38 Wesley, 109.

which would contract our hearts into an insensibility for all the human race, but a small number whose sentiments and practices are so much our own, that our love to them is but self love reflected. With an honest openness of mind let us always remember that kindred between man and man, and cultivate that happy instinct whereby, in the original constitution of our nature, God has strongly bound us to each other.[39]

Here we can see that Wesley calls all Christians to consider everyone as their neighbor and seek to help those in need. In Luke 11:2–4, Jesus teaches his disciples to pray, making, for Wesley, the Lord's Prayer "the badge of a real Christian."[40] This is because the Lord's Prayer not only focuses on the coming Kingdom of God, but also emphasizes both God forgiving sins and humans forgiving one another. For Wesley, Jesus spoke to his disciples about prayer, and he also directed us to imitate the prayer of Jesus in all our prayers.[41]

Jesus told three parables—the Parable of the Lost Sheep, the Parable of the Lost Coin, and the Parable of the Prodigal Son (Lk 15:1–32)—and Jesus reminded the Pharisees and the scribes of God's love for sinners and the tax collectors. Wesley also sees that these three parables teach the way God forgives and receives the sinners.[42] In the Parable of the Prodigal Son, when the prodigal son came back to his father's house, the elder brother refused to join in the celebration (Lk 15:28). Wesley comments, "Let no elder brother murmur at this indulgence, but rather welcome the prodigal back into the family."[43] Wesley realizes the unconditional love God has for humanity and that the same love should be shown to everyone in order to welcome them back to God's family. At the same time, Wesley insists that we should keep God's commandments and should

---

39 Wesley, 117.

40 Wesley, 118.

41 Wesley, 118.

42 Wesley, 125.

43 Wesley, 127.

not wander. He says, "And let those who have been thus received, wander no more, but emulate the strictest piety of those who for many years have served their heavenly Father, and not transgressed his commandments."[44]

Wesley draws attention to the last seven words of Jesus recorded by the four Evangelists.[45] It shows that Wesley closely studied all four Gospels, and he did not find all seven words of Jesus recorded by any one particular Gospel writer. Luke records only the three last words of Jesus (Lk 23:34, 43, 46). Wesley remarks, "Hence it appears that the four gospels are, as it were, four parts, which, joined together, make one symphony. Sometimes one of these only, sometimes two or three, sometimes all sound together."[46]

Wesley studied the Greek text of the Gospels in order to render a correct English translation in many instances. The centurion who witnessed Jesus's death said, "Certainly this man was innocent" (Lk 23:47). Wesley renders the English translation of the Greek text as "Certainly this was a righteous man."[47] The Greek word *dikaios* used in the text should be translated as "righteous," in contrast to *athōos*, which could be translated as "innocent." Therefore, we can credit Wesley with providing a correct translation in English. After the resurrection, Jesus told the disciples that everything written about him in the law of Moses, the prophets, and the psalms must be fulfilled (Lk 24:44). Wesley affirms that the prophecies concerning the Messiah are found in the books of Moses, the prophets, and psalms, and draws attention to the omission of the historical books.[48] That is, Luke does not show Jesus explicitly referring to the fulfillment of the prophecies mentioned in the historical books, such as Joshua, Judges, Ruth, 1 and 2 Samuel, 1 and 2 Kings, 1 and 2 Chronicles, Ezra, Nehemiah,

---

44 Wesley, 127.

45 Wesley, 139.

46 Wesley, 139.

47 Wesley, 140.

48 Wesley, 141.

and Esther. It would be worth exploring the fulfillment of prophecies concerning the Messiah in these historical books of the Old Testament.

Teaching and Preaching from Luke

Teaching

Many of Jesus's teachings were presented in parabolic form. The word *parable* in Hebrew is *mashal*, which means "riddle" (cf. Ez 17:2; 24.3). The word *parable* in Greek is *parabolē*, which means "a laying beside." In the context of his ministry, Jesus used parables to teach important lessons.[49] Jesus told the Parable of the Barren Fig Tree to teach about God's patience (Lk 13:6–9). He told the Parable of the Mustard Seed to teach about the growth of the Kingdom of God (Lk 13:18–19). The story of the rich man and Lazarus could be considered a parable even though it is not introduced by the words "Jesus told another parable" (Lk 16:19–31). In it, Jesus urged people to help the poor and the needy by means of wealth they accumulated on earth.

Teachers may use the following outline: (1) context of the passage; (2) references or allusions to the Old Testament; (3) text in parallel with other Gospels; (4) the author's message; (5) the meaning of the text; and (6) any additional explanation. The passage chosen for both teaching and preaching is a well-known parable, such as the Parable of the Good Samaritan (Lk 10:29–37), which has a preamble. A lawyer came to Jesus and asked, "What must I do to inherit eternal life?" (Lk 10:25b; cf. Lk 18:18). Jesus asked the lawyer what he read in the Torah (Lk 10:26). The lawyer responded by referring to God's command to love God and to love neighbor (cf. Dt 6:5; Lv 19:18). The question about the greatest commandment is also found in Matthew 22:34–50 and Mark 12:28–34. Jesus told him to keep the law in order to have

---

49 Parables may be classified as similitudes, proverbs, allegories, stories, and so on. But a strict classification of parables into several categories did not exist in the first-century context. Klyne R. Snodgrass has given some suggestions for interpreting the parables of Jesus. See K. R. Snodgrass, "Key Questions on the Parables of Jesus," *RevExp* 109 (2012): 173–85.

eternal life (Lk 10:28). But the lawyer wanted to know the definition of "neighbor" (Lk 10:29). A neighbor could be understood in a limited sense as a relative or member of one's race (Lv 19:17–18). It could also be understood more broadly to include the alien sojourning in the land (Lv 19:34). But Jesus did not give a direct answer. Instead, he told a story to answer the question, "And who is my neighbor?" (Lk 10:29); and, in so doing, made a broader point by answering a question the lawyer did not or perhaps could not ask.

A man, who remains anonymous in the story, is making the eighteen-mile journey from Jerusalem to Jericho. He is stripped and beaten by the robbers and left half-dead on the road (Lk 10:30). There are four characters in the parable, including the man who fell into the hands of the robbers. A priest and a Levite, both of whom were probably returning home after their service at the Temple in Jerusalem, pass by without doing anything to help this wounded man. Probably they thought that he was already dead, and since the law of Moses prohibited them from having contact with a dead corpse (Lv 21:1–2; Nm 5:2), they did not want to be bothered or made unclean. A third passerby was not a Jew, but a Samaritan.

At the time of Jesus, Samaritans were considered as half-Jews because they intermarried with the Gentile people imported by the Assyrians, who conquered the Northern Kingdom in 721 BCE (cf. 2 Kgs 17:6–24; 2 Chr 30:6–11). Moreover, the Samaritans worshipped God on Mount Gerizim, whereas the people of Judah worshipped God in Jerusalem (cf. Jn 4:20). So the Samaritans were not really Jews, they had the wrong heritage, and they worshipped God at the wrong place. In short, they did not keep the Law. Luke alludes to the hostility of the Samaritans that led to the rejection of Jesus by the Samaritan villagers (Lk 9:51–56). The allusion, however, is an understatement of the outright hatred these peoples had for each other.

So it would have surprised no one if the Samaritan had passed by just like the priest and the Levite. But instead, he is moved with compassion and goes to help the wounded man (Lk 10:33–34). He even uses his own resources such as oil, wine, animal, and money to extend help to him. The Samaritan takes the man to the inn and promises the innkeeper that he will come back and take care of any expenses (Lk 10:35).

At the end of the parable, Jesus asks the lawyer, "Which of these three, do you think, was a neighbor to the man who fell into the hands of the robbers?" (Lk 10:36). Earlier, the lawyer had asked about the neighbor as if a neighbor is an object, something that gets love. But Jesus presents the neighbor as the subject who extends love. The Samaritan is portrayed as the quintessential neighbor who cares for an enemy, someone to whom the lawyer would not even give the time of day. In the parable, the neighbor becomes the center of the lesson. Jesus uses the parable to show the lawyer something his own limited, rule-based religiosity did not incorporate. He needed to see how much more God intends, which is to love others as ourselves. This is the spirit and intent of the Law.

To underscore this point, Jesus later commissions the disciples to go to Samaria to proclaim the gospel (cf. Acts 1:8). Luke reports in Acts that Philip undertook a mission to Samaria, and Peter and John ministered there (Acts 8:4–25). Jesus's teaching helped the disciples and, by extension, Luke's readers to transcend ethnic boundaries and become true neighbors to others to whom we never expected God would call. The challenge the parable poses is how far one should go to help someone in need, even if it involves risk-taking.

Preaching

Preachers may incorporate many of those elements from teaching into the Parable of the Good Samaritan. An outline of preaching this parable may consist of: (1) introduction; (2) setting the parable in context; (3) the priest and the Levite; (4) the Samaritan; (5) Jesus's response to the lawyer; and (6) the practice of Jesus's command. The message could be titled "Stepping Beyond the Boundary." Jesus taught that loving God and neighbor is central to living in God's Kingdom. Like the lawyer in the Parable of the Good Samaritan, people thought they knew how to love God, such as through the acts of worship, prayer, fasting, offering, and devotion; but how one should live one's life entirely beyond our traditional boundaries is the focus of the Parable of the Good Samaritan.

Jesus told the parable to illustrate how loving compassion should be extended to the vulnerable, needy, and oppressed. The priest and the Levite could have helped the wounded man. After all, they were not going to Jerusalem to do service at the Temple. In fact, they were going down (away) from Jerusalem. But they lacked one thing: compassion. Both of them feared ceremonial uncleanliness or were afraid the robbers were still around. The most unlikely person, the hated Samaritan, was filled with compassion (Lk 10:33). It was compassion that led the Samaritan to stop and help the wounded man. It was compassion that led the Samaritan to be generous; the Samaritan paid for shelter, food, and rest. He also promised that he would pay anything else that was owed when he came back (Lk 10:35). In other words, the Samaritan left an open account with the innkeeper. Jesus says to the lawyer, "Go and do likewise" (Lk 10:37). This is the command that is not just given to the lawyer, but to all who seek to understand the gospel of Jesus Christ. Jesus wants us to be compassionate: "Be merciful, just as your Father is merciful" (Lk 6:36; cf. Mi 6:8). Jesus also introduces compassion into the Parable of the Prodigal Son. When the father saw the younger son from a distance, he was "filled with compassion" (Lk 15:20). It was not the father's status as a keeper of the law that was important. It was only compassion that led the father to welcome back his son.

Jesus demonstrated compassion in his ministry. He proclaimed the gospel to the poor (Lk 4:18). He healed many who were sick, and he cast out demons (Lk 4:40–41). Luke reports that Jesus had compassion on the widow at Nain who lost her son: "When the Lord saw her, he had compassion for her and said to her, 'Do not weep'" (Lk 7:13). Jesus sent out the Twelve and then the seventy to heal and preach the good news, presumably offering compassion (Lk 9:1–6; 10:1–12). The church as a community of faithful neighbors is called to be a compassionate traveler on the road of life. The church is called to demonstrate Jesus's compassion to all who have been victimized. It is Jesus's command that the church, as God's people, go out and extend compassion to those in need and find ways to take risks to fulfill this command. Our love for one another should truly reveal our love for God. Everyone is our neighbor because God created everyone in God's own image.

Preaching that the church itself needs to be transformed by the love of God in order to show love to everyone can be risky, especially if the church prides itself on being caring. So it is helpful to invoke the apostle Paul when he exhorts the believers in Ephesus to be the imitators of God: "Put away from you all bitterness and wrath and anger and wrangling and slander, together with all malice, and be kind to one another, tenderhearted, forgiving one another, as God in Christ has forgiven you" (Eph 4:31–32). Preachers can share many illustrations or stories that demonstrate compassion that comes from the most unexpected places. Compassion overcomes any unnecessary boundaries and helps us step away from self-preoccupation and into God's preferred future.

The following texts can excellent for both teaching and preaching:

1. Luke 2:8–20 (The birth of a Savior)
2. Luke 14:15–24 (The Parable of the Great Dinner)
3. Luke 19:1–10 (Jesus meets Zacchaeus)
4. Luke 19:28–40 (Jesus's entry into Jerusalem)
5. Luke 24:13–35 (The risen Jesus's walk to Emmaus)

Summary

1. The Gospel of Luke witnesses to the life of Jesus. The companion volume, the Acts of the Apostles, focuses on the witness of the early church to the gospel of Jesus Christ.

2. Both Luke and Acts come from the same author. Although the author remains anonymous in his writings, the early church identified Luke, the traveling companion of Paul, as the author of both volumes. Luke possibly composed the Gospel anywhere between 61 and 64 CE, before the destruction of Jerusalem. Luke's

Gospel could have been written in one of many places, such as Macedonia, Achaia, Ephesus, Caesarea, Rome, or Antioch.

3. Luke structures his Gospel in seven sections. In each section, he emphasizes the fulfillment of God's plan of salvation in the life and ministry of Jesus.

4. Luke's theology is history-oriented. For him, Jesus accomplished God's salvation in fulfillment of Scripture and in accordance with the events of history. Luke looks at theology from the point of view of human history in that he portrays God acting through Jesus of Nazareth in public view of the course and context of history.

5. John Wesley exhibits his in-depth study of Luke's Gospel in its original context, and he shows awareness the Jewish apocryphal writings, such as the *Book of Tobit*. Wesley talks about the contemporary significance of the Gospel text.

6. Luke's Gospel draws attention to the universal nature of the gospel of Jesus, including those at the margins of society. For Luke, the gospel of Jesus transcends all barriers and invites the disciples to move beyond Jerusalem in order to preach the gospel to all nations. The Parable of the Good Samaritan served as a teaching tool for Jesus to encourage his disciples to minister with compassion to outsiders. Through the narrative, Luke provides ample opportunities for teachers and preachers to challenge people to demonstrate loving compassion to everyone.

For Discussion

1. The Song of Mary (*Magnificat*) is found only in Luke's Gospel (Lk 1:46–55). Mary praises God for God's salvation. If you were to compose a song that praises Jesus for accomplishing God's salvation, how would it go?

2. Only in Luke do the shepherds appear in the birth story of Jesus (Lk 2:8–18). Imagine the same angels who announced the birth of Jesus to the shepherds also proclaimed the resurrection of Jesus to them. What do you imagine their reaction would have been?

3. Luke attests that Jesus came to actualize the Kingdom of God on earth. In one instance, Luke tells that Jesus said, "But when you give a banquet, invite the poor, the crippled, the lame, and the blind" (Lk 14:13). Who would you invite for Thanksgiving dinner if you followed Jesus's mandate?

4. The story of the walk to Emmaus is unique to Luke's Gospel (Lk 24:13–35). The risen Jesus comes as a stranger and is recognized at the breaking of the bread. Write your own story of the walk to Emmaus and share it with the group. Put yourself in the place of the disciples.

5. John Wesley sees Luke connect the prophecy of fulfillment to the historical books of the Old Testament (Lk 24:44). Can you identify a prophecy concerning the Messiah in at least two of the Old Testament historical books (Joshua, Judges, Ruth, 1 and 2 Samuel, 1 and 2 Kings, 1 and 2 Chronicles, Ezra, Nehemiah, and Esther)? Show how a prophecy from these works is fulfilled in the life and ministry of Jesus.

5

The Gospel According to
John

Introduction

But that John, last of all, conscious that the outward facts had been set forth in the Gospels, was urged on by his disciples, and, divinely moved by the Spirit, composed a spiritual Gospel."[1] Thus writes Eusebius about what Clement of Alexandria said of the fourth Gospel. Clement of Alexandria perceived that John's Gospel reveals the inner theological truths of Jesus's life and ministry. In other words, John's Gospel was not meant to tread the same ground as the other three Gospels, but to demonstrate the spiritual truths about Jesus illumined by the power of the Holy Spirit.

Each Gospel writer views the life and ministry of Jesus from a different perspective. John's Gospel, which comes fourth in canonical order, presents a "higher" Christology when describing Jesus, in that throughout the Gospel, John fully engages in presenting Jesus's divinity. John's Gospel begins with the declaration that the Word identified as Jesus is none other than the Divine in the preexistent state: "In the beginning was the Word, and the Word was with God, and the Word was God" (Jn 1:1; cf. Jn 1:14). The Gospel ends with the culminating statement of Thomas confessing Jesus as Lord and God (Jn 20:28). In John's Gospel, Jesus himself promises that the Holy Spirit will continue to lead the followers of Jesus into greater understanding of Jesus's own words: "I have said these things to you while I am still with you. But the Advocate, the Holy Spirit, whom the Father will

---

1   Eusebius, *Hist. eccl.* 6.14.7.

send in my name, will teach you everything, and remind you of all that I have said to you" (Jn 14:25–26). The Holy Spirit seems to have guided John to compose a Gospel that would disclose the truths concerning Jesus to the subsequent generation.

Authorship

Although John's name is nowhere mentioned in the Gospel as its author, the early church tradition identifies John, the apostle, as such. Clement of Alexandria testified that John, the disciple of Jesus, composed a spiritual Gospel. Irenaeus also attested that John, the disciple of Jesus, published a Gospel: "Afterwards, John, the disciple of the Lord, who also had leaned upon His breast, did himself publish a Gospel during his residence at Ephesus in Asia."[2] Irenaeus refers to the beloved disciple, who appears nameless in the context of the Lord's Supper (cf. Jn 13:23). But John is not identified as the beloved disciple in the Gospel. In his apology to Autolycus, Theophilus of Antioch (120–185), who served as the seventh bishop of Antioch, quotes from John's Gospel and identifies John, Jesus's disciple, as its author.[3] Jerome also attests that John the apostle wrote a Gospel:

> John, the Apostle whom Jesus loved most, the son of Zebedee, and brother of the apostle of James, whom Herod, after our Lord's passion,

---

2   Irenaeus, *Haer.* 3.1.1, in *The Apostolic Fathers with Justin Martyr and Irenaeus*, ed. A. C. Coxe, vol. 1 of *Ante-Nicene Fathers*, ed. A. Roberts and J. Donaldson (Peabody, MA: Hendrickson Publishers, 1999), 414.

3   Theophilus of Antioch was an apologist and wrote an Apology in three books addressed to Autolycus in defense of Christian faith over pagan religion. He writes, "And hence the holy writings teach us, and all the spirit-bearing (inspired) men, one of whom, John, says, 'In the beginning was the Word, and the Word was with God,' showing that at first God was alone, and the Word in Him. Then he says, 'The Word was God; all things came into existence through Him; and apart from Him not one thing came into existence.' The Word, then, being God, being naturally produced from God, whenever the Father of the universe wills, He sends Him to any place; and He, coming, is both heard and seen, being sent by Him, and is found in a place" (*Autol.* 2.22). Quoted from A. C. Coxe, ed., *Fathers of the Second Century: Hermas, Tatian, Athenagoras, Theophilus, and Clement of Alexandria*, vol. 2 of *Ante-Nicene Fathers*, ed. A. Roberts and J. Donaldson (Peabody, MA: Hendrickson Publishers, 1995), 103. See R. M. Grant, "Theophilus of Antioch to Autolycus," *HTR* 40 (1947): 227–56.

beheaded, most recently of all, at the request of the bishops of Asia, wrote a *Gospel* against Cerinthus and other heretics, and especially against the then-arising doctrine of the Ebionites, who assert that Christ did not exist prior to Mary. On this account he was compelled to maintain His divine birth.[4]

In the Gospel itself, however, the author remains anonymous, yet he is an eyewitness to the ministry of Jesus. We see this when he says, "And the Word became flesh and lived among us, and we have seen his glory, the glory as of a father's only son, full of grace and truth" (Jn 1:14). He appears as one of Jesus's disciples as "the one whom Jesus loved" at the Lord's Supper, at the crucifixion, and at post-resurrection events (Jn 13:23; 19:26; 21:20). He also appears as "the other disciple" or simply as "the disciple" in the Gospel in multiple places (Jn 18:15; 20:2–3, 8; 21:7, 24; cf. Jn 1:35–37).[5] Even if John, the disciple of Jesus, wrote the Gospel, he chose to use the epithet "the disciple" in order to keep the readers in suspense.

The synoptic Gospels provide more information about John than John's Gospel. John was one of the sons of Zebedee and a brother of James; both John and James were called by Jesus along with Simon and Andrew (Mt 4:18–22; Mk 1:16–20; Lk 5:1–11). John and James became part of the twelve disciples of Jesus (Mt 10:1–4; Mk 3:16–19; Lk 6:14–16). John became part of Jesus's inner circle, along with Peter and James, and was permitted to witness the raising of Jairus's daughter (Mk 5:37; Lk 8:51). John was a witness to Jesus's transfiguration along with Peter and James (Mt 17:1–2; Mk 9:2–3; Lk 9:28–29). The mother of James and John came to Jesus and asked

---

4 Jerome, *Vir. ill.* 9.1, in *On Illustrious Men*, trans. T. P. Halton, *The Fathers of the Church*, vol. 100 (Washington, DC: The Catholic University of America Press, 1999), 19.

5 Raymond E. Brown provides a short discussion on the identity of the beloved disciple in the fourth Gospel. See R. E. Brown, *The Community of the Beloved Disciple: The Life, Loves, and Hates of an Individual Church in New Testament Times* (New York: Paulist Press, 1979), 31–34. See also C. S. Keener, *The Gospel of John: A Commentary*, vol. 1 (Peabody, MA: Hendrickson Publishers, 2003), 84–89; R. Bauckham, *The Testimony of the Beloved Disciple: Narrative, History, and Theology in the Gospel of John* (Grand Rapids, MI: Baker Academic, 2007), 73–91; A. T. Lincoln, "The Beloved Disciple as Eyewitness and the Fourth Gospel as Witness," *JSNT* 85 (2002): 3–26.

for a special place of honor for them in Jesus's Kingdom (Mt 20:20–28; Mk 10:35–45). At the Garden of Gethsemane, Jesus took John along with Peter and James to have some private moments with them (Mt 26:37; Mk 14:33). Matthew's Gospel places the mother of the sons of Zebedee along with Mary Magdalene and Mary at Jesus's crucifixion (Mt 27:56), although Mark's Gospel mentions Salome along with Mary Magdalene and Mary without referring to her as the mother of the sons of Zebedee in the same context (Mk 15:40). Mark's Gospel places Salome at the empty tomb (Mk 16:1), so presumably Salome was the mother of James and John.

John became a prominent figure in the early church, and he is mentioned along with Peter on several occasions in Acts (Acts 3:1, 11; 4:1, 13; 8:14–17, 25). John is acknowledged as one of the pillars of the Jerusalem church, as are Peter and James (Gal 2:9). This suggests that John, the disciple of Jesus, occupied a special place during the ministry of Jesus and emerged as one of the leaders in the early church. The issue over the identity of the John who wrote the fourth Gospel has become an indeterminacy in biblical studies. In critical studies, it remains unsolved; nevertheless, I think that John the apostle either was the author of the fourth Gospel or an authority behind its composition.[6]

Date, Purpose, and Place of Writing

The Gospel of John is generally considered to be the last of the four canonical Gospels to be composed. If the synoptic Gospels were written prior to the destruction of Jerusalem, John's Gospel would have been written just prior to 70 CE or right afterward.[7] Since

---

6 Ernst Haenchen argues that when John's Gospel was used in the early church to argue against gnosticism, the Gospel came to be associated with the apostle John, who had genuinely transmitted the Jesus tradition. See E. Haenchen, *John 1: A Commentary on the Gospel of John*, trans. R. W. Funk, ed. R. W. Funk with U. Busse (Philadelphia: Fortress Press, 1984), 6–19. German: E. Haenchen, *Das Johannesevangelium. Ein Kommentar* (Tübingen: J. C. B. Mohr [Paul Siebeck], 1980).

7 Raymond E. Brown discusses both the latest date (around 100 CE) and the earliest date (70–85 CE) for the writing of the fourth Gospel. See R. E. Brown, *The Gospel*

presumably John was an eyewitness to the ministry of Jesus (cf. Jn 1:14; 19:35; 21:24), he would have written his Gospel in accordance with the traditions prior to the destruction of Jerusalem's Temple. We can see this because John refers to the Sheep Gate, which stood in the northern wall of Jerusalem prior to destruction: "Now in Jerusalem by the Sheep Gate there is a pool, called in Hebrew Beth-zatha, which has five porticoes" (Jn 5:2). John also refers to the portico of Solomon that stood in the eastern wall of the Temple complex prior to the Temple's destruction (Jn 10:22). John never alludes to Jesus's prophecy concerning the destruction of the Temple, so the evidence suggests that John wrote the Gospel prior to the destruction.

John alludes to the prediction of Peter's martyrdom toward the end of the Gospel. After the resurrection, Jesus appeared to seven disciples and singled out Peter to feed his sheep (Jn 20:15–17). Here Jesus predicts Peter's death by saying, "Very truly, I tell you, when you were younger, you used to fasten your own belt and to go wherever you wished. But when you grow old, you will stretch out your hands, and someone else will fasten a belt around you and take you where you do not wish to go" (Jn 21:18). Here John seems to be aware of the approaching death of Peter. If Peter died as a martyr around 64 or 65 CE under Nero's persecution, it is likely that John wrote his Gospel anywhere between 65 and 70 CE.

John also notes that Jesus not only predicted Peter's future but also foretold the future of the beloved disciple. In response to Peter's question, "Lord, what about him?" (Jn 21:21), Jesus says, "If it is my will that he remain until I come, what is that to you? Follow me!" (Jn 21:22). The community seems to have understood the words of Jesus to mean that the beloved disciple would not die (Jn 21:23a). So we can presume that John corrects the misinterpretation of Jesus's words by adding, "Yet Jesus did not say to him that he would not die, but, 'If it is my will that he remain until I come, what is that to you?'"

According to John I–XII: A New Translation with Introduction and Commentary (New York: Doubleday, 1966), lxxx–lxxxvi.

(Jn 21:23b). It can only be inferred that John lived for a long time.[8] Bishop Irenaeus testified that John lived until the time of Trajan (98–117 CE). He wrote, "Then, again, the Church in Ephesus, founded by Paul, and having John remaining among them permanently until the times of Trajan, is a true witness of the tradition of the apostles."[9] Irenaeus's testimony does not say anything about the writing of the Gospel when John was old. If John wrote the Gospel close to the time of Trajan, then his Gospel could be placed anywhere between 98 and 117 CE.

John's Gospel has a specific purpose statement, which reads: "Now Jesus did many other signs in the presence of his disciples, which are not written in this book. But these are written so that you may come to believe that Jesus is the Messiah, the Son of God, and that through believing you may have life in his name" (Jn 20:30–31). On the one hand, John wrote the Gospel to convince the readers that Jesus is the Messiah, the Son of God, who bestows eternal life on those who believe in Jesus. On the other, John wrote the Gospel to strengthen the faith of the community that they might continue to believe Jesus is the Messiah, the Son of God.[10] In other words, John intended to use his Gospel as an evangelistic tool to lead people to faith in Jesus as the Messiah, the Son of God. Once the people were brought to the Christian community, the Gospel could be used as a teaching book to strengthen and edify the believers in the ongoing revelation of Jesus through the Holy Spirit (cf. Jn 14:26).

In his Gospel, John seems to be familiar with Jerusalem. He

---

8 Jerome mentions that John died of old age in *Vir. ill.* 9.7: "But after Domitian had been put to death, and his decrees, on account of his excessive cruelty, had been annulled by the senate, John returned to Ephesus under Nerva, and, continuing there until the time of the emperor Trajan, founded and built churches throughout all of Asia, and, worn out by old age, died in the sixty-eighth year after our Lord's passion and was buried in the same city." *On Illustrious Men*, 20.

9 Irenaeus, *Haer.* 3.3.4, in *Ante-Nicene Fathers*, 1:416.

10 Some of the ancient Greek manuscripts, such as Papyrus 66, Vaticanus, and Coridethianus, read, "But these are written so that *you may continue to believe* that Jesus is the Messiah, the Son of God" (Jn 20:31a). See D. A. Carson, "Syntactical and Text-Critical Observations on John 20:30–31: One More Round on the Purpose of the Fourth Gospel," *JBL* 124 (2005): 693–714.

places the cleansing of the Temple in Jerusalem at the beginning of Jesus's ministry, whereas the synoptic tradition places it toward the end (Jn 2:13–25; cf. Mt 21:12–12; Mk 11:15–19; Lk 19:45–48). John alludes to Jerusalem as the place of worship (Jn 4:20–21). After the Passover celebration in Jerusalem, Jesus goes to Galilee and returns to Jerusalem for another festival of the Jews (Jn 5:1; cf. Jn 2:13; 4:54). John places Jesus at the Temple in Jerusalem during the festival (Jn 7:14). The raising of Lazarus takes place at Bethany near Jerusalem (Jn 11:18). Given John's interest in Jerusalem, it could very well be that John wrote his Gospel there before the city was destroyed.

Main Themes

The main theme in John's Gospel is to assert that Jesus came to reveal the very essence of God. John states the central theme early on in the prologue, and he stands as a witness to the presence of God as revealed in Jesus, the incarnate Son of God. John testifies, "And the Word became flesh and lived among us, and we have seen his glory, the glory as of a father's only son, full of grace and truth" (Jn 1:14). John goes on to say that it is not anyone, but only Jesus who fully reveals God: "No one has ever seen God. It is God the only Son, who is close to the Father's heart, who has made him known" (Jn 1:18). If Jesus came to reveal God, he also brought with him the life of God, which is eternal life. John states, "For God so loved the world that he gave his only Son, so that everyone who believes in him may not perish but may have eternal life" (Jn 3:16). Throughout the Gospel, John discloses how Jesus reveals God, which results in offering eternal life to all those who believe in him as the incarnate Son of God.

For John, Jesus shared life with God in the preexistent state (Jn 5:26; 11:25; 14:6). Jesus is the source of life (Jn 1:4; 5:26). The life Jesus offers is none other than the life eternal: "The water that I will give will become in them a spring of water gushing up to eternal life" (Jn 4:14). It is through believing in Jesus and his words as Messiah and Son of God that life is obtained. Indeed, this was John's purpose in writing (Jn 20:31). John then develops the theme of Jesus as the revealer of God and the bestower of life eternal through the following structure.

1. Prologue: Divine incarnation (Jn 1:1–18)

2. Book 1: The witness of John the Baptist and the call of the first disciples (Jn 1:19–51)

3. Book 2: The public ministry of Jesus (Jn 2:1–12:50)

4. Book 3: The farewell discourses of Jesus (Jn 13:1–17:26)

5. Book 4: Jesus's trial, crucifixion, and burial (Jn 18:1–19:42)

6. Book 5: Jesus's resurrection and appearance (Jn 20:1–31)

7. Epilogue: Peter and the beloved disciple (Jn 21:1–25)

Prologue: Divine Incarnation (Jn 1:1–18)

The prologue to John's Gospel reflects on the incarnation of the divine Word (Gk: *Logos*). In other words, the prologue asserts the divine origin of Jesus. For John, Jesus existed prior to his human incarnation as the Word, which in some sense shares the very essence of God. The opening words of the prologue seek to explain the nature of the preexistent Logos: "In the beginning was the Word, and the Word was with God, and the Word was God" (Jn 1:1). John defines who Jesus was prior to his birth in order to understand what Jesus brought to his earthly existence. Jesus was with God in the beginning (Jn 1:2). He actively participated in the creation (Jn 1:3, 10). He possessed life (Jn 1:4a). He was the light (Jn 1:4b). He was God's only Son (Jn 1:14b, 18). He was close to God's heart (Jn 1:18b).

John briefly introduces the function of John the Baptist (Jn 1:6–8). John the Baptist only witnessed to the coming of Jesus; Jesus is the light of the world (Jn 1:7). John the Baptist denied that he himself was the light (Jn 1:8); for John the Baptist, Jesus was the true light that came to enlighten everyone (Jn 1:9). He also affirmed the superiority of Jesus (Jn 1:15). But not all recognized Jesus's true nature. Even his own people did not accept him as the Messiah, the Son of God (Jn 1:11). But some people did; and, consequently, they are given power to become the children of God (Jn 1:12–13).

John draws attention to the historic incarnation of the divine Word: "And the Word became flesh and lived among us, and we have seen his glory, the glory as of a father's only son, full of grace and truth" (Jn 1:14). The Word that had been with God from the beginning has now come into history in the birth of Jesus. Jesus lived in the midst of people just as God lived in the tabernacle (cf. Ex 25:8–9; 40:34), and Jesus's followers did experience the glory of God through Jesus. For John, Moses only brought the Law. But Jesus Christ brought grace and truth (Jn 1:17), which was the intent and fulfillment of the Law. John even makes a bold assertion that God can only be seen through Jesus Christ: "No one has ever seen God. It is God the only Son, who is close to the Father's heart, who has made him known" (Jn 1:18). In other words, John discredits those who claimed to have seen God. John is making the claim that prior to the coming of Jesus, God was not fully known, even if the Israelites faithfully followed the Law of Moses (cf. Jn 1:17a). But now, Jesus came to reveal God fully because he was with God from the beginning.

Book 1: The Witness of John the Baptist and the Call of the First Disciples (Jn 1:19–51)

In this section John describes both the witness of John the Baptist and the call of the first disciples. The Jewish authorities send a delegation to discover the status of John the Baptist (Jn 1:19). John the Baptist denies that he is the Messiah, Elijah, and the prophet (Jn 1:20–21). However, he points to the Old Testament prophecy that he came to prepare the way of the Lord (Jn 1:23; cf. Is 40:3). Again, John is asked about his rite of baptism (Jn 1:24–25). He simply testifies that he baptizes people with water in anticipation of the coming of the Son of God who would baptize people with the Holy Spirit (Jn 1:26, 33–34). John the Baptist further testifies that Jesus is "the Lamb of God who takes away the sin of the world!" (Jn 1:29). Most likely John has in mind the lamb provided by God as a substitute for Isaac (Gn 22:8). For John, Jesus is going to remove the sins of the entire cosmos. In other words, Jesus's death on the cross has a universal effect.

Two of John's disciples also hear him say that Jesus is the Lamb of God (Jn 1:36–37). Jesus then calls them to follow him (Jn 1:39). One of them is Andrew, Simon Peter's brother (Jn 1:40). The other one is not named, although he is probably John, the beloved disciple (Jn 21:24). Andrew consequently testifies to his brother that Jesus is the Messiah (Jn 1:41).

Jesus calls Philip directly, and Philip in turn witnesses to Nathaniel, saying, "We have found [Jesus] about whom Moses in the law and also the prophets wrote, Jesus son of Joseph from Nazareth" (Jn 1:45). Philip brings Nathaniel to Jesus (Jn 1:46), who has already seen Nathaniel (Jn 1:48). Nathaniel confesses, "Rabbi, you are the Son of God! You are the King of Israel!" (Jn 1:49). Encountering Jesus makes many believe that Jesus is the Lamb of God, the Messiah, Rabbi, the Son of God, and the King of Israel. John ends this section with Jesus's own testimony about himself: "Very truly, I tell you, you will see heaven opened and the angels of God ascending and descending upon the Son of Man" (Jn 1:51). Echoing Genesis 28:10–17, Jesus sees himself as the Son of Man who stands as a bridge between God and humans, and this is the revelatory Word Jesus would continue to disclose throughout his ministry.

Book 2: The Public Ministry of Jesus (Jn 2:1–12:50)

In this part, John records seven signs that Jesus performed in the presence of his disciples: turning water into wine (Jn 2:1–11); healing the royal official's son (Jn 4:46–54); healing the paralytic at the pool of Beth-zatha (Jn 5:1–15; cf. Mt 9:1–8; Mk 2:1–12; Lk 5:17–26); feeding the five thousand (Jn 6:1–14; cf. Mt 14:13–21; Mk 6:32–44; Lk 9:10–17); Jesus's walking on water (Jn 6:16–21; cf. Mt 14:22–33; Mk 6:45–52); healing the man born blind (Jn 9:1–12; cf. Mt 14:22–33; Mk 6:45–52); and raising Lazarus (Jn 11:1–44; cf. Lk 7:11–17).[11] The signs in John's Gospel can be compared with the miracles Jesus performs in the synoptic Gospels. In John, through the signs, Jesus reveals his glory (cf. Jn 1:14). John also alludes to other signs that are not recorded in the book: "Now Jesus did many other signs in the

---

11 For a discussion of signs in John's Gospel, see B. D. Crowe, "The Chiastic Structure of Seven Signs in the Gospel of John: Revisiting a Neglected Proposal," *BBR* 28 (2018): 65–81.

presence of his disciples, which are not written in this book" (Jn 20:30). The turning of water into wine and the healing of the royal official's son are specifically referred to first and second signs respectively: "Jesus did this, the first of his signs, in Cana of Galilee, and revealed his glory; and his disciples believed in him" (Jn 2:11); and "Now this was the second sign that Jesus did after coming from Judea to Galilee" (Jn 4:54). Each sign displays Jesus's power that leads people to believe. John remarks, "When [Jesus] was in Jerusalem during the Passover festival, many believed in his name because they saw the signs that he was doing" (Jn 2:23).

John also records seven "I Am" sayings that emphasize the divinity of Jesus: "I am the bread of life" (Jn 6:35, 41); "I am the light of the world" (Jn 8:12; 9:5); "I am the gate for the sheep" (Jn 10:7); "I am the good shepherd" (Jn 10:11); "I am the resurrection and the life" (Jn 11:25); "I am the way, the truth, and the life" (Jn 14:6); and "I am the true vine" (Jn 15:1, 5). John mentions other "I Am" statements without a predicate as in John 4:26; 6:20; 8:24, 28, 58; 13:19; 18:5, 7. The title "I Am" is the divine name revealed to Moses in Exodus 3:14 from the burning bush. By taking on this name, Jesus reveals the very essence of God.

John places the cleansing of the Temple at the beginning of Jesus's ministry, whereas the synoptic writers put it toward the end (Jn 2:13–24; cf. Mt 21:12–17; Mk 11:15–19; Lk 19:45–48). John moves this account toward the front of his Gospel for theological reasons—to predict Jesus's death and resurrection. When Jesus says, "Destroy this temple, and in three days I will raise it up" (Jn 2:19), he alludes to his own death and resurrection (Jn 2:21–22). John also draws attention to the testimony of the disciples after his resurrection: "After he was raised from the dead, his disciples remembered that he had said this; and they believed the scripture and the word that Jesus had spoken" (Jn 2:22). John prepares his reader early on for true worship, which comes as a result of Jesus's death and resurrection. Thus, it is natural for John to move the cleansing of the Temple to the front of his Gospel to emphasize how one becomes completely cleansed for true worship, which will be made possible through Jesus's suffering, death, and resurrection. Then in John 3:1–10, John uses Jesus's encounter with Nicodemus to teach about spiritual birth, which comes from above; and in the following chapter, John describes Jesus's encounter with the Samaritan woman to teach about eternal life (Jn 4:1–15).

The story of the woman caught in adultery is found only in John's Gospel (Jn 7:53–8:11), but the story is not attested in the earliest manuscripts, such as P66, P75, Sinaniaticus, and Vaticanus. However, since the fifth century, manuscripts such as Codex Bezae and Codex Fuldensis do include the story, and Jerome included it in the *Vulgate*.[12] It may be that the story was in circulation but somehow was not included in the earliest edition of John's Gospel. Or perhaps the story was composed by a scribe at a later time and was included in more recent manuscripts. The possibilities are numerous. The story recounts an encounter Jesus has with a woman caught in adultery. John continues that the scribes and the Pharisees bring the woman to Jesus to judge her according to the law of Moses (Jn 8:3–6; cf. Lv 20:10; Dt 22:22). But Jesus challenges them to cast the first stone if they are without sin (Jn 8:7; cf. Dt 17:7). When no one comes forward to stone her, Jesus tells her to go home and sin no more (Jn 8:11). Whether the story was part of the original manuscript, it illustrates Jesus's teaching on judgment and forgiveness (cf. Jn 5:19–30).

In John's Gospel, the raising of Lazarus leads to Jesus's arrest and subsequent crucifixion. The chief priests and Pharisees seek to arrest Jesus because many believed in him as a result of raising Lazarus from the dead (Jn 11:47–48). John alone mentions that Caiaphas, the high priest, says that it is better for one man to die than many. This reflects the Jewish leaders' fear of Rome (Jn 11:49–52). John places the story of Mary anointing Jesus at Bethany before Jesus's entry into Jerusalem (Jn 12:1–8; cf. Mt 26:6–13; Mk 14:3–9). Mary's anointing of Jesus foreshadows Jesus's approaching death (Jn 12:7). John's Gospel, like the others, mentions the triumphal entry of Jesus

---

12 For a thorough treatment of the story of the woman caught in adultery, see J. Knust and T. Wasserman, *To Cast the First Stone: The Transmission of a Gospel Story* (Princeton, NJ: Princeton University Press, 2018).

(Jn 12:12–19; cf. Mt 21:1–11; Mk 11:1–10; Lk 19:28–40). But among the Gospel writers, John alone refers to "branches of palm trees" that people carried to meet Jesus as he entered Jerusalem (Jn 12:13a).[13] Jesus riding on a young donkey was seen as a fulfillment of the Old Testament prophet Zechariah (cf. Zec 9:9; Jn 12:14–15). John adds that the disciples understood Zechariah's words of prophecy about Jesus only after Jesus was raised from the dead (Jn 12:16). John concludes the section with a summary of Jesus's teaching (Jn 12:44–50) and how Jesus came to speak what God commanded him to speak: "For I have not spoken on my own, but the Father who sent me has himself given me a commandment about what to say and what to speak" (Jn 12:49). Jesus embodied the very mind of God in his earthly ministry.

Book 3: The Farewell Discourses of Jesus (Jn 13:1–17:26)

In this unit John provides Jesus's discourses or last words prior to his arrest. This section begins with Jesus's last meal with his disciples before the festival of Passover, which falls on the eve of Jesus's *death* (Jn 13:1–20; cf. Jn 19:42), whereas in the synoptic Gospels, the Passover falls on the eve of Jesus's *arrest* (Mt 26:17–25; Mk 14:12–21; Lk 22:7–14, 21–23). The meal Jesus celebrated with his disciples was not the Passover meal in John's Gospel, whereas it was in the synoptic Gospels. This also leads to the different timing of Jesus's crucifixion. In John's Gospel, Jesus is crucified on the eve of Passover (Jn 19:14), whereas he is crucified on the first day of Passover in the synoptic Gospels (Mt 26:17; Mk 14:12; Lk 22:7). Among the Gospel writers, John alone mentions Jesus washing the disciples' feet (Jn 13:3–15). Although Jesus is presented as "Teacher and Lord," John emphasizes the humility of Jesus in this act of servanthood. Jesus says to his disciples, "You call me Teacher and Lord—and you are right, for that is what I am. So if I, your Lord and Teacher, have washed your feet, you also ought to wash one another's feet" (Jn 13:13–14). Then Jesus gives a new commandment to his disciples: "I give you a new

---

13   See W. R. Farmer, "The Palm Branches in John 12.13," *JTS* 23 (1952): 62–66.

commandment, that you love one another. Just as I have loved you, you also should love one another" (Jn 13:34). The new commandment is not meant to be restricted only to the disciples but extended to the world, which is the object of God's love (cf. Jn 3:16; 17:26).

John's Gospel contains three special passages that talk about the giving of the Spirit (Jn 14:16–26; 15:26–27; 16:7–15). Jesus promises his disciples that he will send the Holy Spirit after his departure from the earth. He says, "But the Advocate [Gk: *Paraclete*], the Holy Spirit, whom the Father will send in my name, will teach you everything, and remind you of all that I have said to you" (Jn 14:26). Here the Holy Spirit assumes the role of a teacher who will present the words of Jesus anew to the believing community. The Advocate or the Spirit of Truth will bear witness to Jesus just as the disciples bore witness to Jesus when he was with them (Jn 15:26–27). Another function of the Advocate is to reprove the world's sin, because they did not believe; the world's lack of righteousness; and judgment (Jn 16:8–11). The Spirit of Truth will continue Jesus's work. What Jesus says after his glorification, the Spirit of Truth will echo (Jn 16:15); and just as Jesus spoke what he heard from God, the Spirit of Truth will continue to communicate. For John, Jesus reveals the essence of God and now the Advocate, the Spirit of Truth, the Holy Spirit will disclose the personhood of Jesus in the present age.

John records a lengthy prayer of Jesus on behalf of the disciples in John 17, when Jesus knew his departure was imminent. He asks God to vindicate him after his death. He prays, "I glorified you on earth by finishing the work that you gave me to do. So now, Father, glorify me in your own presence with the glory that I had in your presence before the world existed" (Jn 17:4–5). Not only does John affirm Jesus's preexistence with God from the beginning in the prologue, and his glorious preexistence with God prior to creation, but now Jesus will return to God. And John tells us that the Lord is concerned about his disciples—us. So he prays to God for our protection: "And now I am no longer in the world, but they are in the world, and I am coming to you. Holy Father, protect them in your name that you have given me, so that they may be one, as we are one" (Jn 17:11). Jesus then asks God to sanctify and care for his disciples: "Sanctify them in the truth; your word is truth" (Jn 17:17), so that they will further Jesus's mission (cf. Jn 20:21).

Jesus prays not only for his disciples but also for the unity of those who would come to believe in him through their witness. Jesus prays, "I ask not only on behalf of these, but also on behalf of those who will believe in me through their word, that they may all be one. As you, Father, are in me and I am in you, may they also be in us, so that the world may believe that you have sent me" (Jn 17:20–21). Jesus concludes his prayer by emphasizing God's love for the disciples and the world—bringing everyone to God. Through this we see that Jesus's life, death, and resurrection is for everyone, not only for some: "Righteous Father, the world does not know you, but I know you; and these know that you have sent me. I made your name known to them, and I will make it known, so that the love with which you have loved me may be in them, and I in them" (Jn 17:25–26).

Book 4: Jesus's Trial, Crucifixion, and Burial (Jn 18:1–19:42)

In this crucial section John focuses on Jesus's final days on earth before his vindication. John draws attention to the divine identity of Jesus at the time of his arrest. When Jesus asks the people who came to arrest him, "Whom are you looking for?" (Jn 18:4b), they all say, "Jesus of Nazareth" (Jn 18:5a), and they all fall to the ground when Jesus says, "I am he" (Jn 18:6). It seems that John is telling us that the people recognized the divinity of Jesus when he uttered God's name as "I am he" (cf. Ex 3:14; Is 43:25; 51:12). According to John's Gospel, Jesus was first taken to Annas, who served as the high priest earlier (6–15 CE) and then to Caiaphas (18–36 CE). John emphasizes that Jesus taught in public rather than in secret. Jesus testifies before Annas and says, "I have spoken openly to the world; I have always taught in synagogues and in the temple, where all the Jews come together. I have said nothing in secret" (Jn 18:20).

John seeks to clear up the misunderstanding of who Jesus is in his encounter with Pilate. Pilate asks Jesus if he is the King of the Jews (Jn 18:33). Jesus answers, "My kingdom is not from this world"

(Jn 18:36a). Jesus wants to make clear that his Kingdom came from above and that he enters the world as an offering of grace and truth from God (cf. Jn 8:23; 1:14). Jesus is a King of a new world order that began to permeate the world with his arrival. Jesus gives a new definition of his Kingship when he answers Pilate's question whether he is a king. Jesus replies, "You say that I am a king. For this I was born, and for this I came into the world, to testify to the truth. Everyone who belongs to the truth listens to my voice" (Jn 18:37). Pilate declares Jesus's innocence but instead releases Barabbas at the insistence of the crowd (Jn 18:38–40).

According to John, Pilate hands Jesus over to the soldiers to be crucified on the day of the preparation for Passover (Jn 19:14). Pilate gives the word, and an inscription is placed on the cross that reads, "Jesus of Nazareth, the King of the Jews" (Jn 19:19). Ironically, Jesus is the King of the Jews because he came for his own people (cf. Jn 1:11), and here John draws attention to three prophetic fulfillments that take place at the cross. First, the Roman soldiers take Jesus's clothes and divide them among themselves. They also take his tunic and cast lots for it. Both acts are seen as the fulfillment of the scriptural prophecy that says, "They divided my clothes among themselves, and for my clothing they cast lots" (Jn 19:24b; cf. Ps 22:18). Second, Jesus says, "I am thirsty" (Jn 19:28b). In response, the soldiers give him sour wine to drink. This offering of sour wine is seen as the fulfillment of Scripture, although no text is quoted (Jn 19:28; cf. Ps 69:21). Third, the Roman soldiers do not break Jesus's legs, an act that is seen as the fulfillment of the Scripture, "None of his bones shall be broken" (Jn 19:36; cf. Ex 12:46; Nm 9:12; Ps 34:20).

John records at least three sayings of Jesus spoken from the cross and places four people at the foot of the cross: Jesus's mother, Mary the wife of Clopas, Mary Magdalene, and the beloved disciple (Jn 19:25–26a). Jesus entrusts his mother to the beloved disciple and says, "Woman, here is your son" (Jn 19:26b); then to the beloved disciple, "Here is your mother" (Jn 19:27a). Just before giving up his spirit, Jesus says, "I am thirsty" (Jn 19:28b). Presumably, John includes those words of Jesus in order to show his humanity. When Jesus receives the sour wine offered by the soldiers (cf. Ps 69:21), he says, "It is finished" (Jn 19:30a). Perhaps with these words Jesus is testifying to the truth that his mission is complete (cf. Jn 18:37). According to John, Jesus is buried near the place where he was crucified, because Joseph of Arimathea stepped forward and asked Pilate for the body. He and Nicodemus bury Jesus according to custom (Jn 19:38–40).

Book 5: Jesus's Resurrection and Appearances (Jn 20:1–31)

Finally, John narrates the amazing events that are reported after the burial of Jesus. He focuses on Jesus's appearance to Mary Magdalene, the disciples, and Thomas. John reports that Mary Magdalene came to the tomb. She discovers that the stone has been removed from the tomb, and she runs back to inform Peter and the other disciples that the body of Jesus has been taken and placed somewhere else (Jn 20:1–2). Peter and the "other disciple" go to the tomb but, like Mary, do not find the body. At this point, only the other disciple believes in the resurrection of Jesus, because he remembers Jesus's earlier words (Jn 20:8–9; cf. Jn 2:22; 12:16). The disciples leave the scene, but Mary stays, and it is to her that Jesus first appears. Jesus calls her by name, and she recognizes him, calling him "Teacher" (Jn 20:16). Jesus urges Mary to go and tell the disciples that he will be ascending to God (Jn 20:17). Obediently, Mary goes and testifies to the disciples that she has seen the Lord (Jn 20:18).

Later, on the evening of the same day, Jesus appears to his disciples and says, "Peace be with you" (Jn 20:19). He then commissions the disciples: "As the Father has sent me, so I send you" (Jn 20:21b). He also breathes on them, saying "Receive the Holy Spirit" (Jn 20:22b; cf. Gn 2:7). In fulfillment of his earlier words (Jn 14:15–17, 25–26; 15:26; 16:7–15), Jesus bestows the Holy Spirit upon the disciples. However, when Jesus appeared to the disciples earlier that first evening, Thomas was not with them. Although the other disciple tells Thomas that they have seen the Lord, he doubts (Jn 20:25); but later, Jesus does appear to him and invites him to touch his hands and side (Jn 20:26–27). Thomas then confesses, "My Lord and my God" (Jn 20:28). In the confession of Thomas, John presents Jesus as God after the resurrection, just as Jesus was God prior to his incarnation (cf. Jn 1:1). Jesus provides a blessing on those who would believe without seeing, which is a reference to the future believing community. Jesus says, "Blessed are those who have not seen and yet have come to believe" (Jn 20:29b). John concludes his narrative by explicitly stating his intention for writing the Gospel: "Now Jesus did many other signs in the presence of his disciples, which are not written in this book. But these are written so that you may come to believe that Jesus is the Messiah, the Son of God, and that through believing you may have life in his name" (Jn 20:30–31).

Epilogue: Peter and the Beloved Disciple (Jn 21:1–25)

The addition of chapter 21 to John seems for many to be the work of a later disciple who sought to expand the resurrection appearances of Jesus to include additional information about Peter and the beloved disciple. When Jesus makes this appearance, there are only seven disciples present (Jn 21:2), and they are fishing with Peter and the beloved disciple. When Jesus appears to them by the Sea of Tiberias, the beloved disciple recognizes Jesus as the Lord (Jn 21:7a). Not having any luck fishing, they obey Jesus's command and cast their nets on the other side of the boat, where they catch many fish (Jn 21:8). Jesus cooks breakfast for them (Jn 21:13), which serves to remind us of a very human Jesus as well as the many times Jesus shared such fellowship during his earthly ministry, especially at the feeding of the five thousand and at the Passover (Jn 6:1–14; 13:1–20). However, there is unfinished business to attend to concerning Peter, who denied Jesus (Jn 21:19; cf. Jn 18:15–18, 25–27). Many scholars see this encounter between Peter and Jesus as Jesus reaching out to Peter to reclaim him as a disciple.

The focus then shifts to the beloved disciple, and the concluding words focus on the beloved disciple as witness: "This is the disciple who is testifying to these things and has written them, and we know that his testimony is true" (Jn 21:24). The Johannine author also draws attention to numerous things Jesus did and concludes with a hyperbolic expression: "But there are also many other things that

Jesus did; if every one of them were written down, I suppose that the world itself could not contain the books that would be written" (Jn 21:25; cf. Eccl 12:12).

From the beginning to the end, the beloved disciple stands as a witness to the life of Jesus. Through his testimony, we learn that Jesus was with God from the beginning and he is God incarnated as Jesus of Nazareth. He is sent by God to reveal God and bring eternal life through his life and death on the cross.

Theology of John

John centers his Gospel around Jesus as the Messiah, the human and divine Son of God (Jn 20:31). From beginning to end, John seeks to unveil the mysterious origin of Jesus, who is revealed as the Son of God. John looks at the life of Jesus from a theological point of view. In other words, John attempts to interpret the ministry of Jesus in the context of Jesus's divinity. Yet John also presents Jesus as immanently human. When some people in Jerusalem question his origin, Jesus says, "You know me, and you know where I am from. I have not come on my own. But the one who sent me is true, and you do not know him. I know him, because I am from him, and he sent me" (Jn 7:28–29). Jesus's response clearly demonstrates that he comes from God and yet many do not acknowledge it.

Jesus's divine nature permeates John's theology; and, as we pointed out earlier, this is clear from the Gospel's prologue (Jn 1:1–18). Jesus was with God from the beginning. He is God in the sense that as a spoken Word represents the intent of a person, Jesus shares the intent of God. He takes on human flesh to reveal divine glory. What exactly this means is still up for debate. But the world does not know (Jn 1:10). John goes on to say that it is Jesus as God's Son who reveals God (Jn 1:18). And while John the Baptist testifies to the divine origin of Jesus (Jn 1:30) and affirms that Jesus is the Son of God (Jn 1:34), it is Jesus who is to be followed.

Others also testify to Jesus's divinity. Nathaniel confesses that Jesus is the Son of God and the King of Israel even before he sees

Jesus perform any signs (Jn 1:49). Jesus's encounter with Nicodemus demonstrates that Jesus is knowledgeable about heavenly things. When Jesus tells Nicodemus that he must be born from above to see the Kingdom of God, Nicodemus at first only understands in terms of an earthly birth (Jn 3:3–4). But Jesus says that he came from heaven to explain the heavenly things. He says, "If I have told you about earthly things and you do not believe, how can you believe if I tell you about heavenly things? No one has ascended into heaven except the one who descended from heaven, the Son of Man" (Jn 3:12–13). John again draws attention to the divine origin of Jesus: "The one who comes from above is above all; the one who is of the earth belongs to the earth and speaks about earthly things. The one who comes from heaven is above all" (Jn 3:31).

Likewise, Jesus's encounter with the Samaritan woman reveals Jesus's identity as the Messiah. When the Samaritan woman tells Jesus that the coming Messiah will announce "all things," Jesus replies, "I am he, the one who is speaking to you" (Jn 4:26). John then reports that many Samaritans believed that Jesus was "the Savior of the world" (Jn 4:42).

In John's Gospel, Jesus feeds the five thousand with five loaves and two fish, which gives John the opportunity to draw attention to Jesus's testimony that he came from heaven (Jn 6:1–59). Just like the manna that came from heaven, Jesus as the bread of life also came down from heaven (Jn 6:31–34; cf. Ex 16:4; Ps 78:23–25). Still, people recognize the earthly origin of Jesus but not his heavenly origin. John sums it up in the statement of the Jews: "Is not this Jesus, the son of Joseph, whose father and mother we know? How can he now say, 'I have come down from heaven'?" (Jn 6:42).

Jesus further explains that he not only came down from heaven, but he came to give eternal life. He says, "This is the bread that came down from heaven, not like that which your ancestors ate, and they died. But the one who eats this bread will live forever" (Jn 6:58). John continues to draw attention to people's inability to perceive Jesus's true origin. Only Jesus and his faithful disciples testify to his true origin. When the Pharisees accuse Jesus of testifying on his own behalf (Jn 8:13), he says, "Even if I testify on my own behalf, my testimony is valid because I know where I have come from and where I am going, but you do not know where I come from or where I am going" (Jn 8:14). John presents a Jesus who is fully conscious of his own origin. Jesus himself testifies, "You are from below, I am from above; you are of this world, I am not of this world" (Jn 8:23). In his discussion with the Jews on Abraham, Jesus again testifies to his preexistent state: "Very truly, I tell you, before Abraham was, I am" (Jn 8:58). But John goes out of his way to show that at least some Jewish leaders really do understand Jesus's claim of divine origin, because they label it blasphemy and even attempt to stone him (Jn 8:59; cf. Lv 24:16).

In the healing story of a man born blind, only the healed blind man recognizes that Jesus is from God. The Pharisees question the authenticity of Jesus's healing and tell the man that they do not know where Jesus came from (Jn 9:29). But the man answers, "Never since the world began has it been heard that anyone opened the eyes of a person born blind. If this man were not from God, he could do nothing" (Jn 9:32–33). Ironically, the man born blind is able to see Jesus's divine origin when others cannot, because Jesus not only heals his physical eyesight but also restores his spiritual eyesight. The implication is clear. The Pharisees can see but choose to remain spiritually blind. The man born blind sees Jesus as the Son of God and worships him (Jn 9:35–38).

John not only presents Jesus as the Good Shepherd but as the Good Shepherd who lays down his life for the sheep (Jn 10:11). Again, John reiterates that Jesus's willingness to die for the flock comes from his willingness to obey God's command. Jesus says, "No one takes it from me, but I lay it down of my own accord. I have power to lay it down, and I have power to take it up again. I have received this command from my Father" (Jn 10:18). In other words, Jesus has a mission to accomplish because he is sent by God from above.

In the story of the raising of Lazarus, Jesus reveals himself as "the resurrection and the life" (Jn 11:25). John says that Martha believes Jesus is the Lord, the Messiah, the Son of God when Jesus refers to himself as the Lord of life. Martha says, "Yes, Lord, I believe that you are the Messiah, the Son of God, the one coming into the world" (Jn 11:27). Martha's statement assumes that Jesus came from above; and now he is recognized as the Lord, the Messiah, the Son of God.

In his farewell speech to his disciples, Jesus alludes to his disciples' belief that he came from God. He says, "For the Father himself loves you, because you have loved me and have believed that I came from God" (Jn 16:27). In his prayer for the disciples, Jesus again alludes to himself as the one sent by God. Jesus prays, "And this is eternal life, that they may know you, the only true God, and Jesus Christ whom you have sent" (Jn 17:3). This is the only place in John's Gospel where Jesus refers to himself as "Jesus Christ."

This conclusion is echoed by a reference to ascension. In his encounter with Mary Magdalene at the garden, Jesus reveals himself as the risen Lord and speaks directly to her about his ascension. Jesus says, "Do not hold on to me, because I have not yet ascended to the Father. But go to my brothers and say to them, 'I am ascending to my Father and your Father, to my God and your God'" (Jn 20:17). Before his death and resurrection, Jesus speaks about his ascension: "I came from the Father and have come into the world; again, I am leaving the world and am going to the Father" (Jn 16:28; cf. Jn 14:28; 17:11). After Jesus's ascension, John says that the Holy Spirit will continue the presence of Jesus until he returns to take the believers, presumably up to heaven (Jn 14:16; 15:26; 16:7; cf. Jn 14:2–4, 18).

Thus, the central theological focus of John's Gospel is clear. It looks at Jesus's earthly ministry from the perspective of Jesus's divine origin. Even before creation, Jesus was with God. It is important for John to draw attention to Jesus's divine origin because it helps us understand Jesus's ministry as divinely ordained. Jesus came to dwell among people as the one sent by God to accomplish the divine mission. Jesus came to do the work of God consistently in his earthly ministry. Jesus never acts alone without God's knowledge, and as God's Son, Jesus only does what God prompts him to do. Jesus says, "Very truly, I tell you, the Son can do nothing on his own, but only what he sees the Father doing; for whatever the Father does, the Son does likewise" (Jn 5:19). Because of his preexistence with God from the beginning, Jesus knows God intimately, and now the Holy Spirit will continue the work of Jesus in revealing God to the world through the ministry of the disciples.

John Wesley's Explanatory Notes on John

John Wesley asserts that John's Gospel is about the history of the Son of God.[14] As stated in the purpose of the Gospel, John describes the life and ministry of God's Son (Jn 20:31). Wesley divides the Gospel into three major sections: (1) the prologue and the first few days (Jn 1:1–2:12); (2) Jesus's journeys to and from Jerusalem (Jn 2:13–10:42); and (3) the last days of Jesus (Jn 11:1–21:25).[15]

The Prologue and the First Few Days (Jn 1:1–2:12)

The prologue to John's Gospel discusses how the Word (Logos) became incarnate in Jesus (Jn 1:1–14). It has been widely debated in Johannine studies whether the author of the fourth Gospel was influenced by Hellenistic philosophy of the doctrine of Logos introduced by Philo of Alexandria (20 BCE–50 CE).[16] Philo introduced the concept of Logos as a mediating principle between God and humans. Wesley thought that John's use of Logos came from the Greek Old Testament but not

---

14 John Wesley, *Wesley's Notes on the New Testament* (Oxford: Benediction Classics, 2010), 143.

15 Wesley, 143–44.

16 Philo, known also as Philo Judaeus, lived in Alexandria. He is known as the founder of religious philosophy and for his allegorical interpretation of Scripture. He interpreted the Jewish Scriptures in the light of Greek philosophy. His thoughts influenced the interpretations of Clement of Alexandria, Athenagoras, Theophilus, Justin Martyr, Tertullian, and Origen. Biblical tradition has it that Philo's nephew Marcus married Bernice, daughter of Herod Agrippa (Acts 25:13, 23; 26:30). Eusebius alludes to a tradition that Philo met Peter in Rome (*Hist. eccl.* 2.17.1). Jerome ranks Philo among "ecclesiastical writers" (*Vir. ill.* 11.1). For the complete works of Philo, see *The Works of Philo: Complete and Unabridged, New Updated Version*, trans. C. D. Yonge (Peabody, MA: Hendrickson Publishers, 2006). For a current discussion on the prologue of John's Gospel and Philo's use of Logos, see T. H. Tobin, "The Prologue of John and Hellenistic Jewish Speculation," *CBQ* 52 (1990): 252–69; D. Boyerin, "The Gospel of the Memra: Jewish Binitarianism and the Prologue to John," *HTR* 94 (2001): 243–84.

from Philo (Jn 1:1; cf. Gn 1:1; Ps 33:6; Prv 8:23).[17] He seems to have studied the works of Philo and the Old Testament in depth, which greatly helped him make the bold claim that John did not draw the expression of Logos from Philo but rather from the Old Testament.

Wesley comments that the incarnation of the Word made it possible for us to become partakers of grace and truth (cf. Jn 1:14).[18] Wesley goes further to paraphrase John 1:14 to fully understand the effect of incarnation: "The whole verse might be paraphrased thus: And in order to raise us to this dignity and happiness, the eternal Word, by a most amazing condescension, was made flesh, united himself to our miserable nature, with all its innocent infirmities."[19] The incarnation of Jesus reveals God to the fullest extent because Jesus was in union with God and had "the most intimate knowledge of God."[20] In John's Gospel, John the Baptist testifies that Jesus is the Lamb of God "who takes away the sin of the world" (Jn 1:29). Wesley sees this testimony of John the Baptist in the context of the prophecy of Isaiah and the paschal lamb,[21] which Isaiah prophesied in the "suffering servant" passages (Is 53:7; cf. Ex 12:1–13).

According to John's Gospel, Cana of Galilee was the place where Jesus turned water into wine (Jn 2:1). But Wesley mentions two other towns by the same name (Kanah): one in the territory of Ephraim (cf. Jo 16:8) and the other in the territory of Asher (cf. Jo 19:28).[22] This shows that Wesley critically engaged the text.[23] Another example of exploring the biblical text is Jesus's reference to his mother as "woman." At the wedding at Cana, when the wine runs out, Jesus's mother comes and

---

17 Wesley, *Notes on the New Testament*, 145.

18 Wesley, 146.

19 Wesley, 146.

20 Wesley, 147.

21 Wesley, 147.

22 Wesley, 148.

23 For the identification of the site of Jesus's first sign from an archaeological point of view, see C. T. McCollough, "Searching for Cana: Where Jesus Turned Water into Wine," *BAR* 41 (2015): 30–39.

reports to Jesus that "they have no wine" (Jn 2:3). Jesus replies and calls her "woman." He continues: "Woman, what concern is that to you and to me? My hour has not yet come" (Jn 2:4). Wesley points out that Jesus also calls his mother "woman" in John 19:26.[24] He comments, "[Jesus] regarded his Father above all, not knowing even his mother after the flesh."[25] Perhaps he means Jesus appeared in his glory to reveal God. No human could command him to perform any sign; Jesus would do it in his own time. For Wesley, Jesus rebuked his mother "as if she had a right to command him, on the throne of his glory."[26] Then Wesley interprets further, "Likewise how indecent it is for us to direct his supreme wisdom, as to the time or manner in which he shall appear for us in any of the exigencies of life!"[27] Here Wesley suggests that we should not demand that Jesus do anything extraordinary for us, because Jesus will perform miracles in our lives in his own time.

Jesus's Journey to and from Jerusalem (Jn 2:13–10:42)

For Wesley, the same love works through faith and leads someone to believe in the Son of God who laid down his life on the cross. This love is what Nicodemus encounters in Jesus when Jesus says that one must be born of water and Spirit to enter the Kingdom of God (Jn 3:5). Commenting on the new birth Jesus offers, Wesley sees the birth by the Spirit as the inward change and birth by water as the outward sign—or baptism.[28] For Wesley, the act of sending Jesus into the world to save humanity shows God's love for the world (cf. Jn 3:16).[29]

In his conversation with the Samaritan woman, Jesus says that the water he offers is special. After drinking this water, one will never again thirst (Jn 4:14). Wesley is intrigued by this and comments, "If

---

24 Wesley, *Notes on the New Testament*, 149.

25 Wesley, 149.

26 Wesley, 149.

27 Wesley, 149.

28 Wesley, 150.

29 Wesley, 151.

ever that thirst returns, it will be the fault of the man, not the wa-ter."[30] Jesus's conversation with the Samaritan woman also centers around the right place to worship. The Samaritan woman says that the Samaritans worship God on Mount Gerizim (Jn 4:19–20). Here Wesley draws attention to some historical background on the erection of a temple on Mount Gerizim. The temple on Mount Gerizim was built by Sanballat with the permission of Alexander the Great, because Manasseh, one of the sons of Jehoiada and the son-in-law of Sanballat, was expelled from the priesthood and from Jerusalem for marrying a foreign woman (cf. Neh 13:28).[31] This historical background is attested in Josephus's *Antiquities* and the Old Testament.[32] From Wesley's comments, we see that he was well acquainted with ancient sources such as Josephus and that he was careful to note the historical context. It also suggests that Wesley was interested in extrabiblical verification of the biblical places and events.

Jesus tells the Samaritan woman that one should worship God in spirit and truth because God is spirit (Jn 4:24). Commenting on true worship, Wesley insists that we should emulate "the truly spiritual worship of faith, love, and holiness, animating all our tempers, thoughts, words, and actions" because God is "full of all spiritual perfections, power, wisdom, love, and holiness."[33]

In the healing story of a man born blind, Jesus applies mud with saliva on the man's eyes and says to him, "Go, wash in the pool of Siloam," which is interpreted as "Sent" (Jn 9:7). In other words, the man born blind was sent by Jesus who was, in turn, sent by God (cf. Jn 3:31–36). The blind man did exactly what Jesus commanded him to do and got his eyesight back. Wesley draws attention to the fact that the man's faith and obedience resulted in a blessing.[34] Wesley

---

30 Wesley, 153.

31 Wesley, 153.

32 Josephus refers to the temple on Mount Gerizim in *Ant.* 11.310–311.

33 Wesley, *Notes on the New Testament*, 154.

34 Wesley, 166.

goes on to offer a prayer for all who would choose to receive the way and what Jesus offers: "Lord, may our proud hearts be subdued to the methods of thy recovering grace! May we leave thee to choose how thou wilt bestow favours, which it is our highest interest to receive on any terms."[35] Wesley indicates that when God acts, God sets God's own terms.

Jesus makes a bold statement when he says, "The Father and I are one" (Jn 10:30). For Wesley, the unity that exists between the Father and the Son is of power and nature.[36] Wesley refers to Sabellius, who argued for one indivisible God manifesting as Father, Son, and Holy Spirit. Sabellius was a third-century-CE priest and theologian who was expelled from the church by Pope Callixtus I for errant views on the Trinity. Wesley draws Sabellius into conversation to point out that the Father and the Son are two persons. In the same context, Wesley argues against Arius to show that the Father and the Son are eternally united as one.[37] Arius was a third-century-CE presbyter who argued for the subordination of the Son to the Father. In Wesley's references we can see that he was fully aware of the christological controversy in early Christianity and stood well with the defenders of historic orthodoxy.[38]

The Last Days of Jesus (Jn 11:1–21:25)

Jesus's raising of Lazarus is mentioned only in John's Gospel (Jn 11:1–44). John does not say how old Lazarus was when he died and how long he lived after he was raised back to life. Wesley refers to

---

35 Wesley, 166.

36 Wesley, 169.

37 Wesley comments, "I and the Father are one—Not by consent of will only, but by unity of power, and consequently of nature. Are—This word confutes Sabellius, proving the plurality of persons: one—This word confutes Arius, proving the unity of nature in God. Never did any prophet before, from the beginning of the world, use any one expression of himself, which could possibly be so interpreted as this and other expressions were, by all that heard our Lord speak." Wesley, 169.

38 For a good source book on early Christian Christological controversy, see R. N. Norris Jr., trans. and ed., *The Christological Controversy* (Minneapolis: Fortress Press, 1980).

ecclesiastical history for such information and states that "Lazarus was now thirty years old, and that he lived thirty years after Christ's ascension."[39] It is Epiphanius (c. 310–403), Bishop of Salamis in Cyprus, who made this statement about Lazarus in his treatise on the *Panarion* ("Refutation of All Heresies").[40] In order for Wesley to quote from ecclesiastical history about this tradition concerning Lazarus, he would have had to study the early church history in depth.

The inscription that Pilate put on the cross read, "Jesus of Nazareth, the King of the Jews" (Jn 19:19). John tells us that it was written in three different languages—Hebrew, Latin, and Greek. According to Wesley, it was written in Hebrew because Hebrew was the language of the Jewish nation, in Latin to honor the Roman Empire, and in Greek for the sake of Hellenists who came to Jerusalem during the Passover festival.[41]

In John's Gospel, Jesus dies on the cross after saying, "It is finished" (Jn 19:30). Commenting on Jesus's last words, Wesley states that Jesus's suffering is finished, and through his death, Jesus brings about "redemption" for all.[42] After the resurrection, Jesus greets his disciples with "peace" (Jn 20:21), and Wesley comments, "Peace is the foundation of the mission of a true gospel minister," which is "peace in his soul."[43] The peace Jesus offers is an everlasting peace that resides in the soul and serves as the foundation of the mission of God's servants. When Jesus shows himself to Thomas and invites him to touch him, Thomas says, "My Lord and my God" (Jn 20:28). Wesley draws attention to the unique confession of Thomas, commenting,

---

39 Wesley, *Notes on the New Testament*, 170.

40 Epiphanius, *Pan.* 37:6–7: "And no one should suppose that Lazarus immediately died again. The holy gospel makes it clear that Jesus reclined at table and Lazarus reclined with him. Besides, I have found traditions which say that Lazarus was thirty years when he was raised. But he lived another thirty years after the Lord raised him and then departed to the Lord." Quoted from *The Panarion of Epiphanius of Salamis, Book II and III. De Fide*, trans. F. Williams, 2nd rev. ed. (Leiden: E. J. Brill, 2012), 258.

41 Wesley, *Notes on the New Testament*, 184.

42 Wesley, 185.

43 Wesley, 186.

"Thomas now not only acknowledges him to be the Lord, as he had done before, to be risen, as his fellow disciples had affirmed, but also confesses his Godhead, and that more explicitly than any other had yet done. And all this he did without putting his hand upon his side."[44] Wesley thus sees in the confession of Thomas recognition of the divine essence of the risen Jesus.

Wesley shows awareness of the intricacies of the text of John's Gospel. He sets the text in its ancient context in order to better understand its meaning in his own contemporary setting. Wherever possible, he provides the Old Testament background of the gospel text, including awareness of Hebrew and Greek that lie behind the English translation. Wesley is familiar with the writings of Philo and Josephus as well as the early church controversies. Though Wesley claimed to be a man of one book, he used the resources available to him to exegete the text.

Teaching and Preaching from John

Teaching

John's Gospel provides ample opportunity for teaching and preaching in that it can be used to both strengthen the faith of the believers and persuade others to come and receive the new life offered through Jesus Christ. The Gospel records lengthy conversations of Jesus with several individuals: Jesus engages Nicodemus on the subject of new birth (Jn 3:1–21); he dialogues with the Samaritan woman on the subject of living water (Jn 4:1–42); and he talks to the disciples, Martha, and Mary concerning the death of Lazarus (Jn 11:1–44). All these stories are found only in John's Gospel. Jesus's conversation with Nicodemus is worth considering for its possibilities for teaching and preaching. Teachers may follow this outline: (1) context of the passage; (2) references or allusions to the Old Testament; (3) text in

---

44 Wesley, 187. Earlier, Wesley points out that the name Thomas is a Hebrew name that means "twin," and Didymus is the Greek translation of the Hebrew Thomas, also meaning "twin" (cf. Jn 11:16). Wesley, 170.

parallel with other Gospels; (4) the author's message; (5) the meaning of the text; and (6) any additional explanation.

Nicodemus was a Pharisee and leader of the Jews (Jn 3:1).[45] As a Pharisee, he was a Jew who observed the Law in minute detail. As a leader of the Jews, he was a member of the Sanhedrin, a Jewish legislative body headed by seventy-one sages. He appears in two other places in John's Gospel. Nicodemus reminds the chief priests and the Pharisees of the Law for judgment: "Our law does not judge people without first giving them a hearing to find out what they are doing, does it?" (Jn 7:51). After Jesus's death, Nicodemus appears with Joseph of Arimathea to assist him in the burial of Jesus (Jn 19:36–42). Nicodemus comes to Jesus under cover of darkness (Jn 3:29). John's reference to darkness is telling and symbolic. Using light and darkness as a literary device, John shows that Nicodemus lives in ignorance because he has not yet recognized Jesus as the Light of the world (cf. Jn 11:9–10). Despite coming to Jesus under the cover of night, Nicodemus rightly recognizes the origin of Jesus because of the signs Jesus performs (cf. Jn 2:11). Nicodemus then testifies, "Rabbi, we know that you are a teacher who has come from God; for no one can do these signs that you do apart from the presence of God" (Jn 3:2). Nicodemus's encounter with Jesus is reminiscent of someone ("rich man" in Matthew and Mark; "rich ruler" in Luke) who approaches Jesus in the synoptic Gospels with a question: "Teacher, what good deed must I do to have eternal life?" (Mt 19:16–22; cf. Mk 10:17–22; Lk 18:18–23).

Jesus starts the conversation and tells Nicodemus that in order to enter the Kingdom of God, a person must be born again (Jn 3:3). But Nicodemus misunderstands Jesus, thinking that Jesus means "the birth from above." This is because of a play on words in Greek. But clearly Nicodemus thinks Jesus is making a reference to physical

---

45 For a discussion of the role of Nicodemus in John 3, see N. Farelly, "An Unexpected Ally: Nicodemus's Role Within the Plot of the Fourth Gospel," *TJ* 34 (2013): 31–43; M. R. Whitenton, "The Dissembler of John 3: A Cognitive and Rhetorical Approach to the Characterization of Nicodemus," *JBL* 135 (2016): 141–58.

birth. Nicodemus perceives the new birth as being born a second time from his mother's womb (Jn 3:4). To be sure, there is a play on words, but Jesus goes on to make it clear that he is talking about a spiritual birth: "Very truly, I tell you, no one can enter the kingdom of God without being born of water and Spirit" (Jn 3:5). People have had various views on this statement, but most probably John alludes to John the Baptist's baptism with water and Jesus's baptism with the Holy Spirit (Jn 1:26, 33–34). Presumably, the reader/listener knows the difference, but Nicodemus cannot comprehend, because he fails to see that Jesus is the true light, the true Son of God, the Logos (Jn 3:9).

Even so, Jesus takes time to explain how God makes new birth possible. Here also Jesus refers to himself as the Son of Man, who comes to serve as a link between God and humanity (Jn 3:3; cf. Jn 5:26–27; 6:62; 8:26–27; 12:32–33; cf. Dn 7:13–14). Jesus then alludes to his own being lifted up in death that will bring eternal life just as Moses brought life through the presence of the bronze serpent: "And just as Moses lifted up the serpent in the wilderness, so must the Son of Man be lifted up, that whoever believes in him may have eternal life" (Jn 3:14–15). In the Old Testament, the Israelites who were bitten by venomous snakes looked at the copper serpent to be saved (Nm 21:9). Similarly, John is saying that all humans can now look to Jesus for healing and salvation.

Jesus taught Nicodemus two important lessons that remain applicable to those in the community of faith. First, God loves the world: "For God so loved the world that he gave his only Son, so that everyone who believes in him may not perish but may have eternal life" (Jn 3:16). Second, God sent Jesus not to condemn but to save the world: "Indeed, God did not send the Son into the world to condemn the world, but in order that the world might be saved through him" (Jn 3:17). And that salvation begins in the here and now (Jn 5:24; 6:40, 47; 11:25–26). Just as Jesus offered eternal life to those who believed in him while he was on earth, he continues to offer eternal life to those who believe in him as the Messiah and Son of God today (cf. Jn 20:21). That is good news indeed.

Preaching

Preachers may draw some of these elements from teaching and incorporate them into preaching. The text can be outlined as follows: (1) introduction; (2) setting the passage in context; (3) conversation between Nicodemus and Jesus; (4) the New Birth—what it is and isn't; (5) invitation to the New Birth. The sermon could be titled "Born of Water and Spirit: New Birth through Jesus Christ." Preachers usually focus on New Birth when they preach from the Nicodemus text.[46] The conversation generally centers around New Birth initially. Jesus plainly tells Nicodemus that no one can enter the Kingdom of God without being born of water and Spirit (Jn 3:5). The mention of water alludes to baptism, which makes this text excellent for topics concerning baptism or baptism renewal. But preachers often overlook how the New Birth is made possible. Jesus begins to explain the possibility of New Birth when Nicodemus asks him, "How can these things be?" (Jn 3:9). In response, first Jesus talks about his incarnation and that he was sent as a mediator between God and humanity (Jn 3:13). Jesus is a true representation of God: he represents God to humanity but also humanity to God, because Jesus is fully human and fully divine, and only God can represent God. This is always difficult to explain to congregations, and it has been a point of contention since the early church. Only Jesus gives us an accurate understanding of God and God's intention for us (cf. Jn 1:18).

Second, Jesus refers to his own death on the cross, and just as the people of Israel looked up to the brass serpent for magical healing when they were bitten by poisonous snakes, we obtain the ultimate and real healing when we look to Jesus and "see" his suffering, death, and resurrection. Jesus died because God loves us (Jn 3:14–15). Jesus emphasized that the love of God is the source of New Birth, a birth into God's kingdom. It all begins and ends with God. God sent

---

46 John Wesley preached two sermons on John 3. One is called "The Marks of the New Birth" and the other is "The New Birth." See A. C. Outler and R. P. Heitzenrater, eds., *John Wesley's Sermons: An Anthology* (Nashville: Abingdon Press, 1991), 173–82, 335–46.

God's Son to the world because God so loved the world (Jn 3:16; cf. 1 Jn 4:9). Even before we love God, God loves us because God is gracious. God does not want humanity to be lost in darkness but saved to live in the light of selfless love. Love is the very nature of God (cf. Jn 4:8b). It is because God loved humanity so much that we should love one another, no matter what (cf. Jn 4:11). The New Birth offers a new possibility to love God and love one another. As the author of 1 John says: "Beloved, since God loved us so much, we also ought to love one another. No one has ever seen God; if we love one another, God lives in us, and his love is perfected in us" (1 Jn 4:11–12). We should love one another because God first loved us (cf. Jn 4:19). God's intention is not to condemn but to save the world through God's Son (Jn 3:17). Likewise, the church, as the body of Christ, is called not to condemn but to reach out to save the world in the love of God. The church proclaims the New Birth available through Jesus Christ and invites everyone to experience it.

Jesus came as the true light. Nevertheless, people choose darkness and sin—turning away or fleeing from God. Yet John tells us whether we live in fear, ignorance, apathy, or pain, there is no place where God is not present. There is no person who is beyond salvation. God will go to any lengths to save us, even if it means that God's own Son has to die, because God loves each of us and all of us. John's Gospel puts the choice is stark terms: walk in the light, believe in Jesus, and have eternal life; or walk in darkness, do not believe in Jesus, and forfeit eternal life.

New Birth, being born again, has to be understood in light of what God did through Jesus. God is the one who intended to save humanity through Jesus, who truly represented God on earth. Through Jesus's death on the cross, God made the New Birth possible for all who would come to believe in Jesus as God's Son. New Birth results from nothing more or less than God's love expressed through Jesus. To embrace and experience God's love through Jesus is to obtain eternal life.

Using this text, preachers can invite congregants to testify to the new life they received from Jesus. Preachers may use arts, illustrations, and stories to elucidate and invite people to experience the New Birth through Jesus Christ.

The following texts are useful for teaching and preaching:

1. Jn 2:1–11 (The wedding at Cana)

2. Jn 4:1–15 (Jesus and the Samaritan woman)

3. Jn 9:1–12 (The healing of a man born blind)

4. Jn 15:1–11 (Jesus, the True Vine)

5. Jn 20:24–29 (The risen Jesus reveals himself to Thomas)

Summary

1. The Gospel of John is a fourth witness to the life of Jesus. John's Gospel dwells upon the divine Incarnation of Jesus and his earthly ministry.

2. Like other Gospels, the Gospel of John is anonymous. The early church tradition identifies John the apostle as the author. John's Gospel could have been written either prior to 70 CE or right after 70 CE. It is also possible that it could have been composed by disciples between 98 and 117 CE. John wrote the Gospel with the express purpose of leading people to believe that Jesus is the Messiah, the Son of God. He also intended his Gospel to edify believers in their faith in Jesus in the life of the Holy Spirit.

3. John organizes his Gospel in seven divisions. Using several narrative techniques, John portrays Jesus as God incarnate. Jesus accomplished the mission of God by being one with God.

4. From the beginning until the end, John develops the divinely ordained ministry of Jesus. In every aspect of his ministry, Jesus reveals God's purpose and selfless love. Jesus is recognized as the Messiah, the Son of God, and above all the very presence of God in human flesh.

5. John's theology is divinely oriented. For John, Jesus took on human flesh to reveal the very heart of God. Jesus is united with

God eternally in accomplishing the mission of God. After Jesus's ascension, the Holy Spirit continues the ministry of Jesus in revealing God to the world through the ministry of the disciples.

6. John Wesley seeks to understand the Gospel of John in its original context. Wesley is fully aware of the christological controversies that took place in the early church over the divinity and humanity of Jesus Christ. He shows how he interprets the Gospel in light of erroneous doctrines put forth by Sabellius and Arius. In addition, Wesley gives us ample evidence of his critical engagement with the text.

7. John's Gospel records many discourses of Jesus. Jesus's conversation with Nicodemus is a lengthy discourse that highlights the importance of the New Birth, being born again. Nicodemus's questions and Jesus's explanations provide many opportunities for teachers and preachers to talk about baptism, the Holy Spirit, the ministry of Jesus, the Incarnation, and God's purpose and love for us and the world.

For Discussion

1. John focuses on the incarnation of Jesus without providing an account of the historic birth of Jesus as in Matthew and Luke (Jn 1:1–18; cf. Mt 1:18–25; Lk 2:1–19). If Christmas were to be based on John's account of Jesus's incarnation, how would it look different? Share your thoughts with the group, and try to celebrate Christmas entirely based on John's Gospel.

2. Jesus turned water into wine at a wedding at Cana (Jn 2:1–11). Suppose Jesus was invited to a wedding today. What would people complain about? What would Jesus do to solve the problem? Share your creative story.

3. The act of Jesus washing the disciples' feet is found only in John's Gospel (Jn 13:1–15). Jesus said, "For I have set you an example, that you also should do as I have done to you" (Jn 13:15). How might you incorporate foot washing into the church's liturgy?

4. The prayer in John 17:1–26 is known as the High-Priestly Prayer. What does Jesus mean by "unity"? Compose a similar prayer in a contemporary context.

5. In his encounter with the Samaritan woman, Jesus told her, "God is spirit, and those who worship him must worship in spirit and truth" (Jn 4:24). John Wesley commented that "all our tempers, thoughts, words, and actions" should imitate "the truly spiritual worship of faith, love, and holiness."[47] For Wesley, God is "full of all spiritual perfection, power, wisdom, love, and holiness," and that should be reflected in our daily life.[48] As we come together for worship, what changes in our behaviors, attitudes, actions, and thoughts should we make in order to mirror the spiritual worship? What part does God's grace play in our daily living? How can we share God's grace with others?

---

47 Wesley, *Notes on the New Testament*, 154.

48 Wesley, 154.

Conclusion

The Life of Jesus in Four Dimensions

Now, those four evangelists whose names have gained the most remarkable circulation over the whole world, and whose number has been fixed as four,—it may be for the simple reason that there are four divisions of that world through the universal length of which they, by their number as by a kind of mystical sign, indicated the advancing extension of the Church of Christ,—are believed to have written in the order which follows: first Matthew, then Mark, thirdly Luke, lastly John."[1] Thus writes Augustine, who spoke of the four Gospels as four dimensions of the world. The four Gospels authentically bear witness to the life and ministry of Jesus; consequently, the early church chose only these Gospels to be included in the New Testament canon. The reason for doing so was to have multiple accounts of Jesus that stand in accordance with the apostolic tradition.

The four Gospels not only narrate the story of Jesus from four different perspectives, they also provide the foundation for historic orthodoxy. The early church used the four Gospels to advance loyalty to the gospel by building on the foundation of the apostles and their companions, who faithfully transmitted the Jesus tradition. Thus, it becomes necessary to study and understand the life and ministry of Jesus as witnessed by each of the four Gospel writers. Each writer narrates the story of Jesus for a different audience and a different theological purpose.

---

1 Augustine, *Cons.* 1.2.3, in *The Harmony of the Gospels*, trans. S. D. F. Salmond, ed. M. B. Riddle, vol. 6 of *Nicene and Post-Nicene Fathers*, ed. P. Schaff (New York: The Christian Literature Company, 1995), 78.

Matthew

Traditionally thought to have been authored by the apostle of the same name, Matthew is the first Gospel of the four in the canonical order. The Gospel was written for people familiar with the Old Testament and the Jewish tradition. Matthew makes more references to the Old Testament and to the Jewish customs than any other Gospel writer, so this Gospel functions perfectly to bridge the gap between the Old and New Testaments. In that context, Matthew takes great care to witness how Jesus fulfills the prophecies of Scripture and faithfully follows the Jewish customs, especially focusing on Jesus's role as *Emmanuel*—the promised Messiah, King David's descendant, the Son of God—and the coming of the Son of Man in his future glorious return.

Matthew is a phenomenal work of theological literature, carefully composed in a way that presents Jesus as the ultimate Savior—the seed of Abraham and the messianic Son of David who saves both Israel and all nations. The prologue to the Gospel introduces these big terms, explores them in the large middle section, and then brings them to culmination in the death and resurrection of Jesus.

Matthew reaches beyond the national confines of Israel. Yes, Jesus came primarily to save Israel, but Israel did not immediately accept Jesus as the promised Messiah. So now Matthew foresees the inclusion of the Gentiles in the Kingdom of Heaven after Jesus's resurrection and his commission of the disciples to spread the good news and make disciples of all nations. Internally, Matthew's Gospel is the only one that previews in detail the emerging church (Mt 16). Matthew describes Jesus's instructions for being in Christian community with others (Mt 18). It seems that Matthew intends his Gospel for a larger worldwide community. With the arrival of Jesus, a new era has dawned. Jesus not only teaches the greatest commandment of God but also draws attention to how people might go about fulfilling it. Jesus came not to abolish the law and the prophets but to fulfill them. Matthew shows how the entire life of Jesus serves as a commentary on faithfulness to the law and its fulfillment through his life. The Gospel narratives provide models and inspiration for the

Christian community to demonstrate in practice and proclamation of the gospel of Jesus Christ.

More than any other Gospel writer, Matthew emphasizes the earth-shattering implications of the death and resurrection of Jesus. The darkening of the sky, the shaking of the earth, and the resurrection of the saints would have been clear signs to ancient readers that a new age has begun to arise. After the climactic resurrection, Jesus emerges victoriously from the grave, defeating death and all powers of darkness. He becomes an object of worship by the disciples and other followers with the purpose of bringing others throughout the world to belief. The risen Jesus directs the disciples to go preach the good news, baptize believers, and teach them to obey everything he has commanded. With the commission of the disciples, the risen Jesus keeps the door wide open for the ongoing work of the church. The community that Matthew envisions is one grounded in the life and ministry of Jesus, who continues to reign as the cosmic Lord, as *Emmanuel*.

Mark

According to early church tradition, the Gospel of Mark was written by John Mark, a missionary companion of Paul and Barnabas. Later tradition asserts that he became an interpreter of Peter in Rome. Mark's Gospel appears to have been written for a Roman audience of Christian believers. Mark's Gospel is action oriented and stresses events more than the longer narratives and discourses we find in Matthew and Luke. For this reason, the early church believed that Mark was a condensation of Matthew or of Matthew and Luke together.

Mark's Gospel begins with a brief account of the ministry of John the Baptist, who prepared the way of the Lord. Early in his Gospel, Mark presents Jesus as the Lord who came to embody the very presence of God. After choosing his disciples, Jesus begins a vigorous ministry of evangelism by preaching the Kingdom of God and healing the sick. Even though Mark describes Jesus as a teacher, he nevertheless includes the mighty works that Jesus performs, which emphasizes the power of God. Jesus instructs his disciples that they will perform the works that he performs.

In Mark's Gospel, Jesus does not explicitly reveal his Messiahship to the public or to his disciples until they reach Caesarea Philippi. He cautions those whom he heals and the disciples who are witnesses not to say anything about his identity. Whether Jesus was conscious of his Messiahship from the beginning of his ministry or it is meant to be understood only after his death and resurrection is not made entirely clear. The audience of Mark's Gospel gets a glimpse of Jesus's Messiahship, but they need to wait until his crucifixion to understand its nature.

Mark narrates a coherent account of Jesus's activities during the days preceding his trial and crucifixion. Jesus says that his kingdom will be far greater than David's. On the way to Jerusalem, Mark prepares his readers to understand Jesus not only as the Lord but as a suffering servant. Jesus is human, but his divinity emerges at crucial points such as at his baptism and transfiguration. Jesus is also affirmed as God's Son at his death on the cross.

Mark tells that a young man announced Jesus's resurrection. Although the women are instructed to tell the disciples and Peter about Jesus's resurrection, they flee from the tomb and say nothing to anyone because of fear, which is ironic because earlier in the Gospel people are instructed not to say anything but cannot contain themselves. Here they are instructed to tell others but do not. Or is this really the case? Can they keep silent? The multiple endings of Mark's Gospel raise many interesting possibilities. However, this is where the shorter ending of Mark concludes—the resurrection of Jesus in fulfillment of his own prediction before death is announced. The longer ending, which supplements the shorter ending, reports that Jesus appeared first to Mary Magdalene, then to the two disciples, and finally to the eleven disciples. The risen Jesus emerges as the Lord who commissions his disciples to preach the good news to the world. For Mark, Jesus became the "Lord Jesus" through his mighty acts, teachings, suffering, death, and resurrection.

Luke

In our present copies of the oldest New Testament manuscripts, Luke's Gospel is the third and longest of the four. This Gospel is a thorough account of the events in Jesus's life. It is arranged in chronological order and was presumably written to provide an orderly account of the life and ministry of Jesus and to emphasize the universal nature of the gospel. Church tradition recognizes Luke, a travel companion of Paul, as the author who also wrote the Acts of the Apostles. Luke's clear intent was to gather different sources and organize those materials with his own interpretation to make a complete and unified narrative. Although it is not clear, Luke may be the only non-Jewish author among the Gospel writers, and because of his association with Paul, Luke occupies a unique place in the New Testament.

Luke's Gospel states that the one whom God's people have been expecting so long has finally come—Jesus of Nazareth. In him all the hopes and promises made to God's people will come to decisive fulfillment. For Luke, Jesus is the Savior for all. He is the divine Son of God like Adam; but unlike Adam, Jesus passes his test in the wilderness and does not yield to temptation. Jesus restores all humanity to God, repairing and healing the ruptured relationship that humanity—and God—has endured since the fall of Adam. Throughout his Gospel, Luke emphasizes the fact that Jesus is a friend not only to Jews but to Samaritans and social outcasts, whether they are Gentiles, enemies, or women. Luke also makes it clear that the disciples should serve different communities, because in addition to the sending out of the Twelve, Luke describes the sending of the seventy to carry the message of the Kingdom to different places. It shows that Jesus's mission is for all humankind and not just for Israel.

In some of Luke's special narratives, such as the parables of the Good Samaritan, the Publican and the Pharisee, the Rich Man and Lazarus, the Lost Coin, the Prodigal Son, the Unjust Steward, the Rich Fool, and the stories of Zacchaeus and the ten lepers, Luke emphasizes Jesus's special love for all sinners and outcasts—the least, the lost, the sick, and the shamed. He places the highest value on human dignity regardless of a person's social status, rank, or nationality.

Toward the end of his Gospel, Luke describes the events leading up to crucifixion, highlighting Jesus's innocence of any wrongdoing toward Jews or the Roman government. Pilate, the Roman governor, declares Jesus innocent of any crime; one of the criminals asserts Jesus's innocence; and the Roman centurion testifies to Jesus's righteousness—his right relationship with God.

Luke's Gospel closes with an account of the resurrection and the subsequent meetings of Jesus with the disciples and others. On the road to Emmaus, Jesus joins two disciples and explains to them the fulfillment of the Scriptures in the ministry of the promised Messiah. Again, Jesus meets with the eleven disciples in Jerusalem and draws attention to the fulfillment of Scripture in the events of his own life. Jesus commissions them to bear witness to the things that have taken place in the life of the Savior who came to save all humanity. It is with the power of the Holy Spirit that the disciples would be empowered to proclaim the message of repentance and forgiveness of sins in Jesus's name to all nations.

John

The last of the four accounts of Jesus's life is John, whom the church traditionally associates with John the apostle, the beloved disciple. Whoever he may be, he probably authored his Gospel after the first three canonical Gospels were already written. This Gospel focuses on the divine origin of Jesus more than the other three. Jesus is the Messiah, the Son of God, and God in human flesh. In his prologue, John identifies the Word with God and God with Jesus. The very Word that was in the beginning eternally coexists with God and has become incarnate in a human Jesus.

John's Gospel presents Jesus as the long-awaited Messiah and Son of God who comes to earth to restore God's covenant people. Nevertheless, Jesus is rejected by his own people. But to those who believe in him, he gives power to become children of God. By believing in him, all people everywhere in the cosmos may possess eternal life in his name. John emphasizes the actual indwelling of

God through Jesus's incarnation. In Jesus, God dwells among us, in us, and for us all. For John, to see Jesus is to see God; therefore, Jesus becomes the link between heaven and earth. He is the divine Son of Man who graciously bridges the gap, bringing God to us. Apart from him no one can ever see or know God. In this way, John conceives the restoration of the relationship between the divine and humanity through Jesus. Jesus is the way through whom one can enjoy the very life of God and live into God's true intent for us.

John's treatment of the sign (miracle) stories is significant. Each sign reveals the glory of Jesus, which is the glory of God. In the raising of Lazarus, Jesus is not simply pointing to resurrection and life. He *is* the resurrection and the life. Everyone who believes in Jesus will enter into new life here and now. In the lengthy discourses, John describes the close relationship that exists between God and Jesus. Like God, Jesus is the giver of life. It is Jesus who sends the Holy Spirit, which is the very Spirit of God who lives in believers and is made manifest in their—the church's—ministry.

John describes the events that culminate in the crucifixion. Jesus dies for all. He is sacrificed as a Passover (or paschal) lamb because, as John the Baptist attests, Jesus is "the Lamb of God." Interestingly—and different from the synoptic Gospels—John chronicles the crucifixion as falling on the eve of Passover to signify the sacrifice of the paschal lamb. Jesus's mission culminates—his hour comes—in his suffering and crucifixion as "the King of the Jews," showing the culpability of his own people. Yet on the cross he accomplishes the purpose of the incarnation—to redeem humanity and demonstrate God's love for the world. The Gospel closes with an account of post-resurrection appearances in Jerusalem and Galilee, where Jesus redeems Peter. Finally, Jesus commissions the disciples and empowers them with the Holy Spirit to continue the mission.

John Wesley and the Gospels

Wesley was a serious student of the Bible and an expert in biblical interpretation, having studied at the premier institution of higher learning in England in his day. He can set a worthwhile example for us, even today, as to how to approach the biblical text. While Scripture was primary for John Wesley, he was also concerned about taking its passages out of context. He wanted people to understand the original context before they drew implications for daily living, because he believed that context informs and contributes to an understanding of the entire tenor of the Bible. Just as Wesley was a critical thinker, he expected all Methodists to think—to love God with their minds as well as their hearts, souls, and strength.

Wesley's explanatory notes on Matthew, Mark, Luke, and John clearly demonstrate his voracious appetite for knowledge and linguistic skills. He faithfully exegeted the biblical texts in order to understand the Gospel writers' intention in conveying the message of Jesus Christ. He articulated, then, contemporary meaning of the text by delving into church history and tradition, issues sometimes studied using what we might call "historical criticism." He consulted with the Greek, Hebrew, and Latin texts in order to glean deeper meanings. He was willing to analyze and refer to available biblical manuscripts in order to come up with what he considered the most reliable text for study and reading. In addition, he offered numerous corrections to the Authorized King James Version, which was the Bible he used.

Wesley also studied the apocryphal writings of the Old Testament and was able to relate the Gospel texts to some books of the Apocrypha. He was well versed in the Septuagint. He studied all four Gospels in a parallel format so that throughout his exposition of the Gospels and other biblical texts he was able to point out the differences and similarities. He was familiar with the works of Philo and Josephus, important Jewish writers from the time of Jesus. In his exposition of the Gospels, Wesley drew attention to the patristic writings and the christological controversies of the early and Reformation church. In so doing, he was confident in his preaching and teaching.

While Wesley held Scripture in high esteem, he was not afraid to engage the text, thereby setting a high standard for Bible study, and he encouraged his preachers to learn the original languages of the text. In short, he used all the available means to interpret the Scripture and discern its meaning for daily living. Indeed, Wesley was a Bible scholar *par excellence*, and he wanted no less from all Methodists.

Teaching and Preaching

Teaching and preaching the gospel of Jesus Christ are key to the witness of the church today, but we must remember that the Gospels are ancient documents. They were written for first-century, and perhaps second-century, audiences. So we cannot be surprised that the Gospel writers used several narrative techniques to construct the text and communicate the message in their own contexts. Because of the nature of the Gospel writings, teachers and preachers need to pay careful attention to the original intent of the authors who mediated the gospel tradition. The Gospel writers themselves referred to the original historical context as they knew it in narrating the life and ministry of Jesus. First it is necessary to set the Gospels in their historical contexts to understand the message and then articulate its implication and relevance in our contemporary context. In Luke's Gospel, the risen Jesus commissions the disciples with these words:

> Thus it is written, that the Messiah is to suffer and to rise from the dead on the third day, and that repentance and forgiveness of sins is to be proclaimed in his name to all nations, beginning from Jerusalem. You are witnesses of these things. And see, I am sending upon you what my Father promised; so stay here in the city until you have been clothed with power from on high (Lk 24:46–49).

The four Gospels witness to the life of the Messiah from beginning to end, and we as teachers and preachers are part of this historic tradition. The risen Jesus empowers the disciples with the Holy Spirit and commissions them—and us—to proclaim the good news to all nations and bear witness to the fulfillment of the Scripture in the life, teaching, suffering, death, and resurrection of Jesus. This is the witness of the four Gospels. Let it also be our witness.

CPSIA information can be obtained
at www.ICGtesting.com
Printed in the USA
LVHW030955100221
678919LV00009B/711

9 781945 935923